P9-DBR-859

Also by Bentz Plagemann

*Novels:*

The Steel Cocoon
This Is Goggle
Father to the Man

*Nonfiction:*

This Happy Place
Now to Write a Story

# AN
# AMERICAN
# PAST

## An Early Autobiography

*Bentz Plagemann*

William Morrow and Company, Inc.
New York

Parts of this book have appeared in:
*The New Yorker, Harper's Magazine,*
*The Atlantic Monthly, Reader's Digest,* and
*The Yale Review.*

Copyright © 1990 by Bentz Plagemann

All rights reserved. No part of this book may be reproduced or utilized in any form or by any means, electronic or mechanical, including photocopying, recording or by any information storage and retrieval system without permission in writing from the Publisher. Inquiries should be addressed to Permissions Department, William Morrow and Company, Inc., 105 Madison Avenue, New York, N.Y. 10016.

Recognizing the importance of preserving what has been written, it is the policy of William Morrow and Company, Inc., and its imprints and affiliates to have the books it publishes printed on acid-free paper, and we exert our best efforts to that end.

Library of Congress Cataloging-in-Publication Data

Plagemann, Bentz, 1913–
    An American past / Bentz Plagemann.
        p.      cm.
    ISBN 0-688-09718-9
    1. Plagemann, Bentz, 1913–  — Biography.  2. Authors,
American—20th century — Biography.  I. Title.
PS3566.L25Z463  1990
813'.54—dc20
[B]                                                    90-6054
                                                        CIP

Printed in the United States of America
First Edition

1  2  3  4  5  6  7  8  9  10

BOOK DESIGN BY LISA STOKES

*This book is dedicated
with love to
Marion Bangle Newgard*

I am, myself, the subject of my book.
—Montaigne

# 1

SOMETIME DURING World War II I found myself in the examining room of the Boston Naval Hospital, being examined by Dr. Palmer whose name I have never forgotten. After looking at the report I had brought with me from the shore dispensary in the Boston Navy Yard, he asked me most politely, "Would you mind taking off all of your clothes? I want to call the interns."

I was there because of the doctor's orders on the destroyer U.S.S. *Bell,* where I was a member of the crew, a hospital corpsman, pharmacist's mate third-class. It was my first sea duty. We had been loaned to the British Home Fleet with a mission in mind. We were out to get the German battleship *Scharnhorst,* hiding somewhere in the fjords of Norway. We did not succeed in this exacting assignment, although we tried, mightily, to my apprehension. I did not count myself a coward, but I felt woefully unprepared for active combat where I might be called on to tend wounded and dying men on the open deck. I had spent sleepless nights, memorizing my Hospital Corps Manual.

We were under the command of the British Home Fleet, and we were fed by it. Each late afternoon, cooks would come on board from the mother ship, bearing vats of food. It was always the same food. Brussels sprouts, cooked to the consistency and the color of library paste, and mutton, carved into serving pieces, ladled out from the cooking pot through two or three inches of boiling fat. (I described this feeding routine years later to a visiting Englishwoman, and she said, with a sniff, that they had survived on the same diet throughout the war. I

9

survived but I did not thrive.) Malnutrition contributed to my having serious nosebleeds on the long voyage home, after our mission was completed, or aborted. Nothing could stop my nosebleeds. Not the cold key down the bare back, not packing, not lying still. I had bled and bled, vomiting in a pail that was beside my bunk.

The doctor ordered me ashore when we reached our home port of Boston. I did not want to go. I was suffering under the delusion that I was indispensable, that the crew needed me, that I was liked, that I would be missed. I did not want to miss the ship when she left on our next assignment. The doctor ordered me ashore. "At least go to the shore dispensary and have a blood count," he said.

I walked stubbornly to the shore dispensary, in my hand an order signed by the ship's doctor for a blood count. Vast dark clouds swirled about my head. But I was stubborn. I kept going. The chief at the dispensary ordered an assistant to do a blood count. Blood was drawn and examined, and the report brought to the chief. The chief boiled over. "Are you totally incompetent!" he said to the assistant. "That can't be right! Do it over again! And see if you can do it right!"

More blood was drawn. The procedure was repeated. When the chief saw the report the assistant handed to him, he was contrite, and thoughtful. "Order an ambulance," he told the assistant. To me he said, "You are going to the hospital."

So I was in the examining room at the Boston Naval Hospital, taking off my clothes. Dr. Palmer returned, followed by three or four interns in white coats.

"Would you please stand in front of the window?" he asked me. So I stood in front of the window, all of my skinny, five feet eleven, one hundred and twenty-five pounds, naked, in the unforgiving light of a New England morning.

"Look at this man," Dr. Palmer said to the interns. "He has lost half of his blood supply, but he is standing."

And turning to me he said, "Were your ancestors pioneers?"

I was startled by this unexpected question. I decided later that only a Boston doctor would have had the instinct to ask that question.

"I've never thought about it," I stammered. "But I suppose they were."

"Please sit down," Dr. Palmer said.

I sat down, thoroughly ashamed of myself. I had never thought about my ancestors. I had always taken them for granted. They were my grandparents, well known to me, and my great-grandparents, one of whom was known to me. A blinding realization came over my addled brain, only half-fed by my blood supply. My ancestors *were* pioneers! On one side of the family they had lived in a sod house on the prairie of Wisconsin. On the other side they had lived in a log house in the "wilderness" of Ohio. I had been taught in school that I was counted among the children of immigrants, not quite of the same level, not quite as good, as the descendants of the *Mayflower* and the settlers of the eighteenth century. That we were all "foreign." That we were not truly American. We were Johnny-come-latelies. And we could never catch up. We would never be true Americans.

I had to think about that.

Dr. Palmer admitted me as a patient to the Boston Naval Hospital. There I was put on a high-protein diet, with plenty of steak, that precious luxury commodity in wartime. When I was a little stronger I was assigned to Dr. Palmer's office. There I kept his appointment book, and assisted him in whatever way I could. I had a very pleasant few months in Boston before I was sent to my next assignment.

It is just a coincidence that my early childhood stories began with memories of Boston. Grandfather Plagemann, "Grandpa," was born in Boston. Not all of the mid–nineteenth-century immigrants arrived in New York. My great-grandparents arrived in Boston, although I do not know where they came from in Germany, and I do not know their first names. We were taught in those distant days that it was best to forget your antecedents, to close the door upon them since you never could go back, and to adopt the language and manners and customs of America. There was a rumor, a legend in the family, that Great-grandfather refused to return to Germany to claim a rightful and substantial inheritance. But that would have meant, presumably, that he would have returned, never to come back to America, and he refused.

I remember Grandpa, coming down Lincoln Avenue in Springfield, Ohio, at a little after five on summer days when our parents took us from Euclid Village in northern Ohio to visit our grandparents. He was an old man, although possibly not as old as I remember him as a small boy. I loved him very much. I used to wait for him in the swing on the front porch. The swing, long enough for two or three, was suspended from the ceiling of the porch by chains, and my feet did not touch the floor. But by body movement I would start it swinging, and I could swing there, happily, watching the street. Always on time, Grandpa would appear. He was not a tall man, rather stocky, and walked with a slight limp. He wore baggy pants and an old shirt buttoned to the collar. He had a walrus moustache that smelled deliciously of hay and warm sunshine, and his own sweet smell. He carried a scythe over his shoulder. He had never been educated, beyond early schooling in Boston, and he was not trained for any profession. When he was too old to work in the iron mills he worked as a gardener.

He would greet me. "Just let me wash up, Billy," he would say, "and I will join you."

And join me he did, to swing lazily along with me in the porch swing, and tell me tales of the prairie and the Indians.

The family had lived in Boston until Grandpa was thirteen. They lived close to the waterfront, to Boston Harbor; having come so far, it seemed they had temporarily lost the nerve to go on any farther. Temporarily.

"The ships were so many in the harbor," Grandpa said, "that their masts were like trees in the forest."

Living so near the water, Grandpa had developed a taste for the sea. When he was thirteen, unknown to his father and mother, he signed on as a cabin boy on a clipper ship.

His parents were horrified when he came home with the paper. There was not a moment to lose. They had left their country behind them, so it was not really so difficult after all to leave Boston behind. At all costs, their young son would not ship out as a cabin boy, and experience the rough and possibly immoral life at sea, on a voyage that would last perhaps two or three years!

They stayed up all night and packed. Grandpa remembered a round, brassbound trunk and a violin. They were setting out for a life that would be as rough and unfitting for them as being a cabin boy on a clipper ship would be for Grandpa.

At dawn they went to the railroad station. They bought tickets for the end of the line, which was somewhere in the frontier of Wisconsin. Grandpa remembered it as being Appleton.

He could recall little of the journey. At the end of the railroad line they got down from the train. There were Indians on the platform, drunk on white man's "firewater," who frightened them. Father Plagemann gathered his little brood about him, for there were more than Grandpa, although I don't know how many. Father Plagemann bought a wagon and a pair of oxen. In the wagon they set out for the prairie. They went a few miles out of town and settled. Grandpa said they staked a claim. The legal arrangements, if there were any, were forgotten or were unknown in this tale.

Halfway through the story, or stories, my maiden aunts would come down Lincoln Avenue, returning from their jobs. Grandpa had fathered six children, my father among them. Three girls and three sons. The sons and one of the daughters had married, but Aunt Mary and Aunt Minnie had not married. Their childhood of hardship had made them confirmed spinsters, dedicated to taking care of their mother, who obviously was not properly cared for by their dreamy, unskilled father, rocking away in the porch swing with me.

They would hiss angry words to me, not greeting their father. "You don't have to listen to Grandpa!" they would say, sotto voce. "Get up and go out!" "Go out and play!"

I was too shy and intimidated by them to answer them. They were very successful women, unusual in their time, unappreciated, laughed at by men. One was a court stenographer, the top in a new profession, who typed and took shorthand. The other was a department-store china buyer who made business trips to New York. They wore high-necked shirtwaists, and long skirts, and laced, high-heeled shoes. Their hair was piled on top of their heads. Their lexicon was work. They never smiled. Impatient with me, as no-good as their father, they would shrug and go inside to greet their mother.

Father Plagemann had built a sod house on his claim. A

sod house belongs in fairy tales. It was not meant for prolonged human habitation. Chunks of sod from the primeval prairie, which had never known a plow in the thousands of years after the Ice Age had retreated, were a solid mass of prairie-grass roots that could be cut and laid up to make a sort of house.

The enterprise had a very shaky beginning. It seemed doomed from the start. The winter came and there was never enough to eat. Father Plagemann was not a farmer. He was a town product, profession unknown. But he had determination. They scrimped along. Other more settled, more experienced neighbors helped them. In the spring Grandpa was farmed out. He helped a neighbor in the fields, for five dollars and a pair of shoes. Once he was given some corn, or wheat, to take into town to the mill to be ground. He set off in the horse and wagon about dusk. He did not know the way. When he was halfway there, an apparition loomed up in his path—a gray, amorphous shape, making a strange and bleating sound. Grandpa was too scared to go on, and he didn't have the nerve to turn back to tell the farmer that he had failed. He stayed in the wagon all night, and at dawn the ghostly apparition revealed itself to be a sheep caught in a thornbush. Grandpa freed the sheep and went on to the mill, telling the farmer that he had lost his way.

In spite of their best efforts, though, the Plagemann adventure was not a success, at least not in the beginning. Finally the awful day came when Father Plagemann gathered his brood around him in the sod house, and told them there was not enough to feed them all. The oldest children would have to leave home, and go on their own. Grandpa told me about this without emotion, but I can imagine how tragic it was for all of them, especially for him because he was one of the oldest, now seventeen years old.

He left. "I never saw any of them again," he said, matter-of-factly. "I don't know what happened to any of them."

He took up the story of his adventures, sparing me the emotion. Perhaps they were so traumatic he had locked them away forever.

He went east. He crossed the Mississippi River and came to the Ohio River. It never occurred to me to interrupt his story, to ask him how he traveled, with whom he traveled, what he had to eat, where he had spent the nights. He went up the Ohio River until he came to Cincinnati. "A bunch of shanties sitting on stilts," was the way he described it. But that was at the river's edge. He climbed the hill to the city proper, and he felt he was in a dream. Everything, every building, was draped in purple. All the citizens were running, in one direction. The church bells were tolling. He joined the running people, and they came to the railroad station just in time to see President Lincoln's funeral train pass sorrowfully through, on its way to Illinois. All the people wept. That was 1865.

Grandpa, a healthy young man in spite of his hardships, or maybe because of them, found work clearing the forests of Ohio. When that was finished he found work in an iron mill. He was a merry young man. He enjoyed his life. One day, "skylarking," as he said, with his fellow workers during lunch hour, he fell from the upper gallery of the iron mill to the floor and broke his leg. He was sent to the hospital, where a "very pretty young Irish nurse" cared for him. But her ministrations were not enough for an active young man, and when he was alone, he jumped out of the ground-floor window. His leg never healed properly. That was why he walked with a chronic limp, looking, to my eyes, a romantic, dashing figure, like a sea captain or, with his scythe, a benevolent Father Time. Soon after the fall, he met his beloved "Molly" (Mary Kaiser, my grandmother), and they settled down, poor as church mice but undaunted, to raise a family.

When the early dusk came we would be called to supper. It was my turn to wash up, which I did in the bathroom, where, now that the aunts were home, two joss sticks ("punk," we called them) smoldered in a glass vase on top of the water closet.

Supper was in the roomy kitchen, on a round table covered with a cloth. In the middle of the table was a cut-glass, stemmed goblet, a "spoon jar," which held teaspoons for the ever-present coffee cups that, with their saucers, were to the right of every place. Coffee was drunk throughout the meal. There was a bowl of applesauce, ever present, for dessert, and a coffee cake. Although I had the appetite of a normal boy, I do not remember anything I ever ate at Grandma Plagemann's except for the applesauce and the coffee cake, which was crumbed and dry to the mouth.

The conversation between my grandmother and my aunts was about neighbors and friends, and their ailments, or their deaths. "She's failing," was said, with a shake of the head. "When I saw her I thought she was not long for this world," was another phrase, not necessarily about the same person. "The funeral is on Tuesday." "Well, he was a good worker." The highest praise that could be said about anyone.

My grandmother Plagemann was a handsome woman. She had the "Kaiser Look," slender and erect. She had been fair, but now she was graying-fair, and her softly waved hair was arranged carefully on top of her head. She wore a shirtwaist, buttoned to the collar, but on her it looked right, not a statement. She wore steel-rimmed spectacles on a thin steel cord, which was attached to a little round case on her lapel. The case had a spring in it, and when she removed her glasses she would touch the spring, and the cord would be retracted and the spectacles hung below. I knew she loved me. But her love was measured, and I was a little afraid of her, not as afraid of her as I was of my aunts and her mother, my great-grandmother, but I tried to do her bidding.

Once, I came in on a hot afternoon and flopped down on the horsehair sofa that faced the bay window in the sitting room, where Grandmother was busy with her sewing basket.

"What is the matter?" she asked.

"I'm tired," I said, with a sigh.

Grandmother did not look up from her mending. "Little boys are never tired," she said.

Without a word, I got up and went outside again.

I was not encouraged to talk at the dinner table. My opinion was never asked. My well-being taken for granted. "Don't stare, Billy," Aunt Minnie would say. I looked down at my plate. I stole a glance at Grandpa. He was silent, too.

One Saturday afternoon we went to visit Great-grandmother. She received us in her plain wooden armchair, sitting on the side veranda, looking immortal. I was so overcome with awe and fear in her presence that I had to be drawn forward by the hand, by Grandma, up the three steps of the porch to stand in front of her.

"This is Billy," Grandma said. "Will and Elizabeth's oldest."

Great-grandmother looked at me. She was German, of course—her name was Wilhelmina Kaiser—yet much later when I saw a Chinese ancestor portrait, I recognized her. She was dressed in a simple black dress, and her thin, straight hair, still dark, was drawn back from her brown and weathered face.

Without a word, she reached out to me. There may have been affection in her touch, but I did not feel it there. Her instinct was more fundamental. She retained all of her faculties to the end, but she wanted to feel me. Her thin, strong fingers moved along my arms and legs. I could not have defined it then, but I felt she denied my uniqueness. To her I was merely a specimen. My reaction to her examination was revulsion.

"He has the Kaiser frame," she said at last, and a sigh of relief went up from her court, a murmur of approval. There were two maiden aunts at this house too, Great-aunts Carrie and Minnie, who stood at either side of her chair like ladies-in-waiting.

Everyone relaxed. It seemed that I was accepted, in spite of my shortcomings. The Kaisers were fair and Teutonic, lean, with blue eyes, but through my mother I had inherited other than German blood. My mother, Elizabeth Agatha Josephine Bentz (the first words I learned to say consecutively), was a very beautiful woman, with features that might have been taken from a Roman copy of an Aphrodite. She had the same straight, classical nose, the serene brow, the mysterious smile even in repose, and the Kaisers were fearful of this. I had the dark hair of my mother, the same dark eyes, the same full mouth, and would have, perhaps, what seemed to them the same softness. My limbs were examined for reassurance, for I was the structure in which the family was housed, and by which it would be continued. I was the immortality in Wilhelmina Kaiser.

She gave me an apple then, from a bowl beside her. The interview was over. I held the apple in my hands, with the carefulness of my secret resentment, as we drove away.

\*     \*     \*

17

The afternoon was not finished. We had to make a second call, a duty call, at a house not too far away. The frame farmhouse we approached was bleak and unpainted, associated in some way in my mind with a feeling of vulnerability.

I was left in the car while my father and the two aunts and Grandma went to pay their respects. I was too young to be told the story. I understood, in later years, that the daughter of the house had been seduced and abandoned, and that the elders had lived in shame with her and her illegitimate child. But the elders had come over from Germany, in steerage, with Wilhelmina Kaiser and Joseph Kaiser, and they had shared their life experience and their tragedies with each other.

Great-grandfather Kaiser had died young, in circumstances that the family didn't like to talk about. In the early part of the Civil War, so I was told by my father, recruiting in the villages and countryside of southern Ohio was done in a very informal way. When the call went out for more men, a drum-and-fife corps and a standard bearer were dispatched to march the dusty roads, and men of military age were meant to fall in behind and march to the village recruiting station. But Joseph Kaiser had had enough of war between the states in Germany. That was why he had left. He and Wilhelmina had worked hard for what they had, and he meant to protect it. Wilhelmina had worked as a servant girl and he as a hired hand on a farm until they had saved enough money to buy a farm of their own. They had children. He could not leave it all behind.

So, when the drum and fife were heard over the hill, he hid under a pile of newly cut logs he had cut from the forest, and when the drum corps had passed and they found him, he was dead, crushed by the logs that had fallen in upon him.

After she had buried Great-grandfather, Great-grandmother loaded the farm wagon with produce from the garden, and took it into the marketplace at Springfield to sell. She had children to feed.

When I arrived on the scene so many years later, the struggle had resolved itself into a solid business enterprise. In a competitive market, as the produce market was, she had learned early to specialize. Celery and tomatoes were her best crops. Pascal celery, banked in the rich river-bottom soil, crisp and ivory white. Tomatoes, perfect tomatoes, which she improved each year by having the harvest baskets brought to her and selecting the best specimens for seed. The Kaiser farm was not a farm in the conventional sense. It was the seat of a business, and there was an impersonal efficiency about it. There were no domestic animals, no chores to be done, no chickens scratching in the dooryard. The hired men worked a schedule as they might have done in a factory. They came at dawn, and they departed in the afternoon.

When we returned to Grandma Plagemann's for supper, I stayed behind the others while they went into the house. Then I threw the apple that Great-grandmother had given me under the porch.

I was put to bed in Grandma Plagemann's house in the front room, in an improvised, very uncomfortable bed converted from a horsehair sofa. In the semidarkness I was restless because light and very serious conversation were filtering in from the sitting room. I was very lonesome for my two sisters and my younger brother and my mother. They got to sleep at the Bentzes' house, our other grandparents; there was not enough room, they said, for all of us. Besides, I was the oldest son of the oldest son, and it was proper that I should spend the night in my father's paternal house.

I found the front room, which was used only for family gatherings and funeral postmortems, very depressing. It was done in shades of brown. Brown "oatmeal" paper covered the walls. There was a brown carpet, and brown curtains hung at the window. In addition to the horsehair sofa there were two horsehair chairs, and an occasional table all in brown. On the wall hung a large framed lithograph in sepia of Jesus in the temple among the elders.

Finally I slept, deeply, but I was wakened sometime later by the sound of fire engines and sirens. The whole household was astir. My father came and got me up, and together, except for Grandpa, we ran down the street and through the fields toward the red glare in the sky. The horse barns and the stockpens at the railroad station were on fire. Flames, out of control, leaped

19

in the sky. The whole scene, of frightened, rearing, screaming horses being led blindfolded out of the burning barns by frightened men, the cries of doomed animals, the shouting and running back and forth, all taking place against a background of fire, like a Goya drawing, remained forever in my memory. And the excited satisfaction that the members of my father's family took from the scene seemed to justify their conviction that life was an unremitting, relentless struggle, beset by unpredictable tragedy, ending only in death.

It didn't matter whether or not I had ever eaten the apple. The rectitude of my great-grandmother walked me over the gravel of the Boston Navy Yard. And it seems likely that the one thing that is left to me, whether I will it or not, is the Kaiser frame.

GRANDFATHER BENTZ always went to early mass, to sit with his fellow members of the St. Joseph Society and to take communion with them. To Grandmother, whose parents were Irish, Sunday morning mass was many things, not the least of which was the opportunity to wear her new hat and her voile gloves and her Sunday dress of watered silk, and to chat with her friends afterward on the church steps. She would leave home in a last-minute flurry of instructions and violet cologne. "Yes, yes," Grandfather would say to her as he stood at the door of the frame house on Cecil Street, in Springfield, to bid her good-bye. Yes, he would watch the roast in the oven, he would take a look at the catch on the back screen door, he would go out to see the dropsical hen, hiding gloomily in the chicken house. "Yes, yes." And his gentle voice would be filled with patience, a thin glaze over the feeling of exasperation he had lived with for so long that it had become one of the conditions of life, like rain, or age itself. "My wife, Cecilia," as Grandfather called her, was a volatile, still beautiful woman, worthy of his patience and devotion. She had borne him six children, whom he loved, but she *did* talk a great deal.

When Grandmother had gone to mass, Grandfather would remove the jacket of his dark worsted Sunday suit with deliberation and a sense of satisfaction and anticipation that even I could feel. He would unhook his celluloid collar and roll his shirt sleeves to the elbows carefully. Then he would proceed to the kitchen, where the copper kettle stood at the back of the gas range, and where the old pump emptied into the scrubbed zinc sink.

Grandfather was a short, stocky man with high color, a Roman nose, a clipped moustache, clear blue eyes, and a modest gravity of manner. He was a tinner by trade, and he was also a merchant in hardware with a partner who was a friend of his youth. Although he was born in Ohio, in a neat, small brick house beside the Scioto River in Chillicothe, and although his father had died when he was a small boy, the racial pattern of his Alsatian-French ancestry had persisted in him, as much a part of his being as the migratory instinct is of a bird's.

Beyond the windows, beyond the shutters folded back to let in the morning light, the grapes ripened on the arbors that covered the brick terrace and the long, sloping walk that led to the chicken house. There, out in the sunlight, was Grandfather's domain.

While he meticulously peeled the chilled boiled potatoes and sliced them thick, ready to drop into the hot bacon fat in the iron skillet on the range, I would sit on a small bench at the window, a bench he had made for me, and look out at his little kingdom. The soft red bricks of the terrace and walk had been laid in the familiar arrow design. The walking surface rolled gently. There were treacherous spots, slippery with moss, hidden by the dappled shadows of the heavy green leaves of the grapevines, in the cool green tunnel of the walk. Two varieties of grapes ripened in the sunlight above. There were blue Concords, and there were light Catawbas, like milk-glass marbles flushed with pink. The white wine and the red that Grandfather pressed each year from these grapes mellowed in old green bottles on racks in the earthen cellar under our feet.

Sometimes I think that food, any food, never tastes so delicious as it did when one was a child. When I remember with what pleasure I shared Sunday morning breakfasts with Grandfather Bentz, it astonishes me, since at those breakfasts we had wieners and fried potatoes. They were called wieners, or wienerwurst, in Springfield, although they were identical in appearance with what are now called "frankfurters," "frankfurts," or "franks." Only the casing was tougher. Grandmother was convinced that this casing was actually the intestines of hogs, and she advised me not to eat it. She once showed me how to split the hot wiener, bursting with steam from the boiling pot, and peel away the casing with a fork. Grandfather never bothered about this. At these breakfasts, which he delayed until Grandmother had gone to eleven o'clock mass at St. Raphael's, we ate the wieners, casings and all, in silent pleasure, dipping the solid chunks in generous amounts of a strong mustard made by a neighbor, Mr. Woebber.

Food and wine were the rightful pleasures of life for Grandfather, the gifts of God, to be enjoyed with grave but unqualified delight. Perhaps it is for that reason that I remember those Sunday morning breakfasts with such pleasure, with the two of us alone in the agreeable early heat of a summer day, silent for the most part, but comfortably silent, in a house temporarily free of women, each of us knowing his place, an old man and a boy in whom the same blood flowed.

The climate of conflict in which parents live—that balanced tension present in any successful marriage—is generally perceived by children, but they are not always aware of the atmosphere in which their grandparents live. Not every child sees his grandparents often enough, or long enough at any one time, to realize that in marriage they, too, set up what might be called a magnetic field in which they stand as opposing polar forces. During my first visits with my Bentz grandparents, which were brief, they seemed more like companions than lovers, often merely polite or indifferent to each other. Their private conversations did not flare up suddenly, alarmingly, or unpredictably into quarreling as the conversations of my parents sometimes did. But that summer with them, I heard them quarrel for the first time.

The nature of the quarrel was not clearly understood by me at the time. I did not try to comprehend it because only the fact of the quarrel itself had interest for me. It gave me a peculiar sense of apprehension, as if my existence were threatened; as if, were the quarrel not settled, I should cease to be, canceled out in some way by the failure of their love. I slept upstairs in the back bedroom, over the kitchen, with a window looking down on the grapevine-covered terrace and a window facing east on an alley. There was a hole in the floor beside the bed, a round hole lined with metal, meant to serve in the wintertime as a source of warmth, the heat rising from the kitchen range below. On those nights when I heard Grandmother speaking with passion in the kitchen, I would slip out of bed and lie on the floor with my face above the hole, held slightly to one side of it, so that if they chanced to look up they would not see me.

One night, after I had been sent up to bed, Grandmother, I could see, was busy at the stove and the sink, and Grandfather, as was his custom, was shaving in front of the mirror that hung on the wall beside the sink. He shaved at night for the following day, and he did it deliberately, as he did all things. He stropped his straight razor thoroughly, testing the water in the tin basin as he added more from the kettle, lathering his shaving brush with absorption. Grandmother talked as she moved about. I could not hear her distinctly; she was aware that I might not be asleep or that I might waken, and if sometimes in the heat of the discussion she forgot and let her voice rise, Grandfather would admonish her silently, with a forefinger pointed toward the ceiling. That night I heard the name of my aunt Ella mentioned repeatedly—my headstrong, impetuous aunt, who had rushed into an unacceptable marriage. Tom, her husband, was an ex-cavalryman, a bluff, red-faced giant who awed me to speechlessness. He was not a Roman Catholic. He had married Aunt Ella in a civil ceremony, which in the eyes of Grandmother, and of Monsignor Flaherty, was no marriage at all. Grandmother longed to save Aunt Ella from her life of sin while there was still time, before any children came. "If you would speak to her, Will," Grandmother said. "You know how stubborn she is. And how proud. Just go to her and bring her home."

"She has made her choice," Grandfather said, his gentle voice firm, his hand steady with the razor on his cheek. "She must love him, or she would come home to us."

"But, Will!" Grandmother protested, holding the copper kettle in her hand, her soft cheeks pink, her beautiful hair curled in wisps about her face by the heat of the stove. "She is your daughter!"

"We must not interfere," Grandfather said. "She is a child no longer."

Grandmother was very angry. Still holding the kettle, she went up close to Grandfather and spoke to him with fury. "That's your way," she said. "Just stand there! Do nothing!"

Grandfather's expression did not change. He put his razor down carefully, wiped the lather from his face, and left the kitchen without a word. Grandmother stood still for a moment. Then she put the kettle on the range, covered her face with her apron, and burst into tears.

The next morning, I awoke to the sound of Grandmother's laughter. It was Saturday. Mr. Caspar, the Jewel Tea man, had come. I could hear his voice in the kitchen, and I jumped from bed and ran to the east window to see his hooded wagon in the alley below. When Mr. Caspar left the wagon to come into the kitchen, bringing his metal basket with boxes of tea and allspice and cloves and cinnamon, he heaved a lead weight out, fixed to a chain, to keep the old roan mare from straying. I saw her down there now, her head straining against the weight, her ancient yellow teeth bared, as she tried to reach the coarse grass that grew along the edges of the alley. I threw on my clothes and ran down to help her by pulling the grass and holding it up for her to eat.

As I ran out the door I could see Grandfather out in back, cleaning the chicken house, his customary Saturday morning chore. After that, he would scrub the interior of the outhouse. Grandfather's outhouse was the most superior outhouse I had ever seen, with its clean pine boards and generally with a wasp, sleepy and vexed, circling lazily overhead in the warm air that was redolent of lime. Best of all, the inside was papered with large posters advertising the Barnum & Bailey circus, decorations that Grandmother suffered in silent disapproval. On the posters, beautiful ladies with faces of pink wax balanced on high wires, or stood on tiptoe on white horses in full gallop. The ladies were wearing purple tights drawn up over full thighs to impossibly small waists, and balancing themselves with Japanese parasols that they carried over their mountainous, glossy hair.

After Mr. Caspar had gone, we had breakfast. Then, possibly forgetful of the tension of the night before, or wishing to avoid more of it, I persuaded Grandmother to invite to lunch a neighbor girl named Mary Lou. Mary Lou and I had sworn secret and undying devotion to each other earlier in the summer, in a ceremony in which we touched tongues. Our days were filled with the carrying out of great dares and challenges, climbing trees, running along the tops of walls. When forced to sit still, we whispered and giggled.

Grandmother's cuisine, aside from her excellent baking, was centered on the potato, as befitted her Irish ancestry. She even said the word "potato" differently from the way I have ever heard anyone else say it, softening the consonants lovingly, and as she went about her work, she often sang about the potato, her voice rich with the heritage of County Cork. "Oh, the praties grow so small, we can eat them, skins and all," she sang, and it was not until years later that I knew the song had a name and a history, that it was the song of the Irish potato famine, and not simply a tune she had composed to entertain herself and me. Indeed, we did eat our praties skins and all, cut open on a plate, bathed in melted butter, and sprinkled liberally with salt and some of the pepper from Mr. Caspar's wagon.

On this particular day, we ate our praties in silence, sitting at the large, round kitchen table, which was covered with a round white cloth that fell over one's knees. With the boiled potatoes we had steamed fresh beet tops, dressed with chopped onion and bacon. Grandfather ate his food without raising his eyes from his plate. Mary Lou and I giggled and dawdled until Grandmother, unable to bear the situation any longer, sprang up from the table and ran outside. There she unaccountably slammed to all the shutters of the kitchen windows, imprisoning us in a dim green light, as if we were lunching at the bottom of the sea. Grandfather ate on methodically while Grandmother came back in and ran upstairs without a word and changed into her street clothes. When she came down again, wearing her hat and carrying her bag and gloves, she looked in on us briefly.

"I will go for her myself," she said to Grandfather, either forgetting that Mary Lou and I were there or not caring. Then she left swiftly by the front door, slamming the screen behind her.

After lunch, Mary Lou went home somewhat subdued, and I felt a need to stay close to Grandfather. We cleared the table and washed the dishes, and then he set about preparing the boiled beef for dinner, which he quite often did on a Saturday. While Grandmother sometimes ate merely to keep going, Grandfather loved food and the preparation of food for its own sake. Boiled beef was one of his favorite dishes. The preparation began with a shin of beef, the meat cut away from the bone. Meat and bone were simmered together slowly for hours, with finely chopped onion and a bit of bay leaf or dried celery leaf and three or four peppercorns. Salt, as any cook knows, was not added until later, to avoid toughening the meat.

At dinnertime, shallow soup plates would be set out on dinner plates on the tablecloth, along with a knife and fork and spoon. Clear, hot broth, from which the fat had been skimmed, was then ladled into the soup plates, and into it went a big helping of boiled beef. Horseradish was served, too, a spoonful being put on the wide, sloping rim of the soup plate. Watching Grandfather, I would eat as he ate, cutting a portion of beef, dipping it into the horseradish, then placing the beef in the soup spoon and submerging it in the broth, so that simultaneously one had beef, broth, and horseradish. And on crusty slices of fresh bread we would spread the rich marrow from the bone.

While the beef simmered, Grandfather and I went out to weed the kitchen garden. This garden was located on the east side of the grape arbor and the brick walk that led to the chicken house, so that it would receive the morning sun. It was a tidy garden, each vegetable bed neat within its low margins of lichen-covered limestone. There were lettuces—Black Simpson and a heading variety I cannot identify; pole beans, every tendril neatly tied up with a torn strip of soft old linen; beets, grown for their tops as well as their roots; and long rows of green onions, and of radishes, red where they burst from the ground and white beneath. The soil had been enriched with chicken droppings. Sometimes, at night, I would go down through the garden to say good night to the roosters and hens, decorously asleep on their perches in the low chicken house.

We had finished weeding the garden and were resting in the iron lawn chairs on the west side of the grape arbor, in the cool late afternoon shade of the plum tree, when Grandmother returned. She came in the front door, walked through the house, and stood at the back screen door and called. Her voice was low, and sounded weary, I thought. "Will," she said.

Grandfather got up without a word and went in to her. I followed, as if I were attached to him, to them, to their conflict, by some invisible membrane. I dared not follow him into the dining room, where Grandmother had gone and was waiting, probably sitting on the small horsehair sofa in the corner by the bay window. I stood in the kitchen uncertainly.

Grandmother was crying softly, and at last I heard her speak. "You were right, Will," she said. "I should not have tried to interfere." There was a pause then, filled with her weeping. "She loves him, Will," Grandmother went on. "They quarrel, but she loves him. I must resign myself to that."

Silence followed, and when Grandfather finally spoke, it was in his gentle way. "There now, Cecilia," he said. "Yes, yes. Yes, yes."

The boiled beef had an unusually festive air about it that evening at dinnertime. Grandfather served it with the gravity and the deference it deserved, and we ate in the kitchen with the shutters open on the twilight, and the fireflies, and the crickets. While we ate, a man came up the alley noiselessly on his bicycle to light the Welsbach mantle of the gas lamp on the corner. Grandmother entertained us with twice-told tales of her childhood in Fayette County, Ohio. She was born in a log house—some miles out of Washington Court House, the county seat—where her father's rifle and his bullet molds hung over the huge fireplace with a fire that was never extinguished, and where at night she slept on a trundle bed, pulled out from under the bed of her parents. She laughed until the tears came, remembering what a tomboy she had been, an only girl brought up with brothers, and how they had all plagued poor old Mr. Adams, the schoolmaster, dead these many years now, by playing a game called "Johnny-Over," in which during lunch and recess periods they divided into two teams and rolled a ball back and forth over the peaked roof of the one-room schoolhouse while Mr. Adams sat inside at his desk. Finally, almost driven to distraction by the noise, he would dash out, ringing his brass handbell wildly for silence, and, delighted at their success, the children would run for cover in the woods.

These stories, which had the same reality for me as the fairy tales I had read in Hans Christian Andersen, seemed to amuse Grandfather, too, from the look on his face. His only verbal contribution at the dinner table, however, was the saying of grace, the familiar, unchanging prayer that began, "Bless us, O Lord, and these Thy gifts, which we are about to receive from Thy Bounty. . . ." Sitting between them, secure in their renewed devotion, I had for the first time a feeling about their relationship that it would take me many years to understand fully—that separately Grandmother's gaiety, Grandfather's quiet strength meant nothing, and might never have existed, the gaiety and the strength being qualities that flowered only in opposition to each other.

After dinner, Grandfather, with obvious relish, went to the pantry for the large market basket, and while Grandmother cleared the table and washed the dishes, Grandfather and I walked into the center of town to do the weekly shopping. Each Saturday, from the rich bottomland of the valley, farmers brought in their produce in open wagons to the plaza, or esplanade, and wheeled the wagons into places that had become theirs by custom. This was the same market that Great-grandmother Kaiser had brought her vegetables to so many years ago, before she started a business through a private jobber. Here, under flaring gaslights, Grandfather selected the vegetables he did not grow in his own garden—scrubbed potatoes gleaming in mounds on the open tailgates of the wagons; cooking onions, red and yellow; green corn, grown in the earth where the Shawnee Indians had raised their corn. The farmer, and often his wife, stood nearby the wagon, sometimes wearing the hat and the bonnet of the Plain People. And behind them, dressed carcasses of beef hung on hooks along with freshly slaughtered pigs, and chickens and geese, plucked and pale.

Grandfather shopped slowly, undisturbed by the clamor and the excitement, the Saturday night air of carnival. He had a knowing eye, a sense of satisfaction in the proper contour or texture or shape of each potato or onion or ear of corn. Were they not, after all, gifts of the bounty of God, created to sustain us? And when we finally left the marketplace, there were delicacies in the basket, too—a link or two of liverwurst, a wedge of cheese, a half peck of hickory nuts saved from winter stores, to be cracked with a tack hammer on the bottom of the flatiron at home and used for cakes or for that wonderful confection of powdered sugar, butter, and cream known as sea foam.

Walking home under the heavy leaves of the maple trees, going down Limestone Street and over Madison Avenue to Woodlawn, I experienced an unaccountable feeling of sadness and loneliness. An owl hooted above us, a train mourned in the distance, and I slipped my hand into Grandfather's hand for comfort.

I was homesick.

# 3

IT IS SOMEHOW DIFFICULT to realize that one's parents were very young once themselves. My mother was nineteen, and my father twenty-one when they married. They must have been thought by their parents to be children still themselves. My mother was beautiful, in the most fortunate of ways, by the standards of beauty of her time. She wore her hair piled high over her forehead in a fashionable pompadour, and she had unconsciously the regal air of her mother, and the dignity of her father, and a smiling serenity. Yet there was a kind of life-wonder about her, like that of a child thrust into a roomful of strangers.

With our parents there are always areas of mystery. We are too much a part of them, or they of us, to see them objectively. There was a quality of vulnerability about my mother that always puzzled me. She would seem to have everything that a woman of her interests might want. She was beautiful, she was gentle, she had a knowledge of the arts of housekeeping; she moved in an aura of goodness and simplicity that brought to her any friend she might seek.

It is necessary to say that her vulnerability was not a product of my parents' marriage. She brought it with her. Her family life on Cecil Street was warm and close and filled with love, open to the world, for her mother, Grandmother Bentz, as well as being a volatile and impetuous woman, was a wellspring of comfort to whom anyone could turn. She was never too busy to

30

answer an appeal for help, and would even go with a basket of food to a house where there was a contagious disease, on which occasions she fortified herself in advance by eating a rasher of bacon, confident that the animal fat, in coating the membranes of her throat, would prevent the passage of germs. No, they lived in the present on Cecil Street, with positive actions and a spontaneous generosity of spirit. They lived there under the protective benevolence of God, which had failed only once, when Marie, the youngest daughter, had died. Was that the source of the vulnerability in my mother?

As the oldest daughter, with her mother upstairs, deep in the "brain fever" of her grief, from which at first not even Father Sidley could rouse her, Mother had had to take charge. That terrible winter remained forever in her memory. It was a long, gray day in which hope had died, a day that began before dawn; getting up to go to mass at St. Raphael's before the chores of the day had begun, so that she might pray for her mother, and for the soul of the little lost Marie. She always remembered the bitter cold of that winter, of running along the gray and silent streets with the frozen footprints of the previous day breaking under her hurrying feet, the plume of her breath rising above the collar of her coat, which she had drawn across her mouth and nose to keep away the fearful cold. When she crossed the bridge on Limestone Street the Mad River below was choked with ice, but a sense of relief came to her because now she could see the steeple of St. Raphael's, with the cross her father had placed there gleaming in the cold sky. Perhaps it was that winter which had struck the flaw in her from which she never quite recovered, which gave her that sense of loss and of the past, as if she were forever trying to recapture the sun and the gaiety of the day before Marie died, turning back to protest that it could not be so, refusing to face the present with its intolerable reality, Marie dead, her mother defeated, and the care of the small children and her father all suddenly up to her.

But why did she marry my father? She had many beaux, being a beautiful woman, born to marriage and motherhood, with a figure neither thin nor plump but softly rounded everywhere, with beautiful hands and arms and small, graceful feet, her only vanity.

31

On the other hand, there was no uncertainty or vulnerability in my father. For him the past did not exist. He seemed never to have been a boy. He never spoke of his boyhood. I knew he had gone to the German school in the parish of St. Bernard, where he was instructed by nuns, and found himself, at least in the early years, in the equivocal position of speaking German in school and English at home. German had ceased to be the language of the family when they stepped on American soil. The Plagemanns lived outward, as I had seen, outside of themselves and of houses. The present was almost as elusive for them as for my mother, but if my mother was the past, then it might almost be said that my father was the future.

I suppose it was this my mother saw in him; he called to that need in her. His step in the hall would rouse her. His hand would lead her to a warm and familiar world.

My father was a fair-haired youth, in the old tradition. The world was his oyster. He was not handsome, but he was good-looking. He had a straight nose, a good mouth, a slender, Teutonic face, and fine, bold eyes. In their wedding picture, taken of the heads and shoulders only, my parents turn their eyes to the right to look at a point in the middle distance. My mother, in her high lace collar and pearls, is smiling and serene, but there is a natural aggression in my father's face, an unblinking intensity. What did it matter if he was born of poor but humble parents on the wrong side of town, on the wrong side of the railroad tracks? What did it matter if he had married slightly above himself, a beauty, Elizabeth Bentz of Cecil Street? It was all as it should be, a play with familiar roles, a story already written—the poor but ambitious boy, the pretty girl, together in an age of miracles, where life was a fairy tale. And it was. It was. For this was Ohio at the turn of the century, and there are libraries of practical testimony to bear me witness.

What marvels had begun or had developed there, which Ohio had given the whole world, marvels that today we take so much for granted that it is impossible to imagine life without them. The electric light bulb, for example: Thomas Edison and Charles Brush, who invented the arc light, were both Ohioans; the public square at Cleveland was the first open space in the world to be illuminated at night by electricity. The Wright brothers were Ohioans; the plane that flew at Kitty Hawk had been thought out first in Ohio. The cash register was an Ohio invention. If we stopped right there, we would seem to have a synthesis of the elements of our society: the airplane, electric power, and the cash register. But even so, these things were only a part of Ohio's contribution to the world from that period; the list is endless: early motorcars, the first rubber tire, the "self-starter," even what might be called the world's first "machined" food, rolled oats, the breakfast cereal. But how appropriate indeed is the last example, for the sowing, cultivating, and reaping of the world's grain was revolutionized by machinery invented or perfected right there in Springfield. My father had served his apprenticeship in the International Harvester Company.

With the state like a great Pandora's box, spilling out treasures in prodigality to enrich not only the world but the men who made them, the self-starter of Charles Kettering seems to be the perfect example of its kind, not only in itself, but of the men of the time. It was a generation of self-starters. Grandmother Plagemann always said laughingly of my father that he would spend more time in trying to figure out how to do a given job by some mechanical way than if he had done it by hand. This is a description of his kind, of a whole generation of men.

They were not always easy or pleasant to live with, these dedicated and obsessed men like my father. He seemed never to be aware of his surroundings, or rooms, and their furnishings. His mind was somewhere else. But we felt secure in his love, the four of us. He was "Daddy" to all of us all his life. He demonstrated his affection for us, and pride in us in various ways, not the least of which were in words. But when we were children he never had time for us. He never played games with us. My older sister and I recalled, with astonishment, when we were grown that there had never been a ball in our house. Any ball of any kind. No baseball, no football, no basketball, volley ball, soccer ball, bowling ball, golf ball, not even a Ping-Pong ball. There were no guns either—play guns or real guns. We were not even allowed to point our fingers at each other and go "bang-bang!" We did not notice the absence of ball or gun. It bears out the principle of what you don't have, you don't miss.

There was always a workshop wherever we lived, in a barn in the back, in the cellar, or in a shed attached to the garage. The shop was a miniature machine shop, a place of untidy creativity, where something that did not exist before was meant to be constructed. My father's mind was filled with cogs and wheels and schemes, with dreams of glory from the patent office. Someday he would create a device, a machine that had not existed before, that would bring us fame and fortune. Ohio was filled with men like him, busy in their barn or woodshed, men like James Ritty, lost in the absurd complications of his ridiculous cash register, men driven a little mad by the wonderful possibilities of machines. My father would laugh until tears stood in his eyes, describing for example the poor soul who had come to him with the hopeless jumble of an early typewriter. Think of all the things not yet invented! The areas not yet understood! The problem of friction, not yet mastered, and that of inertia. The idea of perpetual motion, a perpetual motion machine, was for these men in some ways what the dream of the Holy Grail had been for men of the past, glowing in the distance, always just a little out of reach, but surely to be gained in the end by fasting and meditation, and the lonely, all-night vigil in the little workshop.

Meanwhile, we children were supposed to entertain ourselves. "There are four of you," my father would say reasonably. "Surely you can find something to entertain yourselves."

The principal advantage of having young parents is that they are young with you. My mother helped us entertain ourselves, and she had adventures and fun with us. It was she who taught us how to dry cornsilk in the sun, and roll it in brown wrapping paper to make cigarettes, which she smoked with us, sitting on the back-porch steps. She taught us how to roast potatoes in the ashes of a fire, and I see her beautiful white teeth now, revealed in laughter, blackened with the soot of the burned potatoes we were eating. She taught us how to make angels on a snowbank. She pushed us in the rope swing under the cherry tree, to our cries of "Higher!" and "Higher!"; and she led us each spring through the fields in the search for wild strawberries. She helped us build little huts of straw in the fields, and she would crawl inside to lie with us, just as a part of each Christmas was the ritual of crawling back under the Christmas tree, to lie there and look up through the branches at the lights.

And there was reading. Reading became a passion for all four of us children. On Saturday morning, when it came time to do household chores, Mother would say to us, "Bring me whatever you are reading, and I will hold it for you until the chores are finished."

My Saturday chore was scrubbing the bathroom. Later, in navy boot camp, when I drew the dreaded latrine duty, it seemed to me the most natural thing in the world.

# 4

BY THE TIME I was born on July 27, 1913, my parents had moved into a house, from the cramped, rented rooms they had lived in after they were married. This was a new house, in a "new development," which suited their young ambitions. I was the last child of theirs to be born at home. Those who followed—my younger sister and brother—were born in the hospital. It was as if I stood at the end of one age and the beginning of another, and indeed this can be clearly seen in a childhood picture, for my older sister, Coletta, named for my mother's music teacher, and I were the last to be photographed in the old-fashioned way, formally, in a photographer's studio. My sister sits with her small feet together, her hands demurely folded in her lap, in a child's Queen Anne chair. I—in the straight, starched dress then still worn by small boys, with a wide belt just above the knees—stand beside her, holding my father's silver cigarette case, which he had given me to keep me quiet while the picture was taken. We look out, it seems to me, my sister and I, from the last shadow of the nineteenth century, fallen across the threshold of the new century, and in my childhood memories I seem to hear the echoes of that quiet age, dying away.

There was gaiety, though, in those early days for my parents—gaiety in themselves and in that innocent world before the wars when they were so very young. When I was old enough to walk I was allowed to follow a path through the field to meet my father when he came home from work in the late afternoon. I would walk this path to the end and stand on the corner to watch for my father on his bicycle. He would put me up on the handlebars when he reached me, and wheel me home, whistling or singing "K-K-K-Katy," or "Down by the Old Mill Stream," or "I'll Take You Home Again, Kathleen," a sentimental favorite of his, out of deference to the Irish blood in his young bride.

In the early evening, after the supper dishes had been washed, my sister and I would sit on the steps of the front porch while our parents put on their roller skates and skated up and down the center of the new macadam-paved street, along with their neighbors, skating as they did on ice skates in the winter, two by two, with crossed arms, and singing as they swept gracefully along.

There was grace in my parents. They loved to dance. Their courtship had been a period of dancing; that summer they had even won a silver cup in a contest for the waltz, a happy presage for any marriage. They continued to dance after they were married, taking us with them to summer dance pavilions, where we sat at the edge of the dance floor, as we had sat on the porch steps, watching them, and I see them now with delight as they were then, younger than I knew. They danced in the wonderful manner of their time, facing each other but slightly side by side, my father's long and graceful steps carrying them across the floor, with my mother's small and beautiful feet flashing in shorter steps beside. They were intent and proud, smiling, with heads held high, invincible; the eldest son, the eldest daughter of their families, in a new world, a new century, a new land.

I was between five and six years old when the opportunity came for my father to go to Cleveland to the Warner and Swasey company, manufacturers of machine tools and precision instruments. It was an opportunity he sought; he was ambitious, he longed for wider horizons. He also argued, in defense, that Springfield, in his words, would "never amount to anything." The city fathers were too reactionary. They resisted change. They discouraged new industries. He knew of specific instances, he would say ominously, where new factories had gone to other towns. He also wanted a scene of greater opportunity for his children, and furthermore he wanted them to grow up away from the conflicts of diverse family influences.

These arguments and persuasions must have been rehearsed and presented many times because my mother did not want to leave Springfield. It was the past again, drawing away from the future. How could my mother bring herself to leave her family? How could she live away from this warm complex of relationships, the cousins, and the aunts and the uncles? Here among these people was her life; in this milieu like a plum pudding of emotions, laughter and tears were always close together, each day was a long conversation, a reminiscent tale spun across to the golden past. She had never expected that in marriage it would be required of her to leave her home and her life.

And so at first my father went to his new job in Cleveland alone. He would see how it went. He would see if he liked the job, if he was successful there. It must have been an exciting moment for him, this ambitious young man from a small town, with the world opening in front of him. And he was confident; he was always confident, sometimes more than circumstances would seem to warrant, but confidence was a part of his nature. He knew he could not fail, because he was prepared for this step. He was no tyro. His many long years of apprenticeship were completed. He was a tool- and diemaker, with some knowledge of time study, and even some experience at supervision.

Exciting as this moment was for him, it must have seemed rather like the end of the world, I imagine, for my mother.

While my father was away we did not move to Grandmother's house because now there were four children, too many of us to be taken in. We stayed in our house with its mission oak furniture and china lamps with shades of pongee, but we gave ourselves to long visits and Sunday dinners at Grandmother's, to picnics and family gatherings. When my father came home, every other weekend or so, we would be waiting for him, scrubbed and freshly dressed, ranged in a line along the top step of the porch. I remember our sense of shyness with him at first. This laughing, hearty man seemed almost a stranger. But by bedtime our shyness would vanish, and he would have to hold each of us in turn in the walnut rocker while he sang "In the Shade of the Old Apple Tree."

It was not long before we moved to Cleveland. My mother accepted the inevitable with a final grace. After all, this move, as her friends and even her sisters pointed out, would be something of an adventure. They envied her her opportunity. But my mother never really conquered her loneliness and sense of loss. In later years when she realized and admitted to herself that she could not, in a symbolical sense, go home again since the new life had changed her, she felt, I believe, even more isolated, for what tradition had she to take with her in her departure from her home, what household gods were there to pack with the mission chairs? The sense of the past was her sole possession; and this was almost too fragile to be moved, and would scarcely exist at all when removed from the scene of that past; so my mother was, I think, ultimately and finally alone.

We moved at first into a rented house on what was called the West Side of Cleveland, a house on a city street where the houses stood closely together behind small, well-tended lawns, under a row of shade trees. The venture did not go well. Everything was too alien, too crowded, and yet, at the same time, too exposed. The neighbors could be heard if they raised their voices, just as the flushing of a toilet could be heard in the house next door. There was not the sense of privacy of a small town, yet there was a greater sense of loneliness, arising from the necessary protective indifference of one city neighbor for another. The First World War was in its fourth year, dragging on, never, it seemed, to end. And then the great influenza epidemic broke out, as devastating as any plague of the Middle Ages, decimating the population, closing the schools and theaters and public buildings. One by one we children fell ill. To better care for us our mother put us all in the same room, the beds ranged along the wall as in the ward of a hospital. Then Mother fell ill. My father, unable to find anyone to care for us, stayed at home, managing as well as he could until his company found a nurse to free him for his job. But at the end of the first day, when my father came home from work, the house was silent. He found the nurse, unconscious, in the empty bathtub, a victim of the epidemic; she had toppled into the tub when she went to draw a bath.

Grandmother Bentz was summoned. She came, bringing with her the comforting assurance of much experience in such situations, and carrying her valise and two freshly killed chickens. She never forgot, she liked to tell us, the scene that greeted her on her arrival, of standing in the bedroom doorway and seeing all of us ranged in a row. She would laugh telling this, her laughter prompted by the memory of my first remark to her. "If Adam and Eve hadn't eaten that apple," I had explained, looking up at her, "we wouldn't be here in bed." (My exposure to a family book, *The Bible in Pictures,* must be responsible for that remark.)

In spite of Adam and Eve, we recovered. It was the good chicken broth, Grandmother Bentz always said and she would laugh again, remembering the look of disbelief on my father's face when they had at last tried to eat the chickens which had produced so much broth.

The war, suddenly, unbelievably, came to its conclusion. We sat on the steps of the Civil War Monument in the public square in Cleveland to watch the victory parade, too young or too excited to reflect on the irony of the situation, with torn bronze battle flags above us, with bronze horses forever rearing above bronze soldiers forever dying, while before us passed tanks, and doughboys in puttees on parade. The streets were filled with shouting, hysterical people; there was an ugly cartoon of a bleeding, vanquished Kaiser (or was it the god of war?) on the front page of the newspaper, and at home our neighbors brought their Victrola out to the front porch to play ragtime tunes, and I have a blurred and astonished memory of people kissing, of strangers coming to our porch, and our parents holding them, kissing them, and weeping.

We were ready for a new beginning. My father decided we must leave the city. We must find a place to live where we would have privacy, and room to move about in. He approached this problem in his own practical, imaginative way. He went to a mortgage loan bank. He reasoned that the bank might have what he called a "problem" house on its hands which might be made available to him for his limited funds. His reasoning was justified; he found us a house perfect for our purposes.

THE HOUSE WAS in Euclid Village, some twenty miles northeast of Cleveland, slightly inland from Lake Erie. It was several years before I read Chekhov's *The Cherry Orchard,* but when I did I knew at once that the house in Euclid Village was the house of Chekhov's play, wherein a drama of equal, if dissimilar, tragedy had been played out, even if we did not know that at the time.

It was a comfortable, sprawling frame house, not quite a country house, but not quite a farmhouse, either. Great, venerable cherry trees shaded the veranda that ran along the front and one side of the house, bearing in season the species known as oxheart—firm, sweet cherries, dark as blood in color, with an indentation along one side that made them resemble the oxheart for which they were named. The house was pleasantly beige, which seemed its own complexion, as if it had never known or needed paint. In back of the house was a barn. Untilled fields stretched away into grassy meadows on all sides.

The house seemed ours from the moment we saw it, but we had to remain still and listen while the conditions of agreement we must accept if we were to live there were explained to us by a representative of the bank. For the modest rent my father proposed he would be expected to maintain the house and repair it at his own expense and not ask for such things as paint or roofing. That was the first condition. There was another: There were two rooms in the house, locked, that we were not to occupy or enter. One room was upstairs, and one was downstairs.

Since there were more than enough rooms in the house for us, this condition was also acceptable to my father, and for us children, it lent an added touch of excitement and intrigue, as if we were about to live in Bluebeard's castle, although I am not certain how my mother felt about it.

On that day we also had our first and only encounter with the former lady of the house, who had come with the representative from the bank to meet us. She so overwhelmed us that we found ourselves unable to speak. To begin with, she was foreign, but not foreign in a way that would be familiar to us, as an immigrant was foreign. She was an aristocrat, a great lady, of a kind we had never known. She spoke flawless English in a beautifully accented voice. She was highly distraught on that day, but she never lost for even a moment her natural manner of authority and elegance. She wore a lavender, fitted suit and a brimmed hat with a veil over her face, that she kept raising and lowering and adjusting as she talked. She seemed always on the verge of tears, but she was so remote from our experience that we could not identify with her distress. Her husband had died suddenly. That much my father had known, from the bank. She had a son. He was away in the West somewhere, at a boarding school. She would go to be near him, for what could she do alone? Her hands twisted. The mourning veil was raised and lowered. A sort of divine fury seemed to possess her. She needed time to think. To overcome her grief. To make up her mind what to do. We must have been acceptable to her because she shook hands with my mother and father, saying that it was good of us to consent to take care of her house and to allow her things to remain until she could decide what to do.

She sat down for a moment on an empty packing case in the room where we stood. She looked about. She was Madame Ranevsky, whom I would later see and recognize, and I could almost hear her then, saying, "It's as though I'd never really seen these walls, these ceilings before, and now I look at them eagerly, with such tender love."

Then she stood and adjusted her veil again and was gone, with the man from the bank. We were to know more about her later, but for the present the house was ours.

The locked room downstairs was a sitting room or drawing room, and Mother hung curtains over the glass doors that led into it, to prevent our peering into the shaded darkness to try to see what was there. There was another sitting room downstairs, and into this the furniture was moved that had come from our house in Springfield. There were the two pieces my father had made before he was married—a long settee and an armchair, in mission style, from quarter-sawed oak. The seat of the settee, called a davenport, as well as the seat of the armchair, was upholstered in leather. These pieces of furniture were surprisingly comfortable. There was a reading lamp on a table beside the armchair. In this room was also the walnut rocking chair in which my father held us children in turn and rocked and sang to us before we went to bed.

There was a dining room, furnished with our round table and straight-backed chairs, that also served as an academy of learning, for it was there at dinner that our father tested and extended our limits of knowledge by the Socratic method of deductive question-and-answer, concluded by a Delphic pronouncement. Our Socrates was not infallible and implanted in our minds at that time was some measure of persistent folly, along with whatever native wisdom he possessed. ("Hard work never killed anybody." "Don't do anything for money alone, but go where money is." "Save money on anything you can, but always wear shoes that fit.")

It was a comfortable house, easy to live in. We were to grow accustomed to the locked rooms, the curtained room on the first floor, the locked bedroom door upstairs, where we would often try to peep through the keyhole. Nonetheless, a sense of something mysterious and unexplained persisted, like the footsteps that used to mount the three low wooden steps on the veranda outside on certain nights and walk the length of the veranda, and then stop. How many times my father would grow impatient with himself when, reading the evening paper or studying one of his technical books from the International Correspondence School, he would forget and absently go to the door to open it, and find no one there.

"These old floorboards creak so when the night air cools down," he would say.

Here in this house began the lifelong conflict in which my father was involved, between the need of providing for a growing family, and his own need, equally important, to fulfill himself in his work. As with so many conflicts, it was never fully resolved, and sometimes other conflicts intervened to further confuse the basic issue. But, as my father would have said, a man's life is not easy.

Meanwhile, he was making his own plans. He was restless. He really did not like to work for another man. He wanted to be on his own. After all, the great lure of the house in Euclid Village was the sound and spacious barn behind it, an ideal place for a workshop. Here he could experiment and develop the mechanical inventions that would bring us fame and fortune. He had no capital, and he would need subsidy of some kind, so he would open an automobile repair shop to bring in a little steady income.

There was no automobile repair shop for miles in either direction, and now there were more cars on the road. It was a favorite Sunday pastime with us children to sit on the front steps, and count the cars, and try to identify them as they went by.

This repair shop project was discussed with Mother, and it met with her approval. She would no longer be alone all day, with responsibility for the children. My father would be in the barn in case of any emergency in this lonely new environment. He would be able to come into the house for lunch, and give some sense of order to the day. There would be activity around. People would be coming and going in the repair shop.

My father painted a large sign, black on white, and put it

up beside the driveway. It read: PERPETUAL AUTO SERVICE. To celebrate the occasion, Mother packed a picnic supper to take to the park.

Although it was begun with such high hopes, the PERPETUAL AUTO SERVICE seemed doomed from the start, although my father persisted in it, so great was his desire to be on his own, almost to penury. We children used to bring optimistic reports from our vigils on Euclid Avenue. We had seen a Pierce Arrow! A Peerless! A Reo! We had seen a Winton, a Westcott, even a White Steamer! Three cars that were made in Ohio.

We had a Willys-Overland Touring Car. Capital letters! A great ark, an open car with a backseat that curved outward like an opening flower, the tufted seats upholstered luxuriously in leather. A salon could be held in our backseat. On late Sunday afternoons we had our "drive" in this car, our destination being the next village, where we would be treated to an ice cream cone. We children lolled in the backseat, arguing, complaining, persecuting our younger sister, Jane, because she managed to make her cone last longer than the rest of us did, and she would still be eating ice cream, smugly, when the rest of us had finished ours.

When we got too rambunctious, Daddy would turn in his seat and tell us, in no uncertain terms, to "Be quiet!" One Sunday afternoon, Mother, turning to look at us, asked me where my sweater was.

"Oh," I replied obnoxiously, "it blew out of the car a long while back, but I didn't say anything because Daddy told us to be quiet."

Finally, reluctantly, the PERPETUAL AUTO SERVICE sign had to be taken down. There were just not enough cars on the road, not enough cars in existence, to justify a repair business. My father had to take a job to feed us and to maintain the house.

In back of our fields was a large open space where the hangars were in which Glenn L. Martin was building his early airplanes. My father was welcomed there. But my mother made him promise that he would never go up in those fragile, insubstantial planes that buzzed over our house like angry wasps.

One day I looked in on one of the hangars. At a large table, with blueprints spread out in front of them, men, my father among them, were arguing. Disorder and happenstance lay all around them. The argument among the men grew quite heated. I was afraid to go in. But I learned, for the first time, how violent and untidy the act of creation always is.

IT WAS THROUGH Miss Giddings, the daughter of Judge Giddings, that we finally learned the mystery or secret behind the locked doors in the house owned by the beautiful and exotic foreign woman whose name we children learned was Mrs. Prescott. The memory of Mrs. Prescott had captured my imagination, and the locked rooms obsessed me. Even after our mother had hung curtains on our side of the glass-paned doors of the front sitting room, I used to slip behind the curtains when I was not observed to try to make out what was in there in the light that filtered through the shuttered windows.

The room seemed to have been filled during a disaster of some kind, at a time of crisis when unhurried action was impossible. Things were piled on top of one another without regard, even at risk of damage. There were chairs and sofas much grander than our own handmade mission oak. There were many small tables on which other tables were stacked, or on which objects of art, such as vases or figurines, were crowded. Rugs and carpets were rolled and piled in the spaces between the furniture. There were glass-fronted cases crammed with books, and

45

these were the objects of my most intense longing, for reading had become like a drug for me, to which I was addicted.

I could not get to the books in the locked room, but it was not the books alone that tantalized me; it was the mystery of the extraordinary people, so unlike ourselves, who had lived in this house. I also longed to find my way into the locked room upstairs.

On a lower shelf in the pantry I found a cigar box full of keys. They were old keys, monstrous in size, of brass or iron, the bits or webs of the keys so elementary in structure that I felt they might be used interchangeably. Whenever I had an opportunity to be alone I would dart upstairs with the cigar box and carefully try the keys, one after the other, in the lock of the room. I found that the keys only looked interchangeable. When they did not fit or would not turn, no forcing or twisting would make them do so. But then, on one heart-stopping afternoon, a slender black key slid into the lock, silently, and when I turned it I heard the bolt inside move. The doorknob turned freely in my hand. I froze there, afraid to open the door. The enormity of my transgression was apparent to me. We had accepted the locked rooms as a condition of living in the house. My father would be furious with me if I betrayed that trust and went into that room. I did not open the door. I turned the key back again, hearing the tumblers fall back into place, and removed it from the lock. But I kept the key. I hid it in a box in which I kept my treasures, on a shelf in the closet of the bedroom that I shared with my younger brother, Ned.

I resisted all temptation to go into the locked room until one day the meadow caught fire during a dry spell in the autumn. The threat of such a fire was a source of continual worry to our mother ever since the field had caught fire the late autumn the year before. It had been a small blaze, far in the back field, and it had burned itself out when it reached a marshy place, before posing any threat to us.

These fires were caused by sparks from the smokestack of the small engine that pulled two or three open cars along the spur of a railroad line at the south of our rented property; it was taking them to be filled at the bluestone quarry in the hills to the east, on the other side of Euclid Avenue. The fireman always stoked the firebox heavily to generate steam for the climb, and the little train would puff along, blowing its whistle for the crossing, its stack belching forth smoke and flame. The stone quarry did not seem to be in continual operation and we could not be prepared for the train, since it ran on no schedule. Often it would not appear for weeks, but when we heard the shrill sound of its whistle, or chanced to see it puffing through the fields, we would race to the crossing and place pins, crossed, on the rails, to make what we called little scissors.

For our mother these were moments of anxiety. Since the fields had not been cut or cultivated for some time, the dried grasses and bramble and brush stood high. I find it difficult to believe that the house could have been at any time in serious jeopardy from a fire in the fields. The lawns surrounding it were mowed, and the fire could not have progressed over green grass. But the barn stood in some danger, since the fields and the brush grew close to it, and inside were tanks of gasoline and kerosene. The fire engine could always get there in time, my father explained, if the barn was threatened, and besides there was always the garden hose to be pulled back there.

But beneath her smiling beauty and her gaiety and her frequent flashes of Irish wit, our mother lived with a compulsive anxiety and the sense of desolation and loss that had not been exorcised from her. Besides, now that the PERPETUAL AUTO SERVICE was closed, she was alone again a good part of the time.

On this particular day my father was away and, for some unaccountable reason, even though we were all home from school, the fire was almost upon us before we knew it, leaping in high flames above the brush beside the house and in back of the fields.

Mother rushed to the telephone to call the fire department, two miles away in the village. She then ranged us on our knees alongside the mission oak davenport to pray. When we were disposed, with our hands folded, she went outside with a broom and a pail of water to beat at the grassline nearest the field.

The siren of the arriving fire engine finished our devotions, but as we leaped to our feet to run outside, I suddenly stopped, for I realized that from the window of the locked room one would have the best view of the firemen in action. I was a little unwilling to perform such an act of transgression alone. I grasped Coletta by the arm and held her back. As boys sometimes do with sisters, even older ones, I frequently made her a victim of, or an ally in, my misadventures. I whispered to her that I had found the key to the locked room upstairs. "We can get the best view from there," I said.

Coletta's eyes widened for a moment, but she had learned to be ready for any adventure, and without a word she rushed with me up the stairs.

I found the black key where I had hidden it in my box of treasures. We went together to the locked door. My hand trembled as I slid the key into the lock and turned it. The knob turned, the door opened, and we were inside.

For a moment we stood still with disbelief. The room was empty. There was nothing in it. Nothing. There was not even a carpet on the floor.

After a moment of hesitation we crossed the room to the window, and drew up the shade. We looked out and down at the burning fields where the firemen were beating at smoldering embers of brush. Mother stood at the edge of the lawn, watching to make sure all would be extinguished, with Jane and Ned at her side. Two firemen with the hose from the fire truck were busy in the field at the back, wetting the area around the barn. The drama of the fire was over.

We turned from the window, and as we did we saw that beside the door a painting hung turned against the wall. We could see only the back of a stretched canvas, and the frame that held it. We could not quite reach it, and Coletta ran from the room to get a chair. When she had come back and placed the chair beneath the picture, I stood on it and with some effort, for it was a sizable picture in an ornate frame, I turned it toward us.

It was a portrait in oils of a rather distinguished-looking man, painted when he was fairly young. A man of intelligence and noble bearing.

We stood for a moment, silent conspirators, staring at it. Then I turned the picture back against the wall. I got down from the chair. I drew the window shade. I carried the chair out of the room. I locked the door.

"You must never tell anyone we went inside," I said. "Promise?"

Eyes wide again, Coletta nodded.

\*　\*　\*

It was I who could not keep the secret. The mystery of the locked room, far from being resolved, had become even more tantalizing. My curiosity finally overcame my fear of rebuke, and I went to my mother to tell her what I had done. It was always said, with some justice I think, that I was her favorite and could get away with anything, although this did not help me if I incurred the displeasure of my father. In this instance my mother's own curiosity overcame any other feelings. It was unfortunate that I had done what I had done, but it was done, and so she went upstairs with me to see the room for herself. I gave her the key and she went into the empty room and turned the portrait from the wall to look at it, and then she replaced everything as it was and locked the door again.

Mother kept the key, and that afternoon she went to see Miss Giddings. She was gone some time, while we waited at home in suspense.

Miss Giddings lived in one of those houses that were set back on the hill on the right of Euclid Avenue, opposite us. It was a low, rambling turn-of-the-century house, as ours was, and she lived there with her father, Judge Giddings, who spent the last years of his life in self-imposed isolation, shadowed by a great scandal, which I never heard explained but seemed to involve some judicial proceeding that had taken place while he was in office.

Miss Giddings was a pleasant, slender spinster lady, very well-mannered and polite. She had been a friend of Mrs. Prescott, and she did her best to help my mother feel happy in Euclid Village. Miss Giddings tried to act as catalyst in these new surroundings, New England in character, which my mother found so bewildering, so far removed from her cheerful Irish and Alsatian background, but she never quite succeeded. Miss Giddings persuaded my mother to go to two or three ladies' club meetings, where the ladies were addressed about such problems as unwed mothers, child labor, the evils of drink, problems that occupied the volunteer work and interests of ladies like Miss Giddings; however, the meetings so depressed my mother (who said she had enough problems of her own) that she declined to go again. But she and Miss Giddings remained friends.

When Mother returned she looked rather pale. She stood inside the front door, taking off the hat she had worn to make her call, and absently rearranging her hair.

"Mr. Prescott killed himself," she said, not looking at us. "He shot himself in that room. That is his portrait on the wall."

I do not remember what we said, if anything, Coletta and I. I suppose it did not seem real to us. It was all rather like something out of a book. Mother went out into the kitchen to make tea, and over the cups she told us the story that Miss Giddings had told her. Mr. Prescott had been a scholar of some kind, possibly a historian. He had met Mrs. Prescott and had married her in one of those small Middle-European countries that no longer existed after the treaties of 1918. She had a title. She was a baroness, a countess, or a princess. Mr. Prescott had brought her to this house years ago, and they had had a son. Miss Giddings had been Mrs. Prescott's friend. But if she had any knowledge of why Mr. Prescott had shot himself, she chose not to tell my mother.

That evening we heard Mother tell my father about it, in hushed tones. We children never talked about it with him, just as we never talked about the mysterious footsteps on the front porch that stopped at the door. Were they not after all merely the creaking of old floorboards, cooled by the night air?

# 7

EUCLID VILLAGE was a pleasant place in which to live if one belonged there. On Memorial Day, which we knew as Armistice Day and is now Veterans' Day, we marched in a body from the school, led by the school band, to stand with uncovered heads in the cemetery to hear the annual oration, carried in the clear air over gravestones bearing Anglo-Saxon names. On May Day schoolgirls, in white dresses, danced around the maypole, weaving patterns of colored ribbons. But I remember more clearly a particular day when it was demonstrated to me that we could never really belong in Euclid Village.

The village lay in the northern part of the state called the Western Reserve, a grant from days before the state of Ohio was formed, in which the parcel of land known as "the Firelands" was set aside as the Western Reserve of the State of Connecticut, given over to those citizens of Connecticut whose houses had been burned by the British during the American Revolution. At the time we moved there the village still retained its fiercely Protestant-New England character.

It seemed to have a twilight quality about it, a Gothic darkness not unlike the atmosphere of the early Hawthorne tales, with superstition and scandal and even madness always present just below the surface of the apparently commonplace village life. There was even a witch, who lived on the second story of an ancient house in one of the alleys of the village; schoolchildren used to torment her by calling out names from below the window at which she immediately appeared, a toothless old hag with disheveled hair, to call down curses upon the children, myself, I regret to say, among them. At school I fell in love with a classmate named Ruth who used to go, on a dare, into the swamp in back of the school and catch watersnakes and drape them around her neck.

In the spring the carp spawned in Euclid Creek, a small creek that wound its way down from the wooded hills to Lake Erie. My father loved fishing and he took me one night to see the carp run. Men and boys in boots and with lanterns were on the banks of the creek to spear the carp as they fought their way up to the spawning grounds in the creek, swollen by spring rains. The shouting and the excitement and the sheer mischief of the destruction revolted us. The fish were not considered to be edible. The fat carp were slaughtered and held aloft on poles tipped with spikes, after which they were flung on the banks, bloody and writhing. The gleeful faces of the boys and men, sweating and shouting in the lamplight, made us turn away. My father was a rod-and-reel fisherman who loved angling and casting and bringing his catch home to the frying pan. He taught me how to clean and dress fish, reminding me that Jesus might have done so, since He ate fish.

Tradition had it that the village was named by the drummer boy in the company of General Moses Cleaveland when he had been sent out by the Connecticut Land Grant Company to "plat" the city of Cleveland. By day the village had a calm and sleepy aspect. There was no common, oddly enough, for a community settled by New Englanders, perhaps because it lay on such a traveled road, a major highway called Euclid Avenue, which had been beaten out originally, so we were told, by passing herds of wild game and by nomadic Indians on the shelf of land at the edge of the retreating lake. Euclid Village was a crossroads, with a general store and a post office, and, most important in my boyhood, a village smithy, under not a chestnut tree but a spreading elm.

The smith's glowing forge and pleasant face, the reassuring sound of his hammer on the anvil, were my goals when I set out to walk the two miles to school in the mornings. My sister Coletta and I were supposed to walk together, but she was two years older than I and had her own friends, and so I generally walked alone.

For the space of half a mile the houses were set back on the hills to the left, the Giddings house among them. I was certainly not afraid to pass the Giddings house, but shortly afterward I would begin to run, for nearer the road, on my side, I had to pass a haunted house in a tangled, ruined garden, with one gable fallen in and the glass gone from its empty, staring windows. Someone had been murdered in this house, so it was believed, and we were told that on certain nights one might see the ghost of the murdered woman, with a lighted candle, moving from room to room. (I never saw the lighted candle, but one evening, returning late from school at dusk after an afternoon performance of some kind, I had seen the Giddings house alight with a wonderful, glowing light, the last house I ever saw illuminated at night by oil lamp.)

Still another contributing factor that made this place in the

52

road so alarming to pass was that in the spring, in the glade on the opposite side of the road, Romany gypsies used to camp in their dirty, painted wagons. Mother told us that it was nonsense to believe that the gypsies kidnapped children, but one spring a boy older than I jumped out from behind a bush ahead of me, seized me, and tried to twist the gold signet ring from my finger. My finger had grown so large that I could not remove the ring, and I was postponing telling my father because I knew he would have to file it off. The gypsy boy threatened to cut off my finger, and his dark face frightened me so that I was able to pull myself away from him and run, faster than I had ever run before, to safety.

After the haunted house and the gypsies I was almost to the village and to the school; however, I sometimes saw, as a final chapter, the sinister figure of the Widow. The Widow, whose name I never heard spoken, had lost her husband at Ypres. She was never seen from that time until she died, some ten years later, in anything but widow's weeds, black shoes, black stockings, black dress, black gloves, black coat, black hat, and over her face a black veil, so thick that her features were not discernible. I cannot remember that anyone thought this very odd, or made any overture to help her. She was mad, they said simply. Her grief had made her mad.

I was aware that it was a troubled period for our mother, a time of great emotional and moral crisis, for she was being besieged, campaigned, threatened, and attacked by the pastor of our Roman Catholic church, who wanted us to attend the parochial school. We were members of the parish of St. Philomena* in East Cleveland, Ohio, but this was some miles away. To go to school there would have meant a ride on the streetcar for an hour, and our mother was caught in a dilemma. We lived an intensely private life. We were not encouraged to leave the property when we came home from school. We lived in a separate world, bounded by what seemed to us then, for reasons I now better understand, an alien world outside.

This struggle for our souls between Monsignor Smith and

---

* One of the first acts of Pope John XXIII was to declare Saint Philomena non-existent.

Mother, for such I suppose it was, was merely the beginning of a conflict which would take me many years to resolve, if it was ever resolved. In the end our mother's timidity and fears overcame even her religious scruples, and we were sent to the public school in the village of Euclid.

On what is known in the Roman Catholic Church as a holy day of obligation, a day on which one must attend mass under penalty of sin for failing to do so, the principal of the school came to our classroom to excuse the Roman Catholics there. As we left the room, we passed through a whispered chorus of "Redneck!" "Redneck!" It was many years before I learned that in some mysterious way this term of opprobrium had come to this remote village in Ohio from the reign of Mary Tudor in England. Even though I did not know that then, I did know that in some equally mysterious way it was wrong in Euclid Village to be a Roman Catholic. True, we were taught in school that America was a land of religious freedom, but it was a religious freedom framed and tendered by Protestants. In Euclid Village, as in George Orwell's *Animal Farm,* everyone was equal but some were more equal than others.

At about this time I began to long for someone to invent a box of glass which could be worn over the head and enclose one down to the waist. This magical box was to be made of glass that would be transparent in one direction only, so that I could see out but no one could see me within. Since no one did invent this box, I imagined that it existed, and each morning as I left home for school, I put my wonderful box over my head, and I was invisible.

I approached school in my magical box with a mingling of reluctance and eagerness. I had been born with a joy of learning, and providence had happily, in that respect at least, placed me in a community where learning, in the New England tradition, was attacked with joy. There was a sense of vitality in the school, an excitement, a happy exploring of well-known paths, without any tentative doubts or fearful self-examinings. Everyone knew what a good education was. It was based on a knowledge of reading, writing, and arithmetic, with a special emphasis on grammar, spelling, and accuracy. Learning itself began at the beginning, with the Greek myths and the legends of Rome. The monuments of antiquity, through pictures, were as familiar to us as the buildings of the village. Photographs of the Greek Parthenon and the Forum at Rome looked down at us from the classroom walls, along with Rosa Bonheur's *Horse Fair,* and framed copies of the Declaration of Independence. We memorized the Seven Wonders of the Ancient World along with the multiplication tables, the celestial constellations, and the classifications of plants.

For these reasons I went to school with eagerness, in spite of intermittent reminders that it was a world in which I might never belong. One of our pretty young teachers, whose name I no longer remember, once interrupted a history or civics lesson, with what I presume she thought to be a happy impulse, to ask all of us who were the descendants of immigrants to stand. One of our classmates, a girl whose name might have been Peggy O'Neill, did not rise with the rest of us. Our teacher admonished her gently, reminding her that her ancestors had come from Ireland. Peggy flushed, but her face set stubbornly and she did not rise. "Ireland is an English-speaking country," she said. "I am not a foreigner."

Our teacher insisted she stand. "After all," she said, "your ancestors were immigrants."

"And who were your ancestors?" Peggy blurted out. "Indians?"

For her impertinence Peggy O'Neill was banished to the hall and made to stand there until class had ended. The rest of us, whom Peggy had labeled with the shameful word of foreigner, were permitted to sit down.

We were foreigners. We were Americans, of course. We had been born in America, but our status was qualified by degree. We were first generation, or second generation, or even third generation, but we were foreigners and we could never be anything else. It was in the history books that we had no place in the history of our country. Just as everyone knew what a good education was, so everyone knew what American history was. American history was the Pilgrim Fathers, the Virginia Colonies, the Huguenots, the Dutch in New Amsterdam. It was the French and Indian Wars, and the displacement of the French and Spanish. American history was the forming of the

Thirteen Colonies, the great drama of the American Revolution, the Civil War, the opening of the West. American history had already taken place. Its events were recorded. The book was closed. Our ancestors had arrived too late to be included.

In exchange for a history we were supplied with new national prototypes, ancestral and otherwise. Along with most children, I shared a delight in pageants. In our class play at the school in Euclid Village once, we were Indians, and I remember with pleasure our beaded moccasins and painted faces, our feathered headdresses and tomahawks, and our fringed Indian suits of brown-paper muslin. We danced a war dance on the stage, shouting war whoops with our hands cupped over our mouths, circling around a fire made of strips of red crepe paper blown by an electric fan over a lighted electric bulb. I enjoyed that, I suppose, because it was genuine make-believe. I was as Indian as anyone there, including Peggy O'Neill and the pretty teacher with the forgotten name.

On the other hand, I felt a marked awkwardness and discomfort at Thanksgiving time when, with a classmate named Vladimir Pelatoski, I was dressed in a Pilgrim suit. We wore black brimmed hats, and on our shoes false buckles, cut from cardboard and covered with tinfoil. With wooden rifles over our shoulders, we were given a place in a tableau on the stage of the school auditorium. In this tableau, which was called "The Pilgrims Going to Church," we were posed approaching a church door, through cotton snow dusted with powdered mica. But our fathers would not have entered the door of the church in that tableau on pain of mortal sin. The Pilgrim Fathers were not my forefathers, just as the forefathers of the Revolution were not my forefathers, nor the forefathers, either, of Vladimir Pelatoski.

We had no forefathers.

But we had a religion, and for some this religion became the ancestry and the country in which they lived. Now Monsignor Smith again appeared upon the scene. He had been forced to accept my mother's decision to enroll us in the public school, but now it was her turn to defer to him without delay, for we were tardy in receiving our first holy communion. In the Roman Catholic Church, a child is to receive the sacrament when he attains an age defined as the age of reason, thought to be reached at about seven. I was eight, and my sister was ten.

In order to receive holy communion for the first time, however, one is required to go through a period of religious instruction, or indoctrination into the beliefs and the dogma of the Church, a process that consists largely in committing to memory answers to questions in a catechism.

"How is the soul like to God?"

"The soul is like to God because it is a spirit that will never die, and has understanding and free will."

"Why did God make you?"

"To know Him, to love Him, and to serve Him in this world, and to be happy with Him in the next."

Normally this process of religious instruction is conducted in the parochial school, and so at last, our mother's fears outweighed by seemingly larger considerations, we were enrolled as temporary students in the parish school of St. Philomena, and made the anxious trip together each day by streetcar.

My sister was placed in charge of me. Each morning we walked to the streetcar where it waited at the end of the line at a station on Euclid Avenue. I remember it as a period of four or five weeks, and one of unremitting grayness, a kind of temporary exile that I suffered with numbness and disbelief.

It was true that at the public school in Euclid Village I had always felt a sense of being alien, but at the parish school of St. Philomena, I was even more alien. At St. Philomena's the boys and the girls were separated in the classroom and at play. In the classroom a relentless supervision produced a heavy feeling of oppression or suppression, which burst free in the schoolyard in a reaction of such violence that it swept over me and left me feeling helpless and confused. I was too young then to realize, as I was to learn later, that a separate world of Roman Catholics existed within the larger community, in which a place surely must have existed for me. Perhaps I had been corrupted in the eyes of others by having come from a public school. At any rate, no place was found for me at St. Philomena's, where I was never addressed by another classmate.

The classroom in which I, the alien latecomer, found myself, had boys on one side and girls on the other. It was divided by a wider space between the desks at the middle, an aisle patrolled by the nun who taught us, who paced up and down during instruction like a sentry to maintain order. She carried a long ruler with which she struck at random and without warning. There were members of religious orders in our family. I had a great-aunt who was a nun, and a cousin who was a Christian Brother. The nun's habit did not awe or frighten me, but I was so overwhelmed by the strangeness of the classroom, and my fear of this particular nun that what intelligence I had deserted me. When I was unable to answer a question in mathematics, I would be struck across the knuckles with the ruler and made to stand in a corner of the room for the remainder of the period, with my face turned to the wall.

It all seemed a bad dream. Fond as I was of school, I sat in that classroom in bafflement, for this was not school as I had known it since nothing was required of the students but the memorizing of facts. At recess the students boiled into the schoolyard, where a steel fence separated the boys from the girls. The boys at once took up a game of King of the Hill, with bloody noses and bashed heads, falling into the game so spontaneously that it seemed this was their reality, with the work of the classroom only an interruption. From the other side of the fence, where the girls were, arose a constant shrill scream of quarreling.

At lunchtime my sister and I sought out each other from our separate classrooms for a brief, silent respite. Although we had always carried sandwiches to school for lunch in Euclid Village, for the period at St. Philomena's Mother gave us money instead, as a sort of reward, I suppose. With these nickels and dimes my sister and I went across the street from the school to a pastry shop where we stuffed ourselves with lemon meringue pie washed down with soda pop.

When we concluded our period of instruction and my sister and I received our first holy communion, we returned to the public school in Euclid Village.

There, in my memory, it is perpetual springtime, with the sun always shining. It is one particular day when our beloved Miss Bailey suddenly decided it was much too nice to be indoors and we boys and girls took our textbooks to a grassy hillock in back of the school, where we continued our lesson under a flowering apple tree with the white blossoms drifting down upon us in the warm breeze.

There seemed a morning freshness about our learning, a pagan feeling, as if all of it were new. The world we learned about in that school in Euclid Village was a world that had come to us in a single leap across the centuries, from Greece with the pass at Thermopylae, and Rome with Horatio at the bridge, to Lexington and Concord and the rude bridge that arched the flood. The education I received there seems to me even now an excellent preparation for life—a knowledge of reading and writing and arithmetic, an acquaintance with the natural world, and a sense of the grandeur of our own country as rooted in the grandeur of the past.

It was possible to remain at public school in Euclid Village through high school, but when I finished the eighth grade the ubiquitous Monsignor Smith appeared again, and other plans were made for me.

CATHEDRAL LATIN SCHOOL was under the jurisdiction of Cleveland's Cathedral of St. John. It was not merely a parish or neighborhood school. It was a private high school for boys. The prospectus read that it was a college preparatory school for "arts, medicine, law, pharmacy, and the seminary." There were scholastic requirements, and there was a tuition fee. The tuition was modest, but knowing how difficult the sum might be for our household, Monsignor explained to my mother that there were scholarships available for students who did well in the entrance requirement tests. I took the streetcar into town to take the tests, and I was accepted as a scholarship student.

In all honesty it must be said that at fourteen I was ready for a new beginning. I had never made any close friend in Euclid Village. I had never been in the houses of my classmates. I was too young to realize that friendship among children is sometimes best accomplished in the wider social life shared by their parents. It did not occur to me that our isolation as a family among our Protestant neighbors might be responsible, at least in part, for my failure to make friends.

I knew only that I was alone. I went to school alone, I returned home alone. I was subject at that time to great periods of depression, which often seemed without cause and descended upon me without warning. These periods of depression seemed to possess a life of their own and to determine their own cycle. I once attempted, without success, to count these days, so that I might be prepared in advance for the duration of the blackness of my depression, as much beyond my control as a storm or a season of rain.

To go to a different school seemed a welcome opportunity. I think I knew even then how infrequently life might offer one the privilege of entering a new world fresh, without associations from the past. I put aside my unhappy memories of the parish school of St. Philomena and prepared to enter Cathedral Latin.

To enter this new world I composed a motto for myself, suitably solemn and pretentious. The motto said: NO WEAPON CAN PENETRATE A SHIELD OF LAUGHTER. I would smile and joke. I would play jester to my own gloom, hiding my feelings behind a smiling mask.

So intent was I on putting my new character into effect, and so pleased was I to find how successful my first efforts were, or so I thought, that it was several days before I discovered that the effort was unnecessary. At Cathedral Latin I was not entering late, as I had done those years before at St. Philomena's. At this school I entered at the same time and on equal terms with the others, and into a world where the only requirement was to be a Roman Catholic; isolation and vulnerability were left at the

60

door in exchange for the protective feeling of belonging to a special group. It took me years to understand that I was not entering a world of privilege, but a ghetto instead.

At the same time though, I saw to my enormous relief that I was accepted without judgment, with my thin shield of laughter or without it. I was among my own kind whether I liked it or not, and I saw also with some surprise that among my classmates there were boys even less free than I was, since they had never tasted the dry Protestant air.

In its appearance and in its structure the school was not unlike other high schools. It was housed in a large building, vaguely Romanesque in feeling and built, inexorably, of yellow brick, a circumstance that made me wonder if Roman Catholic establishments were designed on the principle that ugliness is a prerequisite of virtue. In the back of the school was a courtyard used for exercise and games, and beyond that was the house in which the Brothers lived, very different in character from the school building, having once been a private house, a copy of an English manor, with half-timbering.

The order to which these Brothers belonged was the Society of Mary, or *Société de Marie,* as we were encouraged to say in French class, difficult as this was for our Ohio tongues. This order had been founded by a French priest, Father Chaminade of Bordeaux, at the time of the Terror during the French Revolution. Father Chaminade, for purposes of disguise, had adopted the dress of the new "citizen" of France, and the order's habit had been adapted from that, being translated in our day as a black business suit, a white shirt, and a black four-in-hand tie. It was possible for a fastidious young man to look quite distinguished in this habit, and many of our teachers did.

The Society of Mary was a teaching order, including both priests and Brothers. A Brother took vows of poverty, chastity, and obedience, but he did not assume Holy Orders. He could not administer the sacraments or officiate at mass and consequently had more free time to devote to his teaching. It was a life similar to that of a nun, but if a Brother felt called to a more exacting role he could become a priest in the order and continue teaching, but with the added duties and privileges of a priest. This choice was a condition understood by Roman Catholics who are familiar with discussions involving degrees of piety. Our Brothers, if asked, might have said that while they felt called to God and the religious life, they did not consider themselves worthy of the priesthood. It was an ingratiating attitude and most of our Brothers were ingratiating men.

If I were asked what it was they shared in common, I suppose I would have to say that they shared nothing in common. Or perhaps what they shared in common was a sense of separateness, which they cultivated. It is a rather familiar sight to see two nuns walking on the street together, but possibly because as women they would not walk alone. The only time I ever saw two of our Brothers walking on the street together was during the afternoon disciplinary patrols. Since we were students at a day school, the rules and discipline could scarcely be extended beyond the classroom or the school grounds. But the school principal set up boundaries in the neighborhood, taking in an area of two to three city blocks around the school property, in which our behavior was watched in the afternoon once classes were dismissed, presumably that we might not reflect discredit on the school.

We were forbidden to smoke cigarettes in this area. It was not a moral issue. The personal use of alcohol and tobacco is not regarded as a moral issue by Roman Catholics. If we smoked cigarettes away from the school it was our own concern, but within this imaginary boundary around the school we were not to smoke, just as we were not to be boisterous or shout or misbehave.

The Brothers who patrolled the area were a rather ludicrous sight. I think the assignment was not popular with them. They would walk briskly side by side, around and around the area, stopping only to peer briefly into the windows of Hoffman's ice cream parlor at the corner of 105th Street and Euclid Avenue. This was a popular meeting place for the boys of Cathedral Latin and the girls of Notre Dame Academy. Inside, we played a sort of cat-and-mouse game, with a boy lighting a cigarette and handing it to one of the girls as the anxious faces of the Brothers appeared at the windows, since their jurisdiction did not extend to the behavior of the girls of Notre Dame Academy.

On these patrols I do not recall ever seeing the two Brothers in conversation with each other, just as I never saw any two Brothers in conversation at school except in conducting school business, or in conference about one of the students. Looking back I cannot remember friendship between any two of the Brothers. Although the manner of their life seemed unnatural to me, they were, to my knowledge, truly ascetic. Their contract was a personal one with God. To fulfill its terms meant the sacrifice of many if not most of their personal relationships, and their deliberate separateness seemed twofold in character: the need to forego personal attachments, and a desire to avoid any suggestion of scandal by their behavior.

They were consecrated men, but they were human and there were, here and there, signs of neuroticism. We, their pupils, were at great pains to ignore these signs, in a way that now seems odd to me. One of the older Brothers, Brother X, was known to be a terror when aroused, a man to be avoided. But he was one of our athletic coaches, and mixed with the fear was a certain affection for him. Brother X was stationed in the corridor one day at noon to see that we maintained order while waiting to enter the dining room. When one of the boys persisted in horseplay after he had been asked to stop, Brother X sprang at him and seized him by the throat with both hands and held his head back against the wall. A silence fell over us. The incident lasted for only a moment. Aware of his behavior, Brother X dropped his hands and quickly walked away down the corridor.

Brother X often indulged in a form of horseplay himself, going to the shower and locker room after a game to be with the players. The boys endured this with forced good humor as Brother X feinted blows with his fists, or slapped them on the back, or walked the length of the showers to flick them on the bare buttocks with a towel. One afternoon one of the players suddenly took offense at this. He whirled about and shouted, "Cut that out!" in tones that left nothing to the imagination of what he deduced from Brother X's behavior. When Brother X left the shower room, the offended player announced to the others that he was "going to tell my father." The other boys tried to talk him out of it. They tried to convince him that he had only imagined improper intent in Brother X's actions. But the boy was firm. He was going to tell his father. And he did.

I do not know why we pretended not to notice or wanted to ignore the symptoms of sexual repression we sometimes saw about us. One of the Brothers most popular with us, Brother Y, young, handsome, virile in appearance, once embarrassed us during a classroom session, in which we were all laughing for some reason or other, by dashing to the door, where he looked carefully up and down the hall, then came back to the blackboard and scrawled with chalk in large letters, OUR CORSETS GIVE SATISFACTION OR BUST.

Another Brother, genial Brother Z, seemed to alternate between periods of outgoing interest in others and withdrawal. He would sometimes walk up and down the aisle of our classroom during the silence of study period, hiding his flushed face behind an open textbook, while an obvious erection showed behind his trousers.

I find it strange that we did not mention or discuss these things among ourselves. Perhaps our religious environment had given us a degree of the same inhibition and repression we observed in our teachers. At any rate, we felt an affection for the Brothers rather like that of a family relationship, including a protective understanding and acceptance of their behavior.

A week or so later Brother X disappeared from the school. No announcement was made of the reason for his withdrawal, nor even any reference to his absence, but it was rumored that he had either left or been expelled from the order. Our reaction, again rather curious, was directed against the player who had spoken of him to his father. He fell under an ostracism that was not lifted during his time at school. It was as if he had betrayed one of us. His righteousness seemed small and offensive. As far as we knew, Brother X had made no unnatural proposal to him. We had assumed his behavior in the shower room was an indication of unnatural tendencies, but our attitude was, so what? Years later when old classmates met they would invariably get around to asking about Brother X in an effort to determine what had become of him.

The affection we felt for our teachers at the public school in Euclid Village might be described as a secular affection, one suggesting the warmth of physical contact. At Cathedral Latin the affection we felt for our teaching Brothers was of a very different nature. The teachers at the public school were dedicated to their profession, but they went home at the end of the teaching day to a separate and private life. The Brothers of Mary were dedicated to God and to us. They had no other life. They guided us and instructed us, in the words of the prospectus, in Religion, English, Latin, French, Algebra, General Science, Physics, Chemistry, United States History, and Physical Training. They expected much of us, but we knew that we did not have to share or compete with other interests in their lives. Their day began with us in the classroom, and ended there. They lived in their separateness with God. In their temporal lives they were related only to us.

# 9

AT CATHEDRAL LATIN we were marched to chapel in a body on Friday afternoons, class by class, to make confession in readiness for communion on Sunday. We would then wait in the pews in the chapel in alphabetical order to enter the confessional, one by one.

On these occasions I found myself invariably seated next to Tom, one of the most popular boys of our class, a light-haired, lighthearted boy who seemed, at least to me, completely uninhibited and way ahead of all of us, or perhaps just ahead of me, in his knowledge and experience of sex.

My proximity to Tom on these Friday afternoons was of extremely doubtful value to me, however, particularly for the purpose of my Examination of Conscience, and because of Tom I was led into my most "grievous" sin of my young life.

Of all the sacraments of the Roman Catholic Church, confession was for me the most deeply satisfying, and yet ultimately the most frustrating and fearful. I had inherited from my mother a neurotic tendency common enough among Roman Catholics to be recognized and even defined as a sin, the sin of scrupulosity. My mother was tormented all her life by the feeling that she had never made a perfect confession, no matter how diligently she tried. As for me, even in the period of penance, my prayers were unwillingly troubled by thoughts of sins I might have omitted in my recital.

My mother washed her hands a great deal. In the winter she washed them until they were red and chapped. In my most familiar memory of her she is standing at the sink in the kitchen, washing her hands after each household task, washing the soap itself before putting it back into the soap dish, and then carefully hanging the towel in a certain way on the towel rack. She told me that once as a young girl she had returned to the confessional after having been given absolution to tell the priest of a sin she had forgotten. She was confronted there by his anger. It is a condition of absolution that the sins confessed then become as if they had never been committed, even including those sins that were forgotten. In a point of theological reasoning confusing to my mother, or perhaps to anyone, these forgotten sins that one remembered could be confessed at the next confession, but for the present they had never been committed. By returning to the confessional, my mother had violated this important tenet and by so doing threatened the validity of her absolution. Whether or not she then went forward to receive communion the following morning, I never learned.

Confession was the great sacrament that lay at the heart of the Roman Catholic Church, and it was surely the most mysterious of all Roman Catholic ritual to an outsider. It has changed in its method and procedure in our time, but in my youth it seemed inflexible and unalterable.

Confession was preceded by a period of reflection called the Examination of Conscience. One sat or knelt in a pew in church and made an effort to search out one's behavior or misbehavior since last confession. There were certain technical classifications into which sins might be divided in an effort to determine the enormity of the offense. There were mortal sins and venial sins. Any sin in each category might be qualified, however, by being actual, formal, habitual, or material, if one could understand just what this meant. And beyond these sins and their qualifications there was a horrifying realm of "Sins Which Cry Out to Heaven for Vengeance," which included murder, sodomy, oppression of the poor, and defrauding the laborer of his wages.

As guidance in the process of sorting out our sins and to help us determine which were venial and which were mortal, a comparison was given by one of our religious instructors. A venial sin was equivalent to having slapped the face of the crucified Christ. A mortal sin was comparable to having driven one of the nails into His hands.

I do not remember my own first confession, so it must not have been a very painful or unpleasant experience. A younger cousin of mine, at his first confession, had come out in tears. He had counted his sins before he went in, and he altered the ritual opening of the confessional, "Bless me, Father, for I have sinned," by saying, "Bless me, Father, for I have sinned ninety-nine times."

The confessor-priest had burst into involuntary laughter. He had been very gentle with my cousin after that, having upset him, and this story was told in my family again and again, even by my cousin, for it was a pleasant, loving story, and there are many pleasant, loving stories about the confessional.

There were those who argued, when psychoanalysis came into popularity, that the confessional was a more ancient and more reliable source of therapy than the analyst's couch. But an error in understanding is involved in this comparison. A man goes to a psychiatrist for help. He goes to a confessional to be forgiven.

He must resolve to mend his ways, it is true, as a condition of forgiveness. The tool given to him for that purpose is prayer.

67

Whether prayer is as effective as psychiatry in the struggle to cope with personal problems the man must decide for himself, but it is important to remember that the primary purpose of the confessional is not rehabilitation, but the forgiveness of sin.

And so I am back again in the confessional, or in the pew for my Examination of Conscience, trying with a feeling of frustration and mounting fear to sort out my sins. I could never be certain which of them were venial and which mortal, and so, tormented by indecision, I would try to group them together in my mind by their seriousness, beginning with the lesser errors. Domestic sins I believed to be venial. Those dealing with impurity or impropriety of thought or behavior, I believed to be mortal sins. But always, in the midst of my effort to try to determine the gravity of borderline offenses, it would be my turn to enter the confessional, not only feeling unprepared but guilty also, although I did not know it then, of the sin of scrupulosity.

The confessional box, placed against a side wall of the chapel, was divided into three parts. The central part consisted of a seat, facing outward and enclosed, for the confessor-priest. In a country where there had been a religious rebellion or a Church war—as in Mexico, for example, where it was believed that civil insurrection had been plotted inside the confessional —the doors had been removed by official decree so that the priest and the confessor were visible on either side, but in the United States the confessional box was enclosed. The priest, in his center seat, sat behind a grilled door or half-door, curtained above to facilitate ventilation, while the cubicle on either side where the confessor knelt was either curtained or kept closed by a door. In many churches the name of the priest in attendance was hung above the central door, lettered on a plaque he could also carry with him, much as doctors or lawyers exhibit their names outside their offices. In a larger parish where there were many priests, the confessor had a choice. He could shop around, just as some people do with doctors or lawyers.

This custom presented an additional problem for me, however, for in my scrupulousness I feared that to seek out a priest who might be more lenient or understanding would constitute an act of sin in itself, since it was understood that in the confessional one was speaking directly to God. The priest, a mortal man, had been ordained as the instrument of transmission. But of the many ears of God, were some more understanding than others? And if this were so, wasn't it taking advantage of His good nature to try to find the most lenient? Even to know the name of the priest to whom one was confessing seemed a contradiction in terms of this doctrine, and I used to try to avoid looking at the nameplate over the door of the confessional when I was in an unfamiliar church. There was also the possibility that if one did choose to stand in line in front of the confessional of a popular priest, another priest or a nun might appear and peremptorily direct part of the line to another confessional where a priest with a lesser following was available. On one such occasion I heard bellowing from a priest inside his confessional—this was a priest to whom one did not go willingly—as he shouted, "Speak up!" "I cannot hear you!" "Louder!" And eventually I saw my younger sister, Jane, known for her shyness, emerge trembling and in tears.

At any rate, it was essential to remember that no matter to whom one went, in the confessional one spoke to God who could not be deceived.

When my time came I would enter breathless with apprehension, my mouth dry, my heart thumping so loudly that I was certain the priest could hear it in his cubicle. As you entered the confessional and knelt on the *prie-dieu,* having closed the door behind you or drawn the curtain, you would hear the panel in the wall in front of you being closed as the priest turned to the confessor on the other side of the confessional. At this moment I would kneel in the darkness desperately trying not to hear. The confessional smelled dryly of stone or wood, and often of the bodily presence of the person who had been there before, the scent of fear or shame. In this atmosphere I would shut my eyes tightly, thinking this would prevent me from hearing what was said on the other side. If I heard words or sentences I sometimes stopped my ears with my fingers, but even so I might still hear the priest asking, "How many times?," the dread question that always filled me with such confusion.

I think I felt that my unwilling interest in the sins of another might distract me from my own preparations. I prayed, sweating and fearful, waiting for the rasping sound of the panel being opened in front of me.

When the panel was opened, the window it revealed was covered with a fretwork of wood or metal and a square of gauze so that the profile of the priest, seated and facing forward, was seen only dimly in the semidarkness, a folded handkerchief held to his nose.

"Bless me, Father, for I have sinned," I began. "It has been a week since my last confession." I took a deep breath in an effort to control my voice.

"Yes," the priest said. "Go on."

I made an effort to begin. I would start with what I thought of as my domestic sins—quarrels with my brother or my sisters, disobedience to my parents, inattention or infraction of rules at school—those venial sins equivalent to slapping the face of the crucified Christ.

"I quarreled with my brothers and my sisters," I said. "I disobeyed my parents."

"How many times?"

The dreaded words. How many times? How was I to answer this? If I spoke sharply to one of my sisters in the afternoon after a quarrel in the morning, was this one sin or two? If we all quarreled at once, was this a corporate sin or merely the sin of the one who precipitated the quarrel? If I was silent when provoked but thought angry thoughts, was this a sin, and if it was, where did patience or forbearance enter, which were said to be virtues?

The problem of parental disobedience was even more complex. I almost never disobeyed my parents, no matter how rebellious I might be in my thoughts. My father's punishment was swift and stern and humiliating to my pride. With him I practiced passive resistance. But if I obeyed him in the letter, but not in the spirit, was this actual disobedience? And if this was sustained over a period of time, was this one sin or many?

I did not know how to ask the priest about this. I could not even describe my confusion. After all, wasn't I speaking to God, from whom nothing could be hidden? Indeed, I wanted to hide nothing from Him. God loved me. I was constantly reassured about that. I wanted to deserve His love. I wanted to be forgiven my sins so that I might be joined with Him in communion, yet I had to strain my sins through this mortal instrument of His beyond the gauze in front of me. How could I be forgiven my sins if I didn't even know how to number them?

"I don't know, Father," I said in anguish. "I don't know how many times."

"Think," the priest said. "Was it once a day? Twice a day? Once every other day?" The relentless interrogation began, and I twisted on my knees beyond the window, biting at the knuckles of my clasped hands.

"Yes, Father," I said. "Maybe once a day. Maybe every other day." We were like a council of ministers, submitting compromises so that a treaty might be signed. But anything to conclude. Anything to be forgiven.

Was my confusion peculiar to me? Was my concern excessive? I had been introduced to the confessional from outside the walls, so to speak, during my brief period of instruction at St. Philomena's parochial school. If I had been a pupil at St. Philomena's from the beginning, as Monsignor had wished, would I have been instructed differently or learned by example a more temperate approach to the confessional? And if all of this was unusual or immoderate, wouldn't the priest tell me that now?

"For your penance," he said at last, having struggled with me to the end, "you will say three Hail Marys and three Our Fathers."

He then began the Latin words of absolution, while I recited the Act of Contrition, beginning with the words, "Oh my God, I am heartily sorry for having offended Thee."

Sitting next to Tom on these Friday afternoons, waiting for my turn in the confessional, I began to wonder if listening to him was, indeed, the "Occasion of Sin" that we had been warned about by the Brothers, since Tom's own approach to an Examination of Conscience was to review for me, in whispers, his sexual experience since his last confession. ("I knew she wanted it. I could tell by the way she looked at my swimming trunks when I walked past her." Or "See, this is how I bent my ring when I socked the queer in the mouth.")

I would want him to stop, but I could not bring myself to tell him to because I was so fascinated by what he said. For was it not true that he who committed adultery in his thoughts was as guilty as he who committed adultery in the flesh?

Carefree Tom went ahead of me into the confessional and, after what seemed an astonishingly brief stay there, came out. It was possibly easier, I decided, to answer the question of how many times on the basis of performance rather than thought. But Tom would look as lighthearted on his way out as he had when he had gone into the confessional. He seemed to me rather like a man who had taken his suit to a shop to be cleaned while-you-wait.

When I went into the confessional after Tom, I spent a much longer time there in my agonized efforts to comb the labyrinthine ways of my innocence to find the subtle sins hiding from me.

I had never had a sexual experience involving another person, yet in myself I seemed to be a monster of depravity. Did I not know that the body was a temple for Christ in the sacrament, not to be profaned even by my own hands? Did I not make the sign of the cross with holy water before I went to bed, and sleep with my rosary beads wrapped around my hand? Did I not try to keep my thoughts pure? The difficulty was that I could not keep my thoughts pure, much as I tried, for in concentrating on the need for purity of thought I would be drawn inexorably to identify those thoughts that I must avoid in order to remain pure. Now I understood the hairshirt and the lash, the cold stone cells and the straw mats of monks, the temptations of St. Anthony in the desert, the Stylites who took to their pillars to escape all human contact, and all Occasion of Sin. I knelt on the cold floor beside my bed in the winter. I ran races with myself in the woods until I was breathless. I prayed until I was exhausted. I did not conquer myself, nor did I conquer my sense of guilt, either. I, too, learned to wash my hands.

Lacking saintly fortitude, I fell into graver error. Seduced at last by the tales of the thousand and one nights of my fellow sinner Tom, even my monumental inhibitions were broken down and I finally asked him to take me along to a brothel on a Saturday night.

The experience itself was anticlimactic, if that is the word I want. I was assigned to a room where a prostitute waited, and when she saw me she burst into laughter. "Hi-ya, schoolboy," she said.

I blushed, and when she saw how awkward I was, she was kind and helped me. "Don't be nervous," she said. "After a while it will seem just like buying a cup of coffee."

Her prophecy was never fulfilled, but the aftermath of that first experience was devastating, for now I had committed a mortal sin, the sin of fornication, and how was I to confess that, and to whom?

Unlike Tom, I could not bring myself to walk blithely into a confessional where the priest might recognize me by the sound of my voice. I had almost a week to think it over, during which time my sin assumed enormous proportions. When the burden of guilt grew almost too great to bear, I was reminded, as if by association, of a famous priest in the city to whom it was said the truly damned went, such as murderers or rapists, when they were driven by conscience to repent.

This almost legendary figure was assigned to a parish hidden in a bleak part of the city that had degenerated into an industrial slum. It was partly because of the obscure location of the church, as well as the reputed wisdom and compassion that the priest was supposed to possess, that the damned sought him out, since they might go unobserved. It was even said that he served as liaison between criminals and the courts of law. While he never violated the secrecy of the confessional, he was sometimes able to persuade criminals to give themselves up to the police, and then plead for clemency on their behalf.

Obviously this was the man for me.

I do not remember how I evaded confession in the school chapel on Friday afternoon, or on what pretext I took the streetcar into town the following morning, but once in town, in the deserted streets of a Saturday morning, I resolved to find the church on foot as a form of penance. It took me some time to locate it, but when I came upon it at last I found it to be an ancient, ugly building of stone, suitably stained and black, as if the city soot had fallen upon it like sin, to which I was bringing my own carnality to add to its burden.

There was only one penitent ahead of me at the confessional, an old man who looked not wicked but merely weary.

When he went into the confessional and came out, I went in, having had very little time for my Examination of Conscience, which was scarcely necessary since it was already rubbed raw by self-torment.

The exertion of the long walk had made me wet with perspiration. Fear and shame rendered me almost incoherent. But the invisible priest beyond the fretwork and gauze of the confessional window was unusually patient with my stammerings, merely murmuring, "Yes, yes, go on," and finally saying nothing at all. The ritual of my confession had become a kind of compulsive, cabalistic act by this time, and even now, no matter what had brought me to this priest, I had to begin with my domestic, venial sins. It took some time to arrive at the point where I could blurt out my great sin, and when I finally did tell of the visit to the brothel, I stopped, spent, and waited for the divine wrath to fall upon me.

Nothing happened. Nothing at all. I waited and waited. When I entered the confessional I had been unable, in my shame, to raise my eyes to the panel in front of me. Now I did. I could see the priest's head outlined behind the gauze. It seemed tilted to one side. A dreadful suspicion came to me. I listened carefully. Yes, it was so. The priest was snoring. He was asleep.

I didn't know what to do. None of my instruction had prepared me for this. I began to stir, hoping to rouse him. I cleared my throat tentatively. At length I whispered, "Father."

At this, the priest roused himself and sat upright. And at once, without any warning or hesitation, he launched into the Latin words of absolution.

There was nothing I could do. That much I did know from my instruction. When absolution was pronounced, and I responded with an Act of Contrition, my mortal sin was not only forgiven, it was obliterated. It became as if it had never been. That was dogma.

I left the confessional and went out into the street in bewilderment, blinking in the sunlight.

On Friday of the following week, after Tom came out of the confessional in the chapel at school, I went in and told my sin over again to the priest. I thought of my mother going back to the confessional to tell the priest of a sin she had forgotten, and being rebuked for that. I was probably compounding my error, violating the condition of absolution, but I felt compelled to do that. Someone had to hear me tell aloud of my visit to the prostitute so that I might be properly forgiven.

The priest in the confessional was also our instructor in French. When confession was over and I stood to leave, he called after me by name.

"When you leave the confessional, Plagemann," he said, "please close the window out there. I am sitting in a draft."

INTO THIS COMMONPLACE LIFE, the Depression came. By that time, my father had established himself with some relative success in his field of work. He was now the superintendent of a factory, and we had moved to a suburban neighborhood, still in Euclid Village, but in an area not so isolated or remote. The house was newer and stood with other pleasant, middle-income houses on a tree-shaded street that ended at the shore of Lake Erie, at a small park and beach where we bathed in summer and gave picnics for our friends. (Our old house fell on evil days. We heard rumors that it had been turned into a boardinghouse; finally it burned to the ground, with all of its secrets and locked rooms intact. It seemed, somehow, a fitting end to the story. My father still had a workshop in back of the newer house.)

In the new house our furniture did not appear to sit so temporarily in rooms where other furniture belonged. We no longer seemed transients in a society rooted in the past.

I believe my mother was happier there. She had never really been happy in the old house, even though some effort had been made to include her in the community. She had been asked to serve as an officer of a parents' group at the school which had as a secondary activity, aside from the welfare of schoolchildren, the welfare of the poor in Cleveland. But she felt an uneasiness, a sense of being patronized, as if by her presence at school meetings she served as a symbol of democratic tolerance, since she was not invited socially to the homes of the Protestant women who had asked her to serve. In the second instance she was troubled by feelings of patronage in herself. The conditions in the houses of the poor depressed her and distressed her.

I remember coming home one afternoon from school to find her in tears after a morning in the city. She could not disassociate herself from the problems of others, and the impersonal approach necessary to large-scale assistance in depressed areas was foreign to her nature. Immigrants had been brought in large numbers from Central Europe to Cleveland in the early days of its industrial expansion, almost like cattle herded in boxcars, and were put to live in slums. Now the descendants of the early families who had profited from their labor set about in committees to improve the living conditions of the descendants of the laborers. I think my mother sensed that this was not her problem. She was after all a provincial girl from a small town, more familiar with the personal, impulsive charity of her mother going for nursing care or with a basket of food to a neighbor in temporary distress. And Euclid Village, small as it was, was more sophisticated than Springfield, since it served as the setting for the country houses of some of the early families who had made industrial fortunes in Cleveland.

In our new neighborhood we were no nearer a Roman Catholic church than we had been before, and we had no immediate Roman Catholic neighbors, but this did not trouble my mother quite so much now since both of my sisters were day pupils in the Convent of the Sacred Heart and I was at Cathedral Latin. We did not share in the social or community life of our neighbors, but we had friends in scattered places and activities of our own beyond the neighborhood.

Roman Catholic families become accustomed to this rather curious sense of dislocation in their daily lives. If their social life is elsewhere and private, if they sometimes live in isolation in their communities, when together as a result of this, they are more fortified in their feeling of strength and unity as a group. It is a condition not without peril for a democratic society, since in the warmth of their insularity, Roman Catholics sometimes tend to think of themselves as separate or even superior to the larger community in which they live. In Roman Catholic homes when local or even national government affairs were discussed, for example, I often heard the body politic referred to not as "we," but as "they." "When 'they' do something about the public schools," I once heard a Roman Catholic father say, "then I might think of sending my children there."

At any rate, into this interlude of our family life the Depression came. Although we, along with everyone else, were to become only too familiar with the grayness of the endless days that followed, two incidents from the beginning of the Depression remain in my mind. One was walking away from the closed door of the bank where my small savings had been kept, money garnered by cutting grass or performing other chores for neighbors, and holding my deposit book tightly and senselessly in my hand, open at the last entry, realizing that the money was gone and that I would never see it again.

The second incident was more immediate and more serious, because my father fell ill. I could not remember his ever having been ill before, and, as is the way with a household under this threatening circumstance, we all went about our business trying to pretend that nothing was wrong. But at length, after a day or so, when my father still remained upstairs in bed, my mother called the doctor. He came in the evening, and when he had seen my father he came downstairs and went into the dining room where the doors could be closed, and sent for me.

My mother, who was with him, was crying. The doctor, however, wore an odd half-smile, and his voice and manner was cheerfully matter-of-fact, even defiantly so, as he wrote a note on his prescription pad. "There is nothing wrong with your father at all," he said to me. "Sometimes we just get too discouraged to go on."

It was then I learned that my father had lost his job, by the closing of the plant where he had been employed. This had happened a week or so before, but he had kept the news from us, going out each day at the regular hour in an unsuccessful effort to find another job.

The doctor tore the sheet from the pad and handed it to me. "This prescription is for a bottle of port wine," he said. "You get it, and get your father to drink it. All of it, if he wants to."

I brought the port wine to my father, and he drank a good part of the bottle. The following morning he went out and found a temporary, makeshift job.

Under these circumstances, it was decided that I must find a part-time job after school to help out with family expenses. I was fifteen, but I said that I was sixteen in order to get my working papers, and I found a job in a grocery store, halfway between school and home, for two afternoons a week and all day Saturday.

I had never known the intimate community life of a neighborhood before, and now in this somewhat better than middle-class neighborhood where the grocery was, my heart ached with envy. My customers seemed to be gracious and unhurried people who lived in a world where all windows and doors were open, a world without self-imposed restrictions, where God and country were somehow the same, or at least not implicitly antagonistic. I came to know them and their family ways well, for from their manner and tone of voice, I knew they assumed that I shared the same way of life. I was awkward and shy and too ardent; their easy way of life in which everything one did was all right but did not come easily to me, even being a grocery clerk was acceptable, since often their sons worked behind the counter.

Although I assumed that unhappiness was an inevitable part of life, or at least of my life, and went about my tasks humming under my breath, "None but the Lonely Heart Can Know My Sadness," there are moments from that experience that I remember with nostalgia and pleasure.

Saturday was a very long working day, much too long for boys of our age. We worked hours that would not be permitted now, but which went unquestioned at a time when the boon of work itself was so precious. On Saturdays our hours were from six-thirty in the morning until ten o'clock at night, although we were there most often until midnight. It is such long days, curiously enough, particularly Saturdays in the winter months, that I remember with the most nostalgia. Being very young, I appreciated the delights of physical sensation. I would be up before dawn, to arrive at the store at six-thirty, and I recall the winter stillness of that hour, of walking in deserted streets over fresh snow, following the plume of my breath. At the store, beating our hands and arms against our sides, we waited on the cold street for the truck that would bring the fresh vegetables, which was the reason for our being there so early. When the truck arrived we would quickly pull down the crates of produce; one of us would station himself at the foot of the stairs to the cellar, and over a long plank, polished with much use, the crates would be slid down below. There we would uncrate the fresh lettuce, shipped from Florida or other parts of the South, the heavy outer leaves stiff with a rim of ice. We cut away those leaves and brought the crisp heads to the vegetable racks in the store above, along with heads of cabbage, scrubbed carrots tied in bunches, washed beets and turnips, heavy winter squash whose heads we cracked with the blow of an ax to sell the fragments separately.

Often we had worked late the night before, stocking the shelves, and now we moved lightly, drugged with fatigue and a sense of unreality. The milk and cream in glass bottles came next; we carried them, rattling in their wooden cases, to the refrigerator. After that the fresh bread and pastry would arrive. We were working against time now, for the light falling on the winter pavement would attract to serve early shoppers, a man, walking a dog, who wanted a loaf of fresh bread, or a housewife, a scarf over her uncombed hair, who had discovered that she was out of coffee or eggs.

If the shipment of fresh eggs had been delayed the previous day, it might fall to me to candle and box them when they arrived, a task I enjoyed since it seemed freighted with mystery, and since also it left me in solitude in the cellar of the store. The eggs came in cases of many dozens; beside the larger cases I would sit on a stool, under an unshaded electric bulb, and hold each egg up to the light to look at the opaque shell for the telltale shadow of blood, like a wisp of smoke, which meant that the egg would have to be put aside and not sold for first quality.

Sitting there on winter mornings in the cellar, which was dark except for the light against which I held each egg with fingers whitened by cold, I would feel like a prisoner in a dungeon, condemned to perform this curious rite of discarding the imperfect egg. On the floor above me I would hear the feet of early-morning shoppers, and I knew the sun would be flooding the store windows now, melting the frost, to reveal the pyramids of canned foods and the display of produce, like a horn of plenty, which we took turns in arranging to exercise whatever artistic talents we possessed.

The sunshine and the plenty seemed not for me. I felt irretrievably trapped in the grayness of my life with its piety and study, its compulsion to be good, to win, always, the approval or approbation of my teachers, or of my father, or of God. Not for me the easy, careless ways of the other boys who worked along with me, who laughed and wrestled and spoke foul words from fresh young lips, who shrugged off rebukes, and who accepted discipline or obeyed orders only after a token hesitation to demonstrate their young male pride. I envied them, but I felt that I could never be one of them.

**11**

IN THIS MANNER I came under the influence of a teacher who was to be of much importance to me. I shall call him Brother Robert.

Brother Robert was slight and neatly constructed, with black hair and ruddy coloring. I suppose he could not have been much more than thirty years old. He was a quiet man, but in him this did not seem to indicate repression or inhibition. He seemed someone who had resolved all inner conflict, and for this reason and the fact that he took an interest in me I admired him and was drawn to him.

It was Brother Robert who encouraged me, on the basis of a short story I had submitted in an annual short-story contest of which he was one of the judges, to think of becoming a journalist or a writer. He assigned me to the staff of the school newspaper, which was under his supervision. He discussed editorials with me and outlined feature stories for me to write, sending me into the city for interviews he arranged with local public figures.

All of this was an interest and an occupation I fell into willingly. I had always read widely. The atmosphere of the public school at Euclid Village had encouraged reading, and it was still remembered by the Brothers that when I had come to Cathedral Latin and been requested by our English teacher to write the name of a favorite book, I had put down, not one of the Tom Swift books but Bulwer Lytton's *The Last Days of Pom-*

*peii.* I seized upon the idea of writing as if it were the answer that had always been waiting for me for the direction of my life.

There was no important American Roman Catholic contemporary writing. The writing in the Roman Catholic periodicals that came to us at home and at school was didactic or weak and insipid. Brother Robert acknowledged that he was aware of this. It made my own choice of profession more exciting and important.

I did not confide to Brother Robert that I sometimes had the disquieting feeling that the absence of any Roman Catholic writing of any importance could possibly be the result of more than mere chance. It was not until I had come to Cathedral Latin that I had learned of the Vatican Index of Forbidden Books. The existence of this list astonished me. How could any man be corrupted by a book if he did not wish to be? Didn't every man take to his reading the free will that God had given him?

Yet such a list did exist, and the writers of these books had been excommunicated by the Church. If I meant to become a Roman Catholic writer, then I must learn for myself what limitations were imposed by the Church on the Roman Catholic writer. I resolved upon a preposterous step that I knew Brother Robert would have found indefensible, so I did not share my decision with him. I made up my mind to read all of the books I could find that had been proscribed by the Holy Office of the Vatican so that by example I might find out what I was not supposed to do.

To assist me I had the Cleveland Public Library, spoken of as the largest open-shelf library in the world. Every afternoon after class when I was free of my job in the grocery store, I took the streetcar into town to this vast quarry of books.

For a good part of two years I spent my free afternoons at the library in a state of such complete absorption that time would be lost to me. I would look up to see the light fading in the windows and, realizing that I would be late getting home, I would start up suddenly and make my way to the now almost deserted city streets outside, the office workers having already gone home. I would hurry along to the streetcar, lurching a bit, dizzy from having been so long over a reading table, drunk and bemused with words and ideas.

In the library I proceeded without any plan. It was possible to go unchallenged into the stacks, and I remember that moment of excitement and anticipation when I would walk back into the darkness, reach up to pull a light cord, and stand within walls of books revealed. I cannot imagine how I ever hoped to accomplish my purpose, since I had only rather sketchy ideas of what writers or what books were on the Index, and often I didn't know if I was reading forbidden work or not. I believed that I understood in general terms that certain books were forbidden on grounds of immorality because of erotic or pornographic passages, and even I could detect these in Boccaccio or Balzac. But in the area of heresy, or of ideas dangerous to faith, I was at sea. Dutifully I plunged into the novelists of the nineteenth century—Flaubert, Victor Hugo, Anatole France, Dumas, Zola—totally unaware at any time of what insidious wickedness might be presenting itself to me in terms of fiction. In between I read writers at random, early and late, from Ovid to Freud. I read the plays of Shaw. The poetry of Swinburne and Rimbaud. But then, as if drawn downward or backward by the force of a vortex, I came to Voltaire.

I knew that Voltaire was forbidden. Had he not written *"Écrasez l'infame"*? Crush the infamy, destroy the Roman Catholic Church itself? Here I was on firm ground, in Satan's camp so to speak, and yet I found so much delight in Voltaire that I began at last, no doubt belatedly, to have misgivings about the propriety of my project. I decided that I must confess the error of my ways to a priest.

It was apparent that I could not go to just any priest to discuss my transgressions, just as I had sought anonymity for my sin of fornication. I went instead, at some distance, in a kind of pilgrimage, to a priest at John Carroll University, a Roman Catholic institution in Cleveland. This priest, a member of the faculty, was known to me only by reputation. He was said to be a witty man, intelligent and tolerant, and it had become something of a fashion to go to his confessional to discuss what were called "intellectual doubts," those questions that sometimes arise among the faithful about dogma and belief.

Inside his confessional, where I had stood in line on a

Friday afternoon among the students, I pronounced the customary, ritualistic preamble about my sinful nature and the length of time it had been since my last confession. I then told him, to begin what I thought would be a discussion, or at least a series of questions into the purpose of my defection, that I had been reading Voltaire.

Beyond me in the darkened box again there was silence. I was puzzled. I knew the priest was there because I could see his seated figure outlined in the shadow. After a moment I could make out a sort of muffled sound, and to my astonishment and dismay I realized that the priest was not asleep, but was holding his handkerchief to his mouth to stifle laughter.

I waited and after he had controlled himself he spoke to me. His voice was gentle and pleasant. He had been amused, he explained in a tone of apology, because only the day before, walking down the street, he had passed a young man who had raised with defiance the book he was carrying so that the name of Voltaire could be seen on its spine. It was the coincidence that had made him laugh. I no longer remember his actual words, but in effect he told me that my reading Voltaire was quite probably a simple form of youthful rebellion.

Unaccountably I suddenly found myself blushing painfully in the darkness, feeling as a child might feel when he has spoken with candor to an adult and is not accepted on equal terms. For it was obvious that it was as a child or at least a youthful innocent that the priest regarded me, too young, too unlearned to be harmed or to have sinned by my reading. I was not to be taken seriously.

I could not go on. I was unable to tell the priest that my reading Voltaire was merely part of a larger plan, since I feared that further revelations would merely provoke more benevolent laughter.

Apparently accepting my silence as a conclusion to confession the priest pronounced the absolution and gave me for my penance—the customary perfunctory three Hail Marys and Our Fathers. I left the confessional, to be replaced by another from the line of those waiting.

I never went to confession again.

\*    \*    \*

Life intervened. I graduated from Cathedral Latin. To what? The year was 1931. The Great Depression had reached its lowest ebb. There was no thought of my going to college. There were no jobs. Grown, able-bodied men stood on street corners selling apples, or pencils.

But I was fortunate, so I was told. I had a job. With hard work, and if I applied myself, the part-time job in the grocery store might become a full-time job, with a future.

I ADMIT IT was my own idea to take a Greyhound bus when I ran away from home, but I didn't pack a lunch. A friend of mine did that for me, and I would never have run away except for Mr. Gogarty.

Mr. Gogarty was the manager of the grocery store where I worked, weighing potatoes and butter and waiting on customers with a cynical smile.

When I began to work for Mr. Gogarty I was confident that one day someone would come in, some patron of the arts idly tapping a riding crop against his breeches, and exclaim with amazement, "What is this young Voltaire [or Goethe or Shakespeare] doing here?" and forthwith whisk me away to Weimar-on-the-Ohio or some small principality near Cleveland, where I would begin to pen the great, biting, witty thoughts that foamed in my head like near beer.

The passing years had disillusioned me about patrons, and there I was, finished with my schooling, out in the world, still

standing behind the grocery counter and smiling with a knowing eye at the people who asked for pink salmon for the cat, or
oleomargarine for frying, aware of the sham of the world, its
petty hypocrisies. "Where youth grows pale, and specter-thin,
and dies," I used to mutter from Keats, dipping morosely into
the peanut butter barrel.

But if Mr. Gogarty was no patron of the arts, at least I was
forced to admit he was no tyrant. He was a rotund man, with
apoplectic coloring and the manner of a professional Irishman,
which indeed he was. And while it was incomprehensible to me
in my philosophical detachment, he also took pride in being a
good grocer, and he wanted me to be a good grocer, too. He
had tried, with some pain and embarrassment, to teach me his
sales technique. This was in the days before the self-help su-
permarket, and he was concerned with something called the
"plus-sale." The good grocer always sold the customer something more than she had come in for. Mr. Gogarty's approach
was peaty and romantic. "Any cheese, teas, or peas?" he would
shout cheerfully when the customer came to the end of her list.
"Any leeks, beets, or sweets?"

I was a considerable disappointment to him because I could
never master this rollicking technique, which always threw the
ladies into panic spasms of laughter, although I was a constant
advertisement for the goods of the store, my mouth always
stuffed with a dill pickle, a marshmallow, a maraschino cherry,
or a bit of Roquefort cheese.

Mr. Gogarty tolerated me, I suppose, because I was quick
on my feet, tirelessly young, and docile to the point of idiocy.
(The great man bows before destiny.) I was, depending on the
busyness of the season, one of a staff of six or eight pimply-
faced contemporaries. It was a large store, with a counter running the length of one wall and across the back, and each of us
had a certain portion for ourselves where our regular clients
presented themselves.

Although I am at a loss to understand why, I was not an
unpopular member of the staff. I had nothing but contempt for
my business associates, who were only interested in football,
practical jokes, and girls, in that order. I was interested in these
things, too, but I also had my lofty side. Although many of my

fellow clerks have gone on to greater things—I can count a doctor, a lawyer, a public health officer, and a banker among them—only the future public health officer seemed then to possess so much as a glimmering of sensibility.

He and I were members together of the *Cercle Français,* a social group that met on occasional Wednesday nights to discuss the weather in French, and he alone was not amused by my ostentatious reading of Plato or Shaw's *Prefaces* while I ate my lunch in the cellar of the store. It was his sister who packed the sandwiches for me when I ran away from home on the Greyhound bus.

It all began with Pat Walsh, one of the clerks who did not, as far as I know, go on to greater things. Pat was Mr. Gogarty's Achilles' heel, a handsome son of the Old Sod, lazy as sin, the map of County Cork on his face, and the blue of Irish skies in his eyes. The lyrics are Mr. Gogarty's; for his money Pat could do no wrong. Most of us loafed when Mr. Gogarty was not looking; Pat loafed even when he was. And got a smile of indulgence in return. All this did not help him in our esteem, a fact which troubled Pat not at all. He knew which side his bread was buttered on, and I don't suppose it surprised any of us when we learned that Mr. Gogarty had asked Pat to stand as godfather for his new, and first, son.

Certainly it was no business of mine whom Mr. Gogarty asked to be godfather to his son, but on Saturday afternoon that week I learned (in some devious way I now forget) that Pat had a dollar more in his pay envelope than I did, and for the same number of hours. I was a man slow to anger (timid would be a better word), but all the rest of that day my soul seethed with righteous wrath. It had been a bad day from the start. At noon I had telephoned my mother to discover that five of my short-story manuscripts, from my early or Poe period, had been returned without a word by callous, indifferent magazine editors who, I was certain, hadn't even read them, probably because I had no influence in their crass world. All day I moved about among the butter tubs, a cheated and misunderstood genius. I suppose it might all have stopped right there had it not been for the incident of the spinach can.

After the store closed that night and I was on my knees replenishing a lower shelf, a number four, or large-sized, spinach can fell from a higher shelf onto my head. Friends rushed to my aid, and helped me to the back room where I lay stunned, rather like General Wolfe at the battle of Quebec, on a pile of burlap bags. There the iron entered into my soul.

I waited until all had gone home but Mr. Gogarty. Then I emerged, an apocalyptic figure, to face Mr. Gogarty over the counter.

"You gave Pat Walsh a dollar more than you gave me," I said.

Mr. Gogarty had been working on his perpetual inventory, large sheets of paper spread out before him. We faced each other in our aprons.

"So I did," he said. "And what of that?"

It seemed to me that he flushed, if it was possible to observe such a phenomenon under Mr. Gogarty's natural coloring, and I began to flush and tremble at my own temerity.

"It isn't fair," I said.

"I decide that," Mr. Gogarty said. "I decide what's fair."

Then I played my trump card. I delivered the line I had rehearsed on the potato bags. "It says in my prayer book," I said, capitalizing as I went, "that one of the Sins that Cry to Heaven for Vengeance is Defrauding the Laborer of his Wages."

There was a moment of absolute, stunned silence.

Mr. Gogarty without a word flung himself across the counter. He seized me by the neck and shoulders and shook me like a wet rag.

It is difficult to say who was sorrier afterward. I began to cry, and Mr. Gogarty turned away, dabbing at his own eyes with the end of his apron. But I didn't stand there long.

I went into the back room for my sweater, and I took off my apron, and then I ran out of the door, never to see Mr. Gogarty again.

That night I made my plans. My friend, the future public health officer, met me in the dead of night. I would say at home that I was going to mass with him, but instead I would take the bus for New York City. With my weekly pay, and some money he would lend me, I could buy a ticket and have enough left over to get me started on a new life.

I wrote a note to my parents before I left in the morning, impaling it, in the traditional way, on my mother's pincushion. They would not find it until it was far too late to follow, since they planned to go on to a cousin's for dinner after early mass. "Like Oscar Wilde," I penned (I always penned in those days), "I must be allowed to make my own mistakes." It is fortunate that neither my parents nor I knew at that time the exact nature of the mistakes made by Mr. Wilde, so there could have been no sinister suggestions to follow upon the initial shock of the note.

My friend was waiting for me at the bus station. He had confided in his sister and she had prepared a lunch, which he was holding awkwardly in a brown paper bag. "You can throw it away if you want to," he said. "She made me take it." But I was touched. My friend, his sister, and I knew that I was moving inevitably toward the kind of messy destiny that awaits all great, misunderstood men. It might be the last home meal I ever had. I took the brown paper bag with dignity.

Our farewell went off on a satisfactorily high key. Dry-eyed, we clasped hands. On the steps of the bus I turned back and raised my hand, Lord Byron Leaving England Forever.

The trip to New York was one of those tedious episodes best omitted from any biographical account. For a while, I was interested in a young woman sitting opposite me; she seemed to carry with her a kind of tawdry glamour, but as the trip progressed her glamour faded and the tawdriness increased. She spent the night with her head shouldered on the convenient clavicle of a traveling salesman.

There was also a young man who, like myself, was going to seek his fortune in New York. I avoided him after he confided this to me over a cup of coffee during one of our night stops, because I wanted to play that role myself and not share it with anyone.

We arrived in New York City about ten in the morning, at the Greyhound bus station on Thirty-fourth Street. The Sloane House YMCA was nearby, and I headed for it like a homing pigeon, filled with panic and awe at my own courage. I would just stay there until I got settled, I told myself. Besides, it was only fifty cents a night.

\*　　\*　　\*

I spent my days roaming the streets of Greenwich Village, which I found by asking the way to the Provincetown Theater. I had to ask a good many people because there wasn't any Provincetown Theater, but when I found the building where it had been, I stood in front of it, cursing the destiny that had brought me too late into the world.

I had fifteen dollars, over and above the cost of my round-trip ticket. (Well, everybody knows it's cheaper to buy a round-trip ticket, and you can always turn in the other half if you don't use it.) At the end of the first week I began to spend most of my time hanging around the general delivery window of the post office, the address I had thoughtfully written in my farewell note, under the line from the wit and wisdom of Oscar Wilde. On Saturday there was a letter from my father. There was no money in it. He just told me to come home.

I took the bus the next morning. A large, comfortable woman who looked like one of my aunts took the seat beside me, and she bought me hamburgers when the bus stopped, to keep her company, she said. I told her I wasn't hungry. I had lived on hamburgers and hot dogs all that week, and I could see by looking into a mirror that I was becoming green in color.

My mother put me to bed when I got home and called our doctor.

When I was well enough to get out of bed I went into town and got a job as clerk in a bookstore.

SEVERAL YEARS PASSED during which I sold books, or tried to sell books, or pretended to sell books in bookstores in Cleveland, Chicago, and Detroit. Not a great deal is required of a bookseller, which is why one finds so many vague, lost young people behind the counters of bookstores. It helps to be well read, which I certainly was, to the detriment of almost all other social graces. And the bookseller must know the stock of the bookstore so he can get the book requested or order it if it is not in stock. It was my period of higher learning, I said to myself as I took home books to read in the evening, between attempts at short-story writing. After all, not much debauchery can be indulged on a bookseller's salary.

My father had given me advice when I took my first job away from home. "If you can't afford a good restaurant," he said, "stay away from the bad restaurants. Eat instead in a tavern, or bar and grill, where they offer food for sale. They don't have to make any money on the food. They make enough at the bar. You get good value."

I am unable to think of any better advice to a penniless young man going out into the world. On the debit side, I regret to say, it left me ever after with an abiding distaste for pastrami, corned beef, knockwurst, sauerkraut, and boiled potatoes.

In Chicago, where I went on my first job away from home, I went at once to the YMCA, as I had done in my abortive running away to New York. It was expected of a good young

man of my background. It was called, I think, the "Family
YMCA," a name guaranteed to reassure my family back home.
The interior was painted that drab color often found in hospitals. The floors were cement. The inner rooms looked down on
a bleak, cement courtyard in which garbage cans were kept. I
loved it very much.

Plato himself had said that the wise man should live so that
if the city were besieged he could depart with all of his possessions on his back. All of my possessions fitted into an old-
fashioned valise and a Gladstone bag.

I walked to my job each morning with an anticipation mingled with dread. My job was that of a clerk in the large bookstore of Adolph Kroch on Michigan Avenue, in the smart
shopping district. Kroch's Bookstore was the leading bookstore
in the city and, some said, in the country. It was also said that
supposedly Adolph Kroch was the first bookseller in the country to have made a million dollars selling books. He had advertised for book clerks some weeks back in *Publishers Weekly,* a
trade publication. I had replied. He had interviewed me in
Cleveland on a stopover during a business trip to New York
and seemed satisfied with my credentials. He offered me more
money than I was making in my present job. I accepted his
offer, stifling a feeling that I was a fraud.

I was not the least interested in selling books. My heart was
in my writing, and I was convinced that my name would some
day come just before Edgar Allen Poe's in the *Biographical Dictionary of American Writers.*

Mr. Kroch owed his financial success to employing certain
aggressive and innovative techniques, one of which was of
course the plus-sale. Mr. Kroch's approach to the plus-sale was
not as petty and poetic as Mr. Gogarty's, but it was much more
serious, and if I had known about it when he offered me a job,
I would have taken the next bus back home. When a customer
came into the store and asked for a certain book, the clerk was
to think instantly of another book, similar in interest, which the
customer would also like. The customer then left with two books
instead of one, and his name and literary interests were placed
in a card file by the clerk so that the customer could be mailed
future books he would be certain to want. Vast numbers of

people were forever caught in this net, deluged with books and the bills from which they would never hope to escape except by leaving Chicago.

Common decency, as well as a lack of interest, prevailed at my desk. I was no more successful with the plus-sale for Mr. Kroch than I had been for Mr. Gogarty.

Meanwhile, back at the Y I learned from the clerk at the front desk that the "Family YMCA" was not so much a haven for the genteel as a refuge for the dispossessed. There was an elegant Y in town, designed as a club residence especially for young men like myself. It was relatively expensive, something like eight dollars a week, but I moved there feeling required to do so by social pressure. Indeed, it was much more elegant. The scent of the disinfectant that permeated the building had a better quality, a bouquet and body like a good wine. My room had a washbowl and a medicine chest with a mirror, and there was a rug on the floor and carpeting in the hall.

But I was less happy in the clublike atmosphere of this superior YMCA because the same sort of middle-class industry flourished there that I had left behind at home. I was vaguely depressed by the cretonne in the public rooms and the young men who sat there doing homework assignments from night school or reading *Judge* magazine. I was uncomfortable with the brash neatness, the even teeth and scrubbed faces, the short cuts to fashion displayed by the young men. They all looked like clerks or office boys unsuccessfully disguised as junior stock brokers or insurance salesmen, and while their goals did not seem unworthy, still the very definition of their ambition made me feel untidy and isolated.

The unique feature of the establishment, which made it much talked of whenever these worldly young men gathered together, was a soda fountain on the second floor, closed to the street level, to which you might come down before bedtime in your nightclothes for a bite to eat before going to sleep. Its purpose was to make everyone feel at home, and while I could not imagine why anyone would wish to feel at home after they were old enough to leave it, I tried it one night to see what it was like. Suitably attired in leather slippers, pajamas, and the flannel bathrobe that had been given to me when I went out into the world, I descended in the elevator with the air whistling around my bare ankles, but when I got out into the brightly lighted, gleaming room, filled with cigarette smoke and dozens of young men lounging about in pajamas and dressing gowns, the whole spectacle seemed so ludicrous that I bought a candy bar and took it back to eat in the wonderful loneliness of my room.

I tried very hard to like the YMCA, thinking the lack in myself. I bought a straw hat (a sennit straw, it was called). It was stiff, with a narrow stiff brim all around and a dark ribbon. I wore bow ties and tried to look like a junior bond salesman, too. But my heart wasn't in it and I began to wonder what other roles I could play.

On weekends, and after the bookstore had closed in the late afternoon, I explored the city, walking or riding streetcars or the elevated train, getting off impulsively when a neighborhood or a street caught my fancy. I carried no map, purposely, because of my delight at being lost in the city, and I remember now my later disappointment when suddenly it all fell together like the pieces of a jigsaw puzzle and I could no longer turn a corner and be lost.

But on one of these explorations I discovered the University of Chicago, coming upon the old World's Fair midway with something of the awe Balboa must have felt when he first saw the Pacific Ocean. Even Central Park in New York City, perhaps because of its trees and shrubbery, did not give one the same dreamlike sense of suspension in a metropolis, and I decided at once that I would have to live nearby in order to walk like Heathcliff upon the moors.

I roamed the neighborhood looking for signs reading ROOMS TO LET, being careful to avoid those establishments that looked like boardinghouses for students, not because I disapproved of students, or even of education, but having decided that until I could go for longer periods without consulting the mirror to verify my existence, I ought to be alone.

Finally I found what seemed to be the ideal place, an ambiguous sort of building, in every sense of the word, being neither boardinghouse nor apartment, which advertised HOUSEKEEPING ROOMS FOR RENT. It was seedy and not very clean, and the woman who answered the bell would have discouraged a more knowing seeker than myself. She seemed rather astonished that I wanted to see a room, but she shrugged and led the way upstairs, holding her wrapper about her with one hand and reassuring herself with the other hand that her kid curlers were still in place on the back of her head.

I was shown a large, dingy room with an alcove where a sink and a gas ring were hidden behind a curtain that fell short of the floor by about two feet. The room itself had a double frame bed covered with a length of monk's cloth, and the pillows were stuffed into matching covers, the effect intended to suggest a divan. There was a brown upholstered chair that sagged, a scarred writing table, and a floor lamp with an imitation parchment shade pasted with scenes of Italian cities. The bathroom was down the hall, a grubby hole where the flush chain hung over the toilet, which always sang because of a faulty plunger. I was so delighted with all of it that I paid a week in advance and went back to the YMCA at once to surrender my room with its rug and medicine chest, and to bid farewell, with relief, to the young men with shining teeth and rayon bathrobes.

In my new quarters I fought for some weeks a sinking feeling that perhaps my decision to move had not been very wise. At night as I lay on my monk's-cloth divan, trying to read *Thus Spake Zarathustra* by the light filtering through the scenes of Italian cities, the housekeeping rooms around me sounded with shrill laughter, sudden drunken shouts, and sinister bumps and thuds. In the hall on my way to the bathroom I would hurry past large, lurching men who pounded on locked doors or stumbled by me toward the stairs with stained hats pulled down over flushed faces. The rooms themselves all seemed occupied by equally large, fleshy women with soft, pink faces and fragile hair exhausted by hot irons and strong dyes.

No one there, either male or female, ever spoke to me or even seemed to see me at all. My incredible innocence doubtless served as a cloak, but my only conclusion at the time was that my personality was still so unformed that I was scarcely visible to the naked eye.

At the same time, at the bookstore I had begun to make

friends in the staff, and I discovered little by little that some of them lived lives of incredible sophistication in rooms with bookshelves and batik, where they entertained friends who sat on covered daybeds and drank red wine out of cheese glasses. I was admitted into this company of the elect, as I had been into the bookstore, because I had never done anything all my life but read, a drawback I felt constrained to point out to my new friends. I had not even left Euclid Village to go to college, and while it was true that I had read the *Odes* of Horace in the original, I could not pay a streetcar conductor, or order a bowl of soup in a restaurant, without watching someone else do it first.

My new friends were amused by this paradox. They took me in hand kindly. They taught me discreetly, by indirection and example, such complicated social graces as how to come into a room and sit down in a chair, what not to wear (the sennit straw hat went), and how to carry on a casual conversation about nothing in particular with a lady, a much more difficult achievement than reading Horace in the original Latin.

They were appalled when they discovered where I lived. I must leave there at once, since they had assumed responsibility for me, and join my peers in the little colony on the near north side of Chicago, where artists and writers and other people of the New Quality lived. It did not take much to persuade me. Especially since, now and again, it had seemed that I caught fleeting, tantalizing glimpses of my own identity in their company. I joined in the search for suitable quarters and moved at last into a room of my own choosing.

This was an English basement in a brownstone house on one of those pleasant, shaded streets that ran between Lake Shore Drive and Rush Street. I had taken the room because it had its own entrance and thus obviated the necessity of smiling or grimacing at people in the hall or the way to the bathroom. To enter the room you passed under the arch of the outer steps, which climbed to the front door. There was an iron grille set under these steps that had to be opened with a key, a further defense against intrusion. Beyond that you went down two steps to another door, which led into a large room with three small windows set at eye level, from which you could see the feet and ankles of people who passed by on the sidewalk.

My friends helped me decorate this room, which contained the inevitable frame bed covered with (as a concession to the New Quality) an Indian print, a bureau and writing table, and one or two sagging upholstered chairs. They made new covers and curtains and painted a bit here and there to brighten things, and when this was finished I gave, to my surprise, a party, where my guests sat uncomfortably on the edge of the bed and drank red wine from small glasses while we talked about Floyd Dell, Rupert Brooke, Margaret Anderson, and the life of the artist, which is like the life of the fabled phoenix, forever rising from the ashes of its dead self.

In Chicago I did not always attend mass on Sunday, but I still thought of myself as a Roman Catholic. It was a period of great torment for me. Better to sin by not attending mass, I reasoned, than to attend mass and sin by doubting. I did not want to leave the Roman Catholic Church and become one of those homogenized Americans who left the church of their fathers for no church at all, an American without a past.

I corresponded with Brother Robert, as I had done ever since leaving Cathedral Latin School. Brother Robert had left the school shortly after I did, having decided to go on to the priesthood of his order, a decision that took him abroad for study. Ours was an impossible correspondence, I realize now, for Brother Robert. I wrote to him about my religious doubts, my troubled state of mind concerning my faith. In return he wrote to me of mountain climbing, or of his studies, with suggestions appended for my reading, which I fear I ignored.

Even if he did not respond to the issues I raised he did address me, as he had always done, as a peer, and this prompted me to write freely to him, surely a mistake, a discourtesy to him, since I was well aware of the conditions that circumscribed his life.

When a letter came from him I would put it in my pocket to savor the pleasure of reading it at the end of the day, when I would go to Grant Park and sit on a bench under the trees. And it was there, sitting on a bench in the warmth of an early summer evening, that I learned—shatteringly—that I had fallen disastrously from grace, so that when I picked myself up again to walk away it would be to proceed in a very different direction.

This letter from Brother Robert was in reply to one of mine in which I had written that I was reading Shaw again. I had always preferred the prefaces to the plays, probably because I had never seen a play of Shaw's performed, but the preface to *Androcles and the Lion,* in which Shaw had speculated about the divinity of Christ, had set me thinking. Was it not possible, I had asked in my letter, that everything was divine? Wouldn't it be wonderful to think that? If the earth was the creation of God, then wasn't it possible that everything in it or of it was divine, not only Christ and ourselves, but every leaf and tree and stone?

I had gone too far. There was nothing for me now but the thunderbolt. I was ignorant and uninformed. I was apparently so ignorant that I did not even know that what I had written was heresy—and heresy in one of its most elementary forms, pantheism, the pagan belief in the divinity of nature.

I was to cease these idle speculations at once and remember that the only consideration of any importance to me was the salvation of my immortal soul. I must pray for humility. Brother Robert would pray for me. And he signed the letter in the formal manner, with the initials of his order following his name.

After the first moment of shock and disbelief I began to weep, grateful for the shadows on my bench under the plane trees. I wept for our lost friendship. I wept because I knew I could never retrace my steps. I wept because I knew that the past was lost to me. From that moment I ceased to be a Roman Catholic.

To become what? To become whatever it was determined I would become on that day so many years ago when Monsignor had lost his first battle with my mother and she had taken us to the public school in Euclid Village instead of putting us on the streetcar for the parochial school.

I was free. It was a kind of joyless freedom, but on the other hand I had never really been wholly a part of either the country of my birth or the country of my faith.

I folded the letter and put it in my pocket. I stood up from the bench in Grant Park and walked away, to try to find my place in a trackless America.

MR. KROCH HAD my new destiny well in hand. He owned several other bookstores in the Middle West, and at this point he decided to send me to Detroit, possibly because he became tired of looking at me every day at my post in the alcove of Poetry and Belles Lettres where I had been put because of my knowledge of obscure poets and essayists. I was a handy ready reference, but I seldom sold anything. Mr. Kroch, who suffered from high blood pressure, had been told by his doctor shortly before my arrival that it would be a dangerous thing for him to lose his temper. At the end of each day he examined my sales book, purpling slowly.

I went off happily with my valise and Gladstone bag, feeling much more sophisticated than when I had arrived. In Detroit I went first of course to the YMCA, performing in the aseptic room my familiar rites: shirts in the top drawer, underclothes in the next. But I knew it was only an interim stop. I had learned the procedure, and within ten days I had found by inquiry where the new quality lived, a gloomy group indeed in Detroit, who kept complaining that the city had no "cultural center." All of them regarded themselves as exiles from New York City, whether or not they had ever been there, and they lived lives of rootless despair, like citizens of ancient Rome sent to one of the provinces of Gaul.

I found a large room in a great warren of a house, filled with incredible people. I didn't know the people were incredible at first, but I was delighted with my room, with its size, with its dormer windows and their view of a garden, and with the furnishings of the room—a double frame bed covered with an Indian print, a bureau, a writing table, two chairs, and a grass rug.

I was also influenced to take the room by the man who showed it to me, the husband of the landlady, Quasimodo himself. He was a dour man, and as he led me up the stairs in the front hall his misshapen back cast alarming shadows on the wall. There were two flights of stairs going up from the hall; they met at a center landing under an enormous stained glass window, where Thalia, the Grace of Flowers, was portrayed in bare feet and flowing gown and hair, with a brace of Burne-Jones lilies in her hand. As we reached this landing, a dark object darted over our heads in the jeweled shadows, and when I asked what it was my guide dismissed it with a wave of his free hand. "Just a bat," he said.

I paid him two weeks in advance, to stave off the threat of an interloper who had looked at the room before me and said he might return.

At night in my new home I was lulled to sleep by the music of Chinese stringed instruments, played from the record collection of my immediate neighbor. I never spoke to this neighbor when I passed him in the hall because he seemed to inhabit some private, violent world that intimidated me. He invariably left his door standing open when he was away, and when I passed by I could see the walls of his room were hung with wildly colored reproductions of Mexico's three great painters— Rivera, Orozco, Siqueiros. I suppose he was a Communist, something I had decided I could never be, because, as I had explained with diffidence to a friend after trying to read *Das Kapital* for the third time, "I just can't seem to keep my mind on it."

The drawing room of the old house, a room impossibly cluttered with marble figures on pedestals, gilt chairs, faded loveseats, and potted ferns hanging on brackets, was occupied by a not so very young lady who was so neurotic her teeth chattered. She invited me to tea on Sunday afternoon, a disastrous occasion during which we both fell into a catatonic state. When I tried to put my teacup down I found I could not uncurl my forefinger and had to remove the cup with the other hand.

Also on the third floor was a tenant who seemed to have reached this haven of the new quality by mistake. He was a healthy-looking young man who actually did sell bonds or insurance, and in his free time lived a life of such glandular activity that he was scarcely ever home, stopping only long enough to change into black tie or a clean shirt. One evening, as I sat alone reading *Marius the Epicurean,* there was a tentative knock at my door and I opened it to find a girl, weeping. She was pretty and was doubtless even prettier when her eyes were not swollen from crying, but her speech was uneducated. "Johnny isn't home," she said. "He promised he'd be here. Can I come in and wait?"

I said of course she could, and she came in and sat uneasily on one of my chairs, still crying. For perhaps half an hour she sat, weeping quietly, until we heard quick footsteps on the stairs, and a door slam. She was on her feet in an instant and ran out of the room, leaving me in my disquiet with *Marius,* who seemed to pale beside this evidence of Life going on so near my door.

After some time I heard her leave and there was another knock on my door, and there was Johnny. We didn't know each other very well, but he was always very cheery on the stairs. "God, I'm in trouble," he said, sinking down in a chair. He was in his shirt sleeves with his collar unbuttoned, his ruddy face damp with perspiration. He kept running his hand through his hair while he desperately smoked a cigarette. "I need fifty bucks," he said to me without embarrassment, as one man of the world to another. "She says it's mine and I can't be sure, but she's got me by the short hair."

We were silent for a moment, or rather I was silent, while I searched back in the card file of my mind, trying to find precedent in my reading for conversation under such circumstances. Were congratulations in order, or merely commiseration?

"Have you got fifty bucks?" he asked. "I wouldn't let her do it if I was sure it was mine, but I don't think it is."

"I've got ten," I said. It was all I had. My precious bulwark against calamity. I went to the dictionary and took the bill out of the pages where it was filed under D for disaster. I handed it to him. "It's all I've got," I said.

He took it with a perfunctory thanks and left, his eyes

already preoccupied with the next touch. The next week he moved away and I never saw him or the ten dollars or the girl again. I don't think I expected to. There is a period in the life of young men when their fear of the scorn of their contemporaries outweighs any other considerations. I suppose I was afraid that if I had refused him my ten dollars, he would have taken that as a priggish condemnation of his behavior.

Two deaths of distinguished men marked my stay in Detroit, one just after I had arrived, and the other just before I left. I had formed the pleasant habit of dropping into a nearby bar for a whiskey and water before I went home or out for the evening. The bar was dimly lighted, a quiet place, well-suited to calm the nerves after a day that had been marked by the absence of customers. A young man played semiclassical and classical music at the grand piano in the bar, with a great emphasis on Chopin. One evening I found him in a sorrowful mood at the piano, playing a vaguely familiar composition, which I eventually recognized as *Pavane for a Dead Infanta* by Maurice Ravel. The pianist had also lighted a single candle in a tall brass candlestick. This was in the days before Liberace, and such a candle meant something. I went over to the piano. The pianist looked up at me, and without stopping his playing, he said quietly, "Ravel died today."

I have often wondered what Maurice Ravel would have thought had he known that his death was marked by a grieving pianist in the far-off industrial wasteland of Detroit during the Depression.

The other death was that of Sigmund Freud. I read about it over my morning coffee at a lunch counter I stopped in for breakfast. When I went to the bookstore I gathered up all the books by Freud. We had copies of his early lectures, *Civilization and Its Discontents,* and *Moses and Monotheism.* I arranged these books in the window, and in front of them I placed a hand-lettered sign saying: SIGMUND FREUD DIED TODAY.

Not a single customer entered the store all day long.

Edsel Ford did come in whenever we had a sale. I had learned, painfully, how to conduct myself with famous or noted people. In Chicago, on my first day at Kroch's Bookstore, I happened to be alone in the front of the store when Frank

Lloyd Wright came in and asked for a particular book on engineering. I panicked, stammered something about having to look it up. Frank Lloyd Wright took a step away from me, and bellowed, "Won't somebody find me someone to help me who knows something?!" Mr. Kroch came running. Several other salespeople came running, and I went into the back room to regain my composure. While there I tried my damnedest to recollect whatever I had thought to admire about the architecture of Frank Lloyd Wright.

I learned from that disaster. On approaching a noted person: Smile, address him or her by name, be friendly, impersonal. Be calm. Don't speak unless spoken to. Don't panic.

In Detroit when we had a sale we remained open a few hours in the evening to accommodate those who worked all day. Edsel Ford would come in about eight o'clock. I would go up to him and greet him, "Good evening, Mr. Ford," and then leave him alone. He would browse among the books put on sale on the middle counter in the store. Almost always he was alone. His armed bodyguard waited outside the street door. When Edsel Ford reached across the sales table for a book, I could notice the outline of a shoulder pistol holster. He always bought a book or two and paid in cash. I wrapped up the purchase and said, "Good night, Mr. Ford."

At one of the three bookstores I had worked in during my apprenticeship, the manager, a woman, came in one morning with her eyes reddened and sleepy. "I stayed up all night reading the most wonderful novel!" she said. "I predict it will be a great success." So I spent considerable time going up and down from the basement storage room, lugging copies of Daphne du Maurier's *Rebecca*. I also spent a considerable amount of time at Kroch's Chicago store carrying up from the basement storeroom copies of Margaret Mitchell's *Gone With the Wind*, a much heavier novel.

We had no such bonanza in Detroit. No best seller. No sales. No customers. In a city whose inhabitants were hard-pressed to feed themselves and their families, there was no money for books.

Mr. Kroch came from Chicago to close the store and to fire

me, whom he thought partly responsible for the failure of the store. I suppose I was.

Mr. Kroch smiled rather sadly in dismissing me, saying, "I think you have good things inside you, but I have been unable to bring them out."

Undaunted, callously free of guilt, I packed my valise and my Gladstone bag, walked for the last time past Thalia in Tiffany glass, and took my interior virtues off to New York City, where I very quickly got a job in Brentano's bookstore, Mr. Kroch's chief competitor and rival.

BRENTANO'S BOOKSTORE, at Fifth Avenue and Forty-seventh Street, is no more, but in 1939 it had served generations, moving uptown from Union Square when fashion moved uptown. It was a large store, with two entrances, one on Fifth Avenue, the other on Forty-seventh Street. It was an institution, immutable, its importance taken for granted.

Arthur Brentano said he really had no opening, but he would hire me because of my experience, to have on hand when I was needed. I was sent to what was called the "Annex," a long, wide corridor lined with books leading to the Fifth Avenue entrance, to work with Mrs. Porter, who was in charge of sex and sporting books. Although my knowledge of life was largely academic, I did not see the irony in this assignment. Mrs. Porter, however, filled her role perfectly. A widow with a rakish sense of humor, and rather like a bawdy duchess, she had an elderly admirer who came for her when the store closed. One evening when he was late she said that he was probably at the Turkish baths, "getting it steamed up."

We sold classic English hunting books in fine bindings, hunting prints, books on equitation. Of the few manuals on sex then in print, or of books on sex in general, we found that the book most frequently stolen was *The History of Prostitution*. It was a period of innocence.

Now that I had found a job it was possible to leave the Sloane House YMCA, which only reminded me of my former failed attempt to make it in New York. I went to share an apartment on Bleecker Street (a heady triumph) with a friend of my brother Ned back home in Ohio. I did not know Freddie Armbruster, but he needed someone to share the expenses of the apartment he had sublet for the summer. The apartment was in a fairly new building, but it was across the street from the Mills Hotel where aging and indigent men were taken in, a rather depressing habitation to see first thing in the morning, but we were young and we simply ignored it.

In New York City I was made more aware of events in Europe, as I had not been before, though I had been in Cleveland or Chicago or Detroit. Hitler's armies were advancing over western Europe, swallowing whatever country lay in their path. Soon they would be in France.

Arthur Brentano, Sr., was in Paris, at the family bookstore where he had spent most of his adult life and where the Brentano bookstore was a meeting place for the literati. Mr. Brentano was eighty years old and did not want to leave Paris. Concern for his safety hung over the New York store like a pall.

Meanwhile, I was having a wonderful time. I got up with the alarm in the morning. Freddie might or might not be there. If he was there, even the alarm did not rouse him, and this was fine with me because I had the place to myself. I showered and shaved and dressed and made myself some breakfast before leaving for work.

The morning air of New York smelled of freshly ground coffee and the sea, and in 1939 it was clean. The streets were clean and in good repair, and Greenwich Village had the air of being truly a village. There were some older tenements and new apartment houses such as ours, but there were also row houses and town houses and shops and cafés and restaurants. The area was Italian in character, and there were Italian restaurants and shops where salami and other sausages hung from the ceiling. I turned left at the first corner, toward Washington Square. I always turned left on this street because I then passed an ancient brick structure where horses of the New York City Mounted Police were stabled. The fragrance of barn smells and horseflesh was like a tonic, and contrasted vividly with the impressions of the city beyond. Young mothers might be wheeling baby carriages on the sidewalks, and the trees of Washington Square, arching over shaded walks lined with park benches, were in full leaf.

Double-decker, open-air buses waited by the Washington Square Arch. Since this was their starting point they, too, would be almost empty, and I would climb the curving stairway at the rear of the bus to have my choice of a seat. The trip up Fifth Avenue was always interesting. Private residences and small hotels and churches gave way to small businesses and commercial buildings beyond Fourteenth Street. At Thirty-fourth Street the Empire State Building proudly announced itself, and on the corner opposite was B. Altman's department store. I got down from the bus at Forty-seventh Street where Brentano's was and my busy day began.

Going back to the apartment at five-thirty, after the day's work, I sometimes felt like a young husband who never knows what new complication might be waiting for him at home. One day Freddie decided that to save money he would wash the bedsheets in the kitchen sink instead of taking them out to the laundry. He was very proud of this feat and announced it upon my arrival. He had hung the sheets to dry on the roof, and together we climbed up to inspect them. Unfortunately, the apartment incinerator had been fired at five, and the bedraggled sheets were covered with soot. Silently we took them down and folded them, and the next day on my way to work I dropped them off at the laundry, where they cost twice as much to launder than if they had been sent there in the first place.

Weekends at home were equally unpredictable, involving invitations extended to acquaintances of Freddie's. In this way I came to meet the legendary Marsha, who was said to possess only the clothes she wore, a rather graceful silk dress, a picture hat, and shoes with high heels. In her handbag she carried her lipstick. She slept where she was asked, a kind of moveable feast. I was shy with women, especially with the Marshas of the world, and she later confessed to me that at first she had thought I was queer, but then she realized she had misjudged me because I was so refined. I still wonder sometimes what I would have replied to that.

Marsha had her own air of soiled elegance. The first Sunday she came to our apartment she brought with her a young man who had just been released from serving time on a marijuana rap. Whether for possessing or selling, I wasn't told. He was a handsome, confident young man, and when he sat down he pulled from his pocket a package of what looked like homemade cigarettes.

"Have a weed," he said, holding out the package to me.

I got up in silent shock, being so refined, and went to the bathroom and called Freddie. When he came in, I closed the door.

"They're smoking marijuana out there," I said.

Freddie looked at me with a kind of exasperated amusement. "Oh, don't be so Ohio," he said. He opened the door and went back to his friends.

I left the apartment and went to a movie. A double feature.

When my brother had written me about Freddie and the apartment, I didn't know that Freddie was a remittance man whose father had given him up as a bad job. He had cashed an insurance policy that he had taken out in Freddie's name when Freddie was born, given him the money, and showed him the door. When the money was gone, Freddie was on his own.

Instead of looking for a job, Freddie was wasting his substance in the bars and haunts of Greenwich Village, which was not much different then as now. Once he phoned me about two o'clock in the morning. There was a hubbub of music and laughter behind him as he talked. He wanted me to join him.

"Where are you?" I asked, half-awake.

"At the Village Dump," he said. "It's fabulous. Come on over."

The Village Dump was a new place in the Village, and I had never been there. I explained to Freddie, shouting to be heard above the din, that I couldn't come to join him because I had to go to work in the morning. It occurred to me as I hung up that someday, when the money was gone, Freddie might very well end up in the Mills Hotel across the street.

One evening Freddie was waiting for me when I came home from the bookstore. He had a different young woman with him, a girl named Lida, with a pretty, selfish face. She, too, was a remittance person, with money from Father. A lot of it, apparently, because the white, open convertible with the red leather upholstery parked in front of our apartment was hers. She wanted to be an actress. Freddie had now decided that he wanted to be an actor. Lida and Freddie were going to drive to Hollywood in the white convertible and become movie stars.

"What about the rent?" I asked. The lease on the apartment had more than a month to go, and on my pay from Brentano's it was not possible for me to pay the entire sum.

"I'll send you the money from Hollywood," Freddie said.

I stood there with my mouth open, and they were gone, just like that!

I didn't wait for the check from Freddie. After all, the apartment had been taken in Freddie's name. So I vacated the next day, locked the door, and took the key to the rental agent.

# 16

I MOVED TO a room in a boardinghouse for young men in the East Forties, between Lexington and Third avenues. It had been a private residence where a spinster or a widow lived in genteel poverty. The house was rather dusty and gloomy, but it spoke of former glory in its furnishings.

The East Forties were lined with brownstones cut up into apartments, or having rooms to let. Some single girls had not yet achieved the independence that would allow them to live alone respectably, so the rooms were generally occupied by young bachelors.

These rooming houses were similar. The woman in charge—it was always a woman—was someone related to the original owner of the house, maintaining it by renting rooms. In my house, the woman in charge never removed her hat, to make it quite clear that she was a lady and not a servant, although I was certain that she made the beds and did up the rooms after we left in the morning. I never saw the first-floor living rooms. A stairway to the left in the front hall led to the musty bedrooms above.

My bedroom was sizable, well-furnished, and cheerful with windows looking down on a garden court in back. It contained a closet, a bed with a table beside it, a bureau, a straight chair, a more comfortable chair for reading, and a reading lamp. The furniture could be rearranged, the table placed under the reading lamp and the straight chair pulled up to it, so that I could sit at my new portable typewriter. The rate was five dollars a week. The bathroom was at the end of the hall.

I hung some of my things in the closet and arranged the rest in the drawers of the bureau, on the top of which I put a figure of Kuan-yin, the Chinese goddess of mercy and abundance, that I had purchased in a curio shop in Greenwich Village. It was made of soapstone and had been broken at the neck and repaired, and I had bought it for seventy-five cents. I considered it my token of good fortune. At the foot of the bed I placed the folded carriage robe I had brought from home. It was quite literally my security blanket, although that phrase had not yet come into being. There was never an abundance of blankets in these furnished rooms, so I felt quite happy under my own when it was needed. There was no telephone in the room, no radio or television. There was little to keep you in the room except for sleeping, unless you wanted to write, as I did. Because these places did not furnish board, it was necessary to have all my meals out.

In the morning I would get up early, slip on a pair of pants, a sweater, and some shoes, and go out for breakfast at a drugstore counter, where I could have two fried eggs, toast, and coffee for twenty-five cents. Having breakfast first was a strategy I had learned. When I returned to the house the others would have gone and I would have the bathroom to myself.

I could walk to and from work in a matter of minutes. And, as in Greenwich Village, the mornings were cheerful; the air in the city was different then, cleaner and brighter; the streets, and the sidewalks, and the curbs were swept and in good repair. Going to work in the morning, strangers smiled and nodded as they passed.

I enjoyed Brentano's as I had enjoyed no other bookstore in which I had worked. As the great and the near-great came into the store, I acquired an air of false self-confidence, or a false air of self-confidence. Lofty young men like me are often clerks in bookstores, which is probably one of the major reasons why so many bookstores go broke.

Members of the old guard usually came in by the carriage entrance, helped from their limousines by their chauffeurs, to walk grandly through the Annex into the store itself.

Jeanne Eagels, the actress, came in repeatedly to ask for help in selecting books to prepare her for a role. It was said that Greta Garbo sometimes had a rendezvous with an admirer or lover at the back of the balcony in the main part of the store, in the children's book department, where people seldom went. One of Mrs. Porter's favorite customers was Vincent Astor, always a little tipsy, sparkling with good humor, and with ribaldry to match her own. On one Saturday morning, while they were exchanging pleasantries, the then Mrs. Vincent Astor appeared and, taking him playfully by the ear, she said, "Come on, Vincent, I'll take you home and pour you back into the bottle."

New York was not a cosmopolitan city then, although we did not know that until it became a cosmopolitan city. There were still private residences below Fifty-ninth Street. Mrs. Vanderbilt was at home at the corner of Fifth Avenue and Fifty-first Street. She gave grand luncheon parties and dinner parties, and it always amused people to walk around the corner on Fifty-first Street to see that the lace curtains at the kitchen window were mended.

Then there was "Winkie" Thomas, also of the Brentano staff, a member of a socially prominent New York family, who knew everyone, who always came to work with a hangover, and who was almost as bawdy as Mrs. Porter. Sometimes he ran down the street to have lunch with Mrs. Vanderbilt. Once Winkie came back from Mrs. Vanderbilt's house to tell us that Greta Garbo had also been at lunch. When Garbo arrived she requested, without explanation, that no one answer the telephone if it should ring while she was there.

# 17

ONE DAY without fanfare, Mr. Brentano, Sr. arrived from Paris, ready to take up his special interest in old and rare books, as if he had just been away on a holiday. With him was his daughter Rowena.

Mr. Brentano, Sr., was a slight, elegant man with the worldly air of one who has spent his life in fashionable drawing rooms. He gave the impression of having been dressed by a manservant. It was obvious that even in Paris he had had an English tailor. His dun-colored hair was brushed back smartly on the sides of his head. He had a shaped moustache, pointed at the ends. Pince-nez were clipped to the bridge of his nose, attached to a black ribbon that disappeared into the breast pocket of his suit jacket. He wore a vest, a gold chain across its front from pocket to pocket. Once, he pulled the chain out absently from one of the pockets and looked at it reflectively, since there was nothing at the end. "When I was younger," he said, "they let me carry a pocketknife on this end."

He said that to me. His manner was as always solemn and faintly mocking. It occurred to me sometime later that he might once have been an Edwardian dandy.

After two weeks of observation of the staff, Mr. Brentano requested that I be assigned to him as his personal assistant. In spite of my experience, I knew very little about old and rare books, and almost nothing about incunabula, another of Mr. Brentano's passions (the word "incunabula" refers to those

112

books published the first century after the invention of the printing press). I was very flattered but a little apprehensive. I need not have been.

Mr. Brentano set up his desk, with his precious old and rare books on the shelves behind him and around him, at the juncture of the two wings of the store where they met at the Forty-seventh Street and Fifth Avenue entrances. I took up my place beside him. My higher education in book selling was about to begin.

A much delayed and even more pleasurable education was also about to begin. The whole store had come alive with the arrival of Rowena Brentano. She was a mischievous and vivacious woman. She was of average height, slender, not pretty but attractive as only a woman who had spent a lifetime in Paris could be. Her face was alive with humor, and she was in constant motion. Because she was on her feet all day she wore pleated skirts, blouses and sweaters, and comfortable shoes. She preferred to work on the busy floor of the main store, surrounded by stacks of current novels and books of nonfiction. She had never married. She had taken care of Papa. She seemed ageless. Everyone fell in love with her. She made friends easily, and soon she was overwhelmed with invitations. But she could not travel about the city alone. She needed an escort.

I was pressed into service, not at all unwillingly. I was in the fortunate social position of being a young, single, unattached man in New York City, where dinner-party guests still went into the dining room two by two, male and female, as if they were entering the Ark. I was reasonably presentable, I had learned manners and how to eat at a dinner table back home in Ohio. (There were, in fact, so many young men from Ohio in New York that I was told an Ohio club had been formed. I did not attend any of their meetings or functions. I did not care to have my provincialism preserved.)

Proper dress plus proper address were presumed to be the secrets of social acceptance for a young man in the city. I had the address, but on my salary I could not possibly afford to be well dressed. A friend took me to an establishment on Madison Avenue where men's clothing, not exactly new but not visibly worn, was on sale at a fraction of the original price. The party line of the store was that the clothing came from trunks and suitcases impounded by hotel managements when guests could not pay their bills. I suspected, however, that much of the clothing came from young men who had come to an untimely end. This did not disturb me. I was content to go along with the party line as long as I could be well dressed.

I bought one suit in particular, a suit of fine English tweed and tailoring, that fitted me perfectly and gave me such a sense of well-being when I wore it that I imagined I had put on the spirit of the original owner.

I could not possibly afford a dinner jacket. They were easy enough to rent, so I bought the necessary accessories: black shoes of patent leather, black silk socks, garters, a dinner shirt with cuff links and studs, a black evening tie, and a cummerbund. I could rent the tuxedo after leaving the store at closing time, and return it to the place I had rented it from before I went to work the next morning. The rental price was three dollars.

Thus equipped, I was ready for anything.

UNWILLING AS HE had been to leave Paris, the elder Mr. Brentano had not come directly to New York. He had gone first to London. And what he had seen there was apocalyptic. In retrospect, we like to think of the English as being steadfast and calm on the brink of World War II, but they were not all so. It is difficult to remember that the chances of victory over what was assumed to be the impending Nazi invasion seemed very

114

slim. England was not prepared. She did not have the military resources that Germany had. France was next, and after that would come England.

Many of the English had already left their country, and many more were preparing to leave. Mr. Brentano had gone to Sotheby's and Christie's, as he had done so often in the past, on expeditions in search of old and rare books. He found both of these institutions in a state of chaos, their interiors piled high with what looked like the wreckage of great estates—a confusion of old books and paintings and china and furniture and tapestries, which their owners, or heirs, had hastily consigned to be auctioned so they might leave the country on the proceeds, or at least that the treasures might not fall into enemy hands.

Mr. Brentano had invested as much as he could in this wealth of old books, and in time these books, crated, began to arrive in the basement storeroom on Fifth Avenue. With what excitement we unpacked these crates! For example, they contained several complete novels of Dickens, in "parts," as they were called, the original serial chapters that were sold, in paper, as they were written. These parts were neatly boxed, the box ornamented and bound in leather.

I was too unlearned to know the value of what was passing through my hands, and there wasn't time to teach me everything, but in the crates there were early editions, sometimes first editions, of the poems of Byron and Shelley. (No Keats. Keats belongs passionately to the English, and even the threat of death or destruction would not tempt them to part with him.)

There were books in French, the letters of Mademoiselle de Sévigné and of Mademoiselle de Staël among them.

The wonders poured out. There was a fifteenth-century Book of Hours, the devotional prayer book that the clergy and some wealthy members of the laity carried about with them to pray from at prescribed periods. This Book of Hours, the *Hours of the Virgin,* was written in French and Latin on vellum, the borders of the text illuminated with painted flowers and fruit and birds in red and blue with gold laid on. Mr. Brentano explained to me that the secret of affixing pure gold to vellum— fine lambskin, or kidskin, or calfskin prepared for writing and decoration—had never been rediscovered. Apparently the liquid gold was poured, or laid on so heavily that when it hardened it could be polished to brilliance with a jeweler's tool, and remained fixed to the page forever.

There was a more utilitarian prayer book, thick, faded, with bookworm holes, that was said to have belonged to Mary, Queen of Scots, and from which she prayed while waiting to be beheaded. (At her beheading, from a contemporary account in another old and rare book, it was said that her lapdog ran to lap up her blood.)

Two or three examples of fore-edge painting turned up among the books. Mr. Brentano had introduced me to fore-edge painting. If a book is placed on a table, and the top cover is moved back slightly, the pages of the book will reveal their edges, on a slant. If the book is clamped in this position, a scene can be painted on the edges, a scene that will disappear when the book is returned to its natural position. If these edges are then carefully gilded, the result is a secret painting known only to the owner of the book, who can reveal it when he pleases to amazed friends. Erotic or pornographic books were favored for this treatment, so that erotic or pornographic scenes could be painted on their fore-edges.

In this permissive age, where almost nothing needs to be hidden, it would be difficult to find a book worth the trouble, but forty or fifty years ago this was not the case. Locked in the safe in the office upstairs at Brentano's was a copy of *Fanny Hill,* forbidden at that time in this country. It had turned up in a group of books bought at an estate auction.

Whatever became of it I do not know. It was an eighteenth-century edition, not with fore-edge painting but illustrated with exquisite engravings, carefully and lasciviously done. The books with fore-edge paintings that had come from London were not erotic or pornographic. The scenes of the fore-edge paintings were taken from the novels they decorated; they were meticulously rendered and of superior artistic quality.

Among the books were manuscripts, carefully protected. There were several pages from an incomplete copy of the Gutenberg Bible, suitable for framing. There were manuscripts of medieval music on vellum, with square notes, and some had

116

illuminated borders, in intricate filigree, of flowers, fruit, and foliage in color.

There was a copy of a large early almanac, which Mr. Brentano had selected partly because of his interest in incunabula but also because it had passed through his hands before. He opened the book at the back cover and showed me his own colophon. Mr. Brentano indicated he had sold the almanac three times before. It was the first realization I had that books could be an investment, ready at hand when capital needed to be raised.

And, treasure of treasures, there was a quarto edition of Shakespeare's *Hamlet*!

Mr. Brentano had already explained to me the categories of book volume, by size. A newspaper, for example, was a folio, or a single fold. Audubon's *The Birds of America* was also a folio. If you folded a sheet once more, it was a quarto, or four pages. If this sheet was folded again, it became an octavo, or eight pages, the size of most of the novels and books we read. A number of these folded sheets would be bound together, with a spine, and the pages cut. Book collectors who specialize in bindings prefer the pages of a book uncut. In a description of a book in an auction catalog, it will specify "uncut." For the collector who had a reading copy of this book, the rare book would sit, virginal, on the shelf in his library. Such books brought higher prices at auction.

And here was a quarto of *Hamlet*. I unwrapped it with reverence. This startling, miraculous glimpse into the past was something I have never forgotten.

When the last of the books had been unpacked, the business of creating a catalog to be sent to special customers was begun. The *Hamlet* did not go into the catalog. Mr. Brentano had shipped this home with a definite collector in mind. It went, as I remember, to the Shakespearian collection of the Bienecke Rare Book Library at Yale University.

Mr. Brentano prepared his little alcove with care. Beside the chair of the desk, at which he seldom sat, he had brought to him a tall-backed chair, with arms, upholstered in velvet of a deep imperial red. This chair was for his special customers.

I was to stand beside him and keep the sales book, recording all his transactions. It was also my duty to bring the books requested, to see that the books bought found their way to the shipping room, with the proper transaction address, and to take any cash or checks, for those customers who were not billed by mail, to the cashier. And in this manner, my education in books continued.

A FULL LIFETIME later I paid a visit to the small park that William Paley had built on the site of the Stork Club to honor the memory of his parents. It was a beautiful park, with shrubs, and graveled walks, and benches. At the far end was an enormous artificial waterfall, whose sound served to blot out the street-noises. It was possible to sit there in peace. I did, and remembered.

It was difficult to believe that this small space had once encompassed the Stork Club. In memory it seemed an enormous, glowing room, brilliantly yet softly lighted, filled with music, with people dancing or sitting at tables eating and drinking, talking and laughing; jewels, expensive clothes, an aura of opulence.

You went to El Morocco to dance, and to be photographed for the tabloids or the society pages. The zebra-patterned upholstery told people where you were. You went to the Blue Angel for the singing, in a darkened, smoke-filled room. But you went to the Stork Club to talk.

It was the day of café society. New York glittered like a Christmas tree as wealthy expatriates and émigrés poured in from Europe. The city became cosmopolitan, with German and French spoken not hesitantly but assertively on the streets and in the shops and nightclubs. The Baron de Rothschild flew in to Idlewild, the international airport, from France, bringing with him nothing but a chamois bag of uncut diamonds. The city was exciting. We had none of the horrors of war or the agony of the dispossessed. Money flowed and sparkled like champagne, which also flowed and sparkled.

Rowena and I seldom made a full night of it. It was necessary to get some sleep because the excitement and the glitter had begun to flow into the bookstore, and we were very busy. We would take leave of Rowena's friends, our hosts, and I would see her back to the small hotel, within walking distance of the store, where she would spend the night when she was in town. The driver, who brought her and Mr. Brentano to the bookstore each morning from East Orange, would have taken him back.

In the morning it was not business as usual but business as extraordinary. One Saturday morning the liner *Manhattan* arrived on its last crossing from France before the war broke out. It docked at ten o'clock and by noon Brentano's was filled with expatriate Americans, all of them speaking French. They had come to Brentano's in New York as a point of rendezvous, just as they would have gone to Brentano's in Paris. It was difficult to push down the unworthy comparison, which kept arising to the surface of my mind, of rats leaving a sinking ship.

As I made my way through the crowd, I heard from behind me what I thought was a woman's voice, one of the most beautiful voices I had ever heard. I turned to find, not a woman, but a man. It was the American poet Charles Henri Ford with his Russian lover, the painter Pavel Tchelitchew.

In the infrequent lulls in business during those busy days, Mr. Brentano would reminisce to me about his life in Paris. He had known Oscar Wilde in his last days of exile. He had visited the bookstore in Paris one day to tell Mr. Brentano that he had no money at all. Mr. Brentano went to the cash register and opened it and said, "Take what you need."

Oscar Wilde did, and within two weeks he was dead.

\*    \*    \*

When Rowena Brentano went out in the evening in New York, gone were the comfortable shoes and the pleated skirts and the blouses and cashmere sweaters, and in their place was the simple elegance, the fine grooming, and the style of a woman who had spent many years of her life in Paris.

We did not always go to the theater, or to dinner parties, or to nightclubs with Rowena's friends. Sometimes we went on our own. When it came to New York, Rowena very much wanted to see the German film *Ecstasy*. The film was the American debut of the young beauty, Hedy Lamarr, and it created a sensation. The story line was taken from, or copied from, D. H. Lawrence's *Lady Chatterley's Lover,* which had long been forbidden in this country. There was the effete, impotent aristocrat in a wheelchair, the ravishingly beautiful young wife (Hedy Lamarr), and the handsome young, virile gamekeeper on the estate. The story almost told itself. The scene that caused all the talk was one of Hedy Lamarr running naked through the woods. I forget the reason for her being naked, if any reason was given or needed, but after all the public outcry the scene was a great disappointment. The film, in black and white, was grainy, and Hedy Lamarr had been photographed at a distance, and only from the back. Little glimpses of flesh were seen now and again through the trees. The virile young gamekeeper pursued her, of course, and he caught her, of course, but again the film chickened out on the reality. Instead of showing them together, it showed what was happening all around them, in time-lapse photography. It was spring, and the plants put out lusty shoots, slowly; flowers opened, meltingly; fat buds dripped moisture.

It was all too much for Rowena. She had a delicious voice, husky and dulcet, with a laugh to match, both of which carried in any room, although she did not speak or laugh loudly.

Every time a plant shoot came forth, or a flower opened, or a bud dripped, she would laugh and say, in her throaty voice, "Ecstasy!" "Ecstasy!" "Ecstasy!"

I was shaking with laughter myself, but presently I became aware of a firm finger poking me in the back.

It was an usher, wearing a very disapproving face. "The management requests you two to leave, at once," he said.

We choked back our laughter with shocked astonishment, held our breaths, and got up and left the theater as quickly as we could. Holding our breaths all the way to the nearest bar, we slid into a booth and ordered drinks.

When the drinks came and we had taken a restorative sip, we exploded. The bar was fairly crowded and fairly noisy, so there was no one to rebuke us for laughing.

We had been thrown out! We had been thrown out! We kept repeating this again and again, with delight. We had been thrown out! It was the most wonderful thing that had ever happened to us! Oh, ecstasy! Ecstasy!

THE SEASON AT Brentano's reached its zenith with the appearance of the Duchesse de Talleyrand. I had no idea who she was, but I was struck into immobility, beside Mr. Brentano, by the apparition she presented.

She had left her limousine and chauffeur on Fifth Avenue and came through the Fifth Avenue entrance preceded and followed by a small retinue of flunkies. She wore no hat or coat. Orange-colored hair was piled high, held in place by a wide black bandeau around her forehead. Her face had been powdered white, and there was a bright circle of rouge on either cheek. Her mouth had been painted into a cupid's bow by scarlet lipstick. She seemed to wear layers of clothing, but the outer layer was of panels of lace, flowing loosely almost to the floor, revealing, when she walked, her high, high-heeled shoes of white kid.

She carried a staff, which appeared to be made of ivory, which she grasped about two thirds of the way up, not for support but to punctuate her steps as she put each foot down firmly on the long promenade to the waiting Mr. Brentano.

When she reached him, she extended her hand. Mr. Brentano drew himself erect, clicked his heels, bowed, kissed her hand, and said, "Madame la Duchesse."

It was Anna Gould, the daughter of the late financier Jay Gould, come to spend her last years on the family estate, Lyndhurst, near Tarrytown on the east shore of the Hudson River.

Madame la Duchesse was ushered into the velvet uphol-stered armchair. Her retinue of flunkies disposed themselves discreetly about her, and I was dispatched to bring out the treasures for her approval.

It was a banner day. In addition to the purchases made by Madame la Duchesse, Baroness Seidlitz bought Mary Stuart's alleged prayerbook as a gift for a friend. Leaving her limousine at the Fifth Avenue door, with a chauffeur at attention beside it, the baroness had come in the carriage entrance in a full-length mink coat, followed by a secretary in last year's full-length mink coat.

Baroness Seidlitz was another American woman who had married a European title. These wealthy women, titled or un-titled, walked in a certain way, which the length of the Fifth Avenue Annex gave them ample opportunity to demonstrate. They walked slowly, as if on parade, putting each foot down in a decisive manner. They never hurried or made an abrupt movement. The passion for almost skeletal thinness had not come into vogue, and these women were well-proportioned. They held their bodies erect and their heads in a certain way, as if they were carrying a book there. And indeed most of them had been made to do so by a governess when they were girls.

Even Mrs. Sara Delano Roosevelt, mother of the president, made the stately promenade, leaving her limousine and chauf-feur at the Fifth Avenue entrance. She paraded down the Fifth Avenue Annex, and, turning left, walked the length of the main store, her destination being the stationery department, just inside the Forty-seventh Street entrance. She was a familiar figure there, and was always served by Miss Guggenheim, one of the older members of the staff. Having completed her business, Mrs. Roosevelt turned and retraced her steps, sailing back to Fifth Avenue.

After that, there was nowhere to go but down.

But of course we did not always serve the glamorous and titled rich. Sometimes we had the poor rich. Private houses on Fifth Avenue above Forty-seventh Street were not all mansions the size of the enormous stone pile that Mrs. Vanderbilt lived in, but they were not exactly row houses, either. (Winkie said that when you were invited for dinner at Mrs. Vanderbilt's, she submitted reluctantly to the new vogue of a cocktail. Each guest was served one dry martini, which you had to drink like medicine while standing. It was also Mrs. Vanderbilt who said to the duke of Windsor when he arrived for dinner, "Oh, my favorite king!")

These lesser mansions were often inhabited by single older women—widows or spinster daughters, who were seldom seen.

One of these women, neatly and carefully dressed in clothing that was no longer new, used to come into the store to offer Mr. Brentano a book from her library—her father's library—in the hope that he might sell it for her.

One day a shy, gray woman offered Mr. Brentano a framed engraving of Edgar Allan Poe's cottage at Fordham, New York. Poe had lived there in stark poverty with his young wife, Virginia, who had died of consumption with, so the story went, a cat on her breast to keep her warm. This episode of Poe's life had caught the romantic imagination of the time, and these engravings of the cottage were popular, but presumably not of great value to a collector.

But Mr. Brentano said not a word. He took the engraving in his hand, and reached for a penknife on his desk. He turned the engraving over and skillfully cut away the brown paper that covered the back. As he did so, a folded, yellowed sheet of paper fell out. He carefully unfolded it, and there in Poe's hand and signed by him was a copy of his poem "Annabel Lee."

"Poe never had any money," Mr. Brentano said to his silent

and awed onlookers—the gray lady and me. "When he wanted to give a gift to a valued friend, he would copy out one of his poems and give it to him."

The pinched, patrician face of the gray lady lightened with a smile of long-ago innocence and happiness. "Papa never mentioned this to me," she said. "Perhaps he didn't know."

" 'Annabel Lee' is thought to be Poe's expression of grief for his lost wife, Virginia," Mr. Brentano said. "It was natural to frame it with an engraving of the cottage at Fordham." He paused. "I could put it on the market of holograph manuscripts, if you like. It should bring a fair price."

The cheeks of the gray lady were flushed with color. "I think Papa would want you to do that for me," she said. She held out her hand. Mr. Brentano took it. She thanked him. He handed her the framed etching, minus its hidden treasure.

She took the etching and, clasping it to her, hurried from the store.

It was apparent after the appearance of the Duchesse de Talleyrand that the stock of old and rare books was depleted and would have to be augmented somehow. But how to do that? Access to the Continental book markets was closed by the war. And now an event happened in England which meant that door, too, was closed.

An enterprising English publisher had thought to bring out a set of the complete works of Charles Dickens, from the original plates. No publisher had ever attempted this before. Dickens had had several illustrators for his works, and even all these plates had been collected for the set. A prospectus was sent out, after printing was under way, with the price of the set.

At Brentano's we took orders for thirteen sets, possibly an ominous number. When these thirteen sets had been packed and were at sea, a Nazi bomb, or bombs, was dropped on London's publishing center. Much more than the original plates of Dickens's work was destroyed. Publishing in London was severely set back, if not eliminated, for the balance of the war. It was fascinating to see what happened to those Dickens sets at sea! It was like watching the stock market. The value of each set increased each day before they arrived.

With book shipments of any kind from England effectively ended, something else would have to be done to replenish the rare book stock.

Mr. Brentano decided he would go to estate sales in New England. He would be in touch with me by letter. His first destination would be Boston, where there were distinguished private libraries in distinguished family houses; some of these libraries came on the market now and then when book collectors died. Mr. Brentano made advance plans, and took off by train for Boston, accompanied by his friend Mr. Burckhart, the treasurer of the store.

After Mr. Brentano had been gone for about a week, I received a letter from him. He had attended one estate sale and had bought a considerable number of books. He had culled from the collection the less important ones and was having them shipped to me. I was to unpack them, riffle them and furbish them, and arrange them on a sale table in the middle of the aisle, the first Saturday after they arrived. He had marked the price of each book on the inside cover, and in the case of sets, the price of the complete set would be marked inside the cover of the first volume.

(Riffle in this instance meant holding a book by the cover upside down and riffling the pages with one's thumb so anything inside could fall out. Some people saved things in books— letters, receipts, recipes, even money. To furbish meant to clean and polish. Old books were dusted with a soft cloth. *Never* the tops! Dusting the top of a book merely rubbed the dust in. The dust must be removed from the top of a book by blowing it off. This sometimes resulted in attacks of sneezing and coughing, especially in a closed room. Brentano's marketed and sold a compound to be used on leather books. This compound was carefully applied with a soft cloth even to books that were only three-quarter-bound in leather. It removed any soil and it contained oils to reconstitute the leather. Central heating is very hard on leatherbound books.)

As luck would have it, the books arrived on a Friday, which meant that I had to unpack them in the basement, and prepare them and bring them up to the sale table before the store closed that day so that they would be there the following morning. (When the old and rare book department was unmanned, other members of the staff kept an eye on it, and helped out if needed.)

I set about my task with pleasure. It was always an excitement to unpack a box of books. There were books on history, biography, travel. There were memoirs and autobiographies, and essays, and books of poetry. But they were not important books either in edition or rarity. They would make an excellent sale table.

I was about halfway through my task of riffling and dusting and furbishing when I reached into the bottom of a box for the last book, and pulled out a copy of the *Kama Sutra*.

I lifted it out with wonder. I had heard about the book, of course, but I had never seen it, as its sale was forbidden in the United States. The *Kama Sutra*! An English translation of the great Hindu book on the art of making love! *Kama*—the Hindu god of love; *sutra*—the teaching, a collection of precepts. And what a collection it was! I sat down on a nearby chair. It contained every known love position. Every known love technique. And most of them unknown to me. After all, I was a country boy from Ohio. And I was young, and my blood heated easily. I forgot all else. I read. I read. I read.

Suddenly I was conscious that much time had elapsed. I looked at my watch. Only a half hour remained before the store would close. I sprang to my feet. I hid the *Kama Sutra* on a shelf until Mr. Brentano returned. The book was unmarked, and must have found its way into the box by mistake.

I rushed the prepared books upstairs to the sale table. After three trips, I returned and looked at the books that were left. I shook my head. There simply wasn't time to prepare them. I picked up one or two of the books. Among them was a five-volume *History of Greece* by the English historian Grote bound in three-quarter blue Morocco. No, there just wasn't time. I had a date with Rowena. We were going to the ballet, and afterward, by invitation, to supper at "21." I had to pick up a tuxedo and go back to my room and shower and shave and dress.

\*　　\*　　\*

Next day the sale went very well. Almost everything was sold. Mr. Brentano would be pleased. On Sunday I slept the sleep of the just.

On Monday morning, a bright, cheerful morning, a beautiful woman came into the store, smiling happily. She was smartly dressed in a piped Chanel suit, and she was carrying a pair of white gloves. A young Park Avenue matron. She came up to where I was standing behind a counter.

"Do you remember the five-volume history of Greece that I bought from you?" she asked.

"Yes," I said.

Her smile deepened. She looked down. She flicked her gloves on the counter. She looked up, still smiling. "It was interleaved with twenty-dollar bills," she said.

And so saying, she turned and left the store.

I did not move for a very long time. I hope my mouth was closed.

I went over all of the ramifications of the situation. Five volumes, interleaved with twenty dollar bills. She hadn't said how many bills. She hadn't given me a chance to speak, even if I had been able to.

My first reaction was one of disappointment in myself for having failed to complete the instructions given to me. Believe me, a country boy from Ohio is brought up with certain principles. I would not have taken the money. I would have put it aside to give to Mr. Brentano on his return. He would see that it got to the proper owner, the inheritor of the books. But a small, unworthy part of me said that it would have been wonderful to have held that money in my hands for a while before giving it up. For possibly no other man in the world has ever paid a higher price for reading the *Kama Sutra*.

MR. BRENTANO RETURNED from his New England trip, followed
at some remove by the cases of books he had bought. When he
returned he seemed more at home and less a former expatriate.
He had built up a following of book collectors who would often
drop by to chat with him. The atmosphere was relaxed, and not
at all hurried as it had been during the season. When I came to
work in the morning, and left in the early evening, I was struck
by the difference between the world within the store and the
world outside.

The world outside was a world of conflict—of wars and
rumors of wars, of distant devastation and horror. But inside
the store we lived in a world of books. We talked about books
among ourselves and with our customers. We read books. We
classified books. We bought books and we sold books. Our entire life was a world of books. When I had begun as a bookseller, I had taken on myself the custom of taking home a book
each night to read, returning it the next morning, and taking
home another book that evening. Like all exercise—which reading is—with practice you become more proficient, and an experienced reader can get through a book in a few hours. But I
had developed a social life too, which I enjoyed, unlike the
lonely years in the Middle West.

Walking to work in the morning, passing a newsstand, seeing the papers' bold, black headlines of the day's disasters, I
couldn't help thinking that we were living in the Dark Ages, or

the Middle Ages, in spite of our modern dress. Certainly the Middle or the Dark ages could not match our times for mindless horror, for war and pillage, for death and destruction.

In medieval days civilization had been kept alive in the monasteries, where monks copied and recopied the classical works of the ancient past. Now the bookstore was in effect our monastery. So far, the disorder of the world had not reached us, but it was on the horizon.

On the evening of the day that Paris finally fell to the Germans, Rowena and I had been invited to have dinner with refugee friends, Trudy and Klaus Bouvier, in their small apartment, which was crowded with the Biedermeier furniture they had been able to ship here from Germany. I was always happy to have a dinner invitation from the Bouviers. Trudy's good German cooking was wonderfully delicious for a young man who took most of his meals in restaurants. In spite of the food that night, the dinner was a gloomy one. When we were finished we went up to the roof of the apartment house, where, in silence, we drank our wine and looked at the sky.

After war broke out in Europe, the United States had taken a position of official neutrality. Under the circumstances it seemed best to try a friend's advice, which was to forget the whole thing, put it out of one's mind, and concentrate on having a good time.

Certainly New York City at night, pulsing, glittering, offered every opportunity to do so. The truth was that I was beginning to be a little unhappy about my forays into the nightlife of New York City, which was beginning to seem faintly obscene. As I walked back to my room in the early morning I reflected that it was not two worlds that we lived in, but three.

There was the world of the semimonastic bookstore. There was the world of war, the half of the globe that was in flames and never far from our thoughts, thanks to newspapers and the radio. There was also a third world, that of hedonistic pleasure, where we danced and drank and ate and laughed as if nothing else existed.

There was a little of the odor of brimstone about this third world. Polished, gleaming, smiling, bejeweled, who knew what particular pacts the rich had made with what particular devils? Some slept the harsh day away in luxurious hotel suites, or in Park Avenue apartments, and appeared at night, well-mannered, resplendent, unrepentant.

The wicked flourished like the green bay tree.

The climax to this feeling of mine came during a night at the ballet with Rowena and friends at the old Metropolitan Opera House, a dress occasion. The ballet had sets by Salvador Dali. It was called "Bacchanale," and was set to the Venusberg music from Wagner's *Tannhäuser*.

There was a feeling of rain in the air, but New York sparkled. Our seats were down front, in the second or third row. The costumes proved to be so fragile that only one performance of the ballet was given, the one we were watching, since it was impossible to put the whole thing back together again. It was easy, afterward, to think that the ballet had been a dream, or a nightmare.

The backdrop, a painted sky, had lines painted on it that converged in infinity. Figures familiar from Dali paintings stood about the stage—figures on crutches, figures with bureau drawers emerging from their abdomens, a limp watch draped over a wall.

The device chosen to represent time was inspired. A dancer dressed to represent an old man, Father Time in a flowing robe, and with a gray beard and gray wig, sat in the middle of the stage. One leg was folded under him, the other leg was outstretched. He was knitting. A pretty little cupid held the ball of yarn and as Father Time knitted, the cupid ran around him in a circle, jumping over the outstretched foot each time, to represent the clock ticking.

The costumes were skimpy. The female corps de ballet came out first and performed arabesques while lying on the floor. The male corps de ballet, wearing black tights and scarlet lobster shells for codpieces, pursued them onto the stage. They lay on top of the female corps de ballet and writhed. At the climax of the music—and what music!—Venus, wearing a flesh-colored body stocking, was carried out, supine, on the upstretched arms of two male ballet dancers. I don't remember what happened after that, but it suddenly struck me that I was witnessing the most tasteless and decadent performance of dance that I had ever seen.

When we came out of the opera house afterward it was raining, and as always it was difficult to find a taxi. The only thing to do was wait in line for our turn. Finally our little party was able to crowd into a taxi. I found myself on the jump seat on the right. Just as we pulled from the curb the traffic light at the corner turned red and we had to stop.

Idly, busy with my unhappy thoughts, I turned to look out the window. I was hatless and I had not worn a raincoat. A derelict, a tipsy, unpleasant man, stumbled toward us as we sat waiting for the light to change. He looked hard at my rented dinner jacket, at my white shirt with studs, at my black tie. Then he stepped back and spat at me, with all the drunken force he could muster. The traffic light changed. We moved forward. Mingled with rain, the spittle ran down the window.

I think no one else in the taxi noticed the incident. They were busy planning what to do next. Someone suggested going to the Stork Club. I leaned back and whispered to Rowena that I wasn't feeling very well. So we were dropped off at her hotel, where I said good night to Rowena in the lobby, assuring her that I would be all right after a good night's sleep.

I walked back to my room in the rain, the blessed rain, the gentle rain from heaven that falls on the just and the unjust, tilting my head back so that I could feel it on my face.

# 22

I CAN'T VERY WELL speak for others, but it was with a distinct feeling of relief that I opened the famous letter from the Selective Service Commission, headed *Greetings*. I was to report for a preliminary physical examination at the French Hospital to determine if I was fit enough to be drafted. I was young enough to be excited about the prospect. It seemed the ultimate adventure.

In retrospect, World War II seems the last war of our times in which the issues of good and evil were so clearly defined, at least for the young, and the need for defense and attack so clearly indicated. Since the incident outside the Metropolitan Opera House, I had a strong desire not to be identified with the noncombatants or the shirkers. I was ready to go.

I didn't regard myself as a passive type. After all, I had left home without any serious qualifications other than ambition. After receiving the letter many of my close friends had already taken matters into their own hands. One of them, a young actor named David White, volunteered for the Marine Corps, and disappeared into one of the Marine Corps training bases. Another friend, Terry, had long ago prepared himself for this eventuality. He was a member of the Reserve Corps of the United States Cavalry, with headquarters in Fort Myers, Virginia. The principal duty of his unit was to provide grandeur at state occasions in Washington, D.C., which was all right with Terry. He was having some unpleasantness with his tailor, who was growing quite tiresome about his bill, and he was glad to get out of town. (Terry was the only man I have ever known to have real buttons and real buttonholes at the ends of his coat or jacket sleeves. When I asked him why, he replied, "In case of a duel, you can fold your sleeves back and have more freedom of movement with your sword.") At any rate, he found another and even more gullible tailor in Washington, and came back to New York to show off his resplendent dress breeches, which he wore with his boots. My mother, who was visiting me in New York, answered the door at his knock and said, "Oh, it's Western Union." A remark that did not please Terry.

And I, taking my cue from Walt Whitman, who had worked as an orderly in the Union Army hospital in Washington during the Civil War, volunteered for the Hospital Corps of the navy, where I might kill someone with my ignorance but I would not be responsible for killing anyone directly.

The navy gave me time to settle my affairs. At Brentano's, where everyone was becoming accustomed to the departure of young men, the staff prepared a farewell party for me. Mr. Brentano was not there, since he never remained in town at night. Rowena was not there; we planned our own private farewell.

And my mother came to New York to say good-bye to me, and to take back with her the clothes that I would not need.

# 23

MOTHER HAD NEVER been to New York City before, but I knew it would not intimidate or even excite her. She was what people used to call a people person, someone more interested in people than in cities.

She had been a beauty in her day, and now she was a pretty, pleasant, smiling woman, not too tall and rounded, like a Renoir figure, "pleasingly plump," as my father used to say. She had weathered the storms of her early life, made a place for herself in Euclid Village. She had a quiet dignity and reserve, and for some reason I could never figure out, strangers were attracted to her and would tell her their more intimate secrets.

At home when I was a boy, I said, when she took the streetcar for the hourlong trip to Cleveland to shop, she always came back with the life story of at least two strangers.

"Sometimes even three or four," I told her.

"Yes, Basil," Mother said. (Because I had a high level of lace-curtain Irish blood in my veins, thanks to my mother, sometimes my manner could be rather lofty. At these moments Mother said I reminded her of the English actor Basil Rathbone. The "Yes, Basil," was meant to bring me back down to earth. It never did, and Mother knew it wouldn't, but we could laugh about it together because both of us knew the mannerisms came from her side of the family and not from my father's honorable, pragmatic German ancestors.)

So Mother came to New York, and my landlady, wearing

an artificial rose on the wide brim of her hat, found her a room just two doors down from mine.

From the moment she got off the train (where she had made several new lifelong friends), we both began to talk at once without stopping, but the visit was an emotional one, my imminent departure for the navy always in the back of our minds. And through an unforeseen incident, I found out during her visit just how far I had come from the village where I had grown up.

She arrived on a Thursday evening, and she would return home on Sunday. On Friday I had to work, so Mother entertained herself by walking in the neighborhood (and talking to the shop people) before she came to meet me at the store at five-thirty. She wanted something from a department store, so we walked down Fifth Avenue to Forty-second Street and turned right to go to Stern's department store, halfway down the block.

The sidewalks were crowded with people hurrying home from offices and shops. Suddenly Mother stopped. There was a man lying sprawled in a doorway, presumably drunk. I took her arm. "I'm sorry, Mother," I said. "It's a familiar sight in New York. He's probably drunk."

Mother did not move. "But he needs help," she said. "He can't just lie there."

"Come on," I said, urging her forward. "It happens all the time."

"But I have to do something to help him," Mother said. "I can't just walk past a man lying unconscious on the sidewalk."

"A policeman will come along," I said. "He'll know what to do. Come on."

"No," Mother said. "No. I must do something." She opened her handbag. She took out her change purse. She reached in it for a twenty-five-cent piece and stooping forward she placed the quarter in the man's outstretched hand. She tried to fold his fingers over the coin to hold it. She tried again and again, but his hand always fell open.

Suddenly a woman joined us, stepping abruptly from the hurrying crowd. She was obviously a nurse, on her way home or on her way to duty. She wore white shoes and white stockings,

135

and the white hem of her uniform showed below her light coat. Wordlessly she stooped and felt the man's pulse. Then she raised one of his eyelids. She straightened and spoke directly to the hurrying crowd.

"This man is dying," she said. "And none of you care."

Instantly everyone stopped. A crowd formed. A man ran to get the traffic cop at the corner. Another man ran to the emergency telephone on a nearby pole. Two other men raised the dying man and propped him against the wall, which may or may not have been a good thing to do.

We waited until we heard the sound of a siren approaching, an ambulance or a police car. Only then was Mother persuaded to leave. She never referred to the incident again. It was just something one did. And I made certain I never again passed a man lying on the sidewalk without stopping and pressing a little offering in his hand.

I took Saturday off and Mother and I did some sightseeing, of sorts. We took the subway down to Battery Park and boarded the ferry to Staten Island to have a closer look at the Statue of Liberty. When we had come back from Staten Island, we took the subway up to Chatham Square and walked the streets of Chinatown. Mother wanted to send some postcards to the people she had become acquainted with on the train, so we found a drugstore and bought some.

I don't know what exactly Mother saw on our sightseeing because she was so busy talking, catching me up on family news, the doings of siblings, aunts and uncles, and a multitude of cousins.

That evening I packed the things that I wouldn't need, keeping a change of underwear and my night clothes and toilet articles. The navy would send these items home after I had been inducted. The rest I packed in the old Gladstone bag, which Mother would take home on the train with her suitcase.

The next day, Sunday, we tried not to be emotional about our parting. I carried her bags onto the train and put them in the luggage compartment at the end of the coach. I saw her to her seat. My father would meet her at the other end, but I was concerned about the baggage. I excused myself and went to speak to the conductor standing at the steps of the car.

"I spoke to the conductor about your bags, Mother," I said, when I returned. "He said he would see that you had a redcap when you got off the train."

Mother looked up at me from her seat.

"Yes, Basil," she said.

We laughed through our tears.

I have seldom felt as lonely as I did when the train pulled out. I knew that my boyhood and my young manhood were irrevocably behind me.

IN ALMOST EVERY way I was unprepared for my first active duty at the Portsmouth Naval Hospital in Norfolk, Virginia, where I was assigned to the gonorrhea cases in the venereal disease ward. In Hospital Corps school, after the hellish punishment of boot camp, we were rushed through an accelerated course in anatomy and physiology, pharmacology, first aid, and minor surgery, with special attention to knowledge of the pressure points of the body to control bleeding and to practical experience in hypodermic needles, both for routine injections and for intravenous procedure. During one day of intolerable pressure I had written on the flyleaf of my notebook *Nil desperandum*, "Never despair," which became a useful motto for subsequent crises.

Almost none of the foregoing training was required in the venereal disease ward. It was a matter of practical nursing, of changing the sheets on the beds, and being helpful to the patients. (In later years I would tease my wife, after looking at a bed she had just made, very neatly, and saying, "That would not pass captain's inspection," to which she would reply, "The hell with the captain!")

The venereal disease patients were housed in separate buildings, confined in a sort of punitive isolation, unable to leave, forbidden visitors, not permitted to walk about the grounds, since exercise in those days before the discovery of penicillin was considered detrimental to their recovery. Even pay was cut off, as a punishment for their misbehavior.

In the main building of the hospital, which stood at some distance from the venereal ward, the real wounded of the war were being cared for. It was at the time of the landings in North Africa, and many of the casualties came from there in such numbers that staff members were told to hold ourselves in readiness to vacate quarters and sleep in tents on the lawn.

Of the casualties who came from North Africa the most tragic were the burn cases. When the magazine of a bombed ship exploded, great sheets of flame flashed through the reaches of a ship, and those who did not die were often left without ears or noses or fingers. The care of these patients was the most harrowing duty at the hospital. The wards where they lay were sealed against visitors, not so much to protect the wounded as to spare the sensibilities of those who loved them, who were urged not to see them until healing or plastic surgery had somewhat diminished the horror. The stench of the burned, rotting flesh could be smelled the length of the corridor when one approached the ward, and I know of only one person, Eleanor Roosevelt, wife of the president, who insisted on being permitted to enter. When the Purple Heart was awarded to these wounded, she went into the wards to pin the ribbon on the jacket of each man as he lay in bed.

Eleanor Roosevelt did not enter the venereal ward. There were no ribbons to be pinned on the men there.

My months of duty in Virginia were marked by a general feeling of innocence, as if the world was younger then than it is now, which of course it was. It came early in the war, and war itself—the experience of war—was still in the realm of romance. None of our contemporaries had any previous experience or memory of war. Early in our hospital training a few veterans of World War I had been in the wards of the hospital at the naval station, but while we were there they had vanished, presumably to whatever veterans' hospitals existed in those days. In navy hospitals very few men came to die, and so very few thoughts were of death. There was a lot of horseplay in the wards, even if forced, and there was a lot of shouting and laughing. They were not ideal places, I suppose, in which to be sick—aside from the sequestered areas as the burn ward.

In the venereal ward no one was desperately sick. No one would die. There was, of course, an underlying despair, which sometimes took the form of querulousness, and this was what we would more than likely find when we arrived for duty in the morning.

We would have been wakened early, before six. To remind us that we were sailors, and sailors first, we maintained the same routine as if we were deckhands at sea. We were roused from our bunks by the bos'un's pipe, and with the master-at-arms advising us to hit the deck. When we had showered and shaved and dressed and made up our bunks, we mustered on the field in front of our barracks before being dismissed for breakfast.

It was winter in Virginia, a mild winter in which, to northern eyes, the landscape seemed moth-eaten and gray. On those still mornings there was also in the air a sickly sweet scent which came from a nearby wood-pulp plant and was the result of a process used to break down the fiber of the wood in vats of chemical solution. Beyond the fences of the hospital grounds sat small, tidy suburban houses, each with its own plot of lawn, hedges, and shrubbery, the sort of houses most of us had known in another life. As we stood for muster, we might see a small boy go off on his bicycle for a loaf of bread. A man would emerge from his house to pick up the morning newspaper. The milkman would come down the street in his truck. It all seemed as far away as a dream. We counted off, and went to breakfast.

Aside from their morning restlessness, the patients in the venereal disease ward were pleasant, even diffident. Now that the world is older and less innocent, we no longer attach the same stigma to venereal disease. It was not so then. Sexual promiscuity was not condoned. There was still in men's minds a kind of Old Testament judgment imposed on the erring. If one danced to the tune, one must pay the piper, and often, as I made my way back from breakfast to the venereal ward, I half expected to see inscribed above the portals THE WAGES OF SIN IS DEATH. While it was true that our patients would not die, they would never leave cured. They were sentenced to a kind of death in life.

Gonorrhea, the oldest known of the venereal diseases, begins in men with an infection of the urethra. In a very short time, this inflammation becomes so painful that normal urination is almost unbearable. It used to be said that one could tell when a victim of gonorrhea had preceded one in a urinal because the pipes overhead would be twisted out of shape by the man standing there in agony. At this stage of the disease a milky secretion would be extruded, and even the most reluctant were driven to treatment.

Treatment was primitive and conjectural. The urethra would be washed out with various substances, none of which could be counted as a cure. The general instruction was bed rest and a bland diet, a particularly irksome routine for otherwise healthy young men. Pepper was denied them, along with any other spices or seasonings. In time the infection would subside. Microscopic slides would be taken each day of the secretion, and when the gonococcus appeared in lesser degree, a certain prescribed limit, the patient could be discharged to duty. Six to twelve weeks was the customary period of hospitalization. But the patient was reminded that he was not cured. The infection could flare up again at any time. He was cautioned against drinking, against excessive sexual practice, against any physical strain. "I'll be seeing you, Doc," was the usual farewell to those who worked in the wards. More often than not it was true. When I went on to other duty stations, I saw my former patients again and again and again. I remember one evening drinking in a bar somewhere—Boston? Halifax? Glasgow?—when a patient of mine recognized me from the other end of the bar, and raised his glass of beer in salute. "Still dripping, Doc," he called. His laughter was taken up the length of the bar.

His round, glowing, healthy face rises up in my memory as the prototype of all the boys whom I knew in the venereal wards. They were lusty, young, extroverted, full of life, and the love of life. Full, indeed, of love. One could not help but like them. They were the animal in all of us at its most attractive, and it seemed unfair that for this they should have been so punished.

During times of peace the navy managed to cope with this problem in its own way. At shipping centers, such as Norfolk, there were well-known red-light districts where, while not legalized, prostitutes gathered by acceptance of the authorities. There, contained in a known area, they were under the surveillance of navy doctors and were examined at regular intervals. Infected prostitutes were confined or hospitalized. When World War II broke out, the red-light district was broken up and closed, under the pressure, they said, of various committees of mothers. The prostitutes did not leave town or cease to ply their trade. They merely practiced it without medical supervision. The most common practice was to go to work as a waitress in a restaurant, where contact was easily established. Infection spread rapidly, like the metastasizing of cancer cells in a larger physical body.

At Norfolk my duties had not taken me to the syphilis ward. This building was next to the gonorrhea ward, and although its patients were not confined to bed, an aura of even greater isolation and dread surrounded them. The very name of the disease had an almost classical association of repugnance and terror, and so critically were its consequences regarded that even the ward attendants there were not permitted to eat with us in the common mess, but were required to eat in the mess hall provided for their patients.

Often I helped boys in the wards at Norfolk to compose a letter. Some excuse for their hospitalization had to be invented, and the choice of this excuse was a delicate one. It must be serious enough to warrant their being hospitalized, but not serious enough to bring the wife or girlfriend to the hospital, where the unhappy truth would be revealed. As my superior, Dr. Robinson, always said, you couldn't get clap from a toilet seat but many a case was dismissed as a bad cold.

AFTER SEVERAL MONTHS at Norfolk, I was given my first sea duty. The U.S.S. *Bell* was a new destroyer of the 600 class, out of Boston, and after a shakedown cruise we were to rendezvous with the British Home Fleet in Scapa Flow in the Orkney Islands, off the coast of northern Scotland.

First, after the shakedown cruise, we stopped in New York Harbor and the off-watch crew had overnight liberty.

I called Rowena at Brentano's from a telephone booth on the dock as soon as I could get off the ship. She began to laugh with delight when she heard my voice. I wanted to see her, I said. I hoped she could stay in town.

"I'm in my sailor whites," I said, to warn her.

Rowena had an ability to transform any experience into something wonderful and ludicrous at the same time. She asked me to meet her at five-thirty at the hairdresser in the Elizabeth Arden beauty salon on Fifth Avenue and Fifty-seventh Street.

I enjoyed walking the familiar streets of New York again. I had left the bookstore clerk far behind me. I was no longer quite the Giacometti stick figure I had been. Navy boot camp, navy discipline, navy chow (!) had filled me out a bit. I enjoyed looking at my reflection in shop windows as I walked. I was fit. I swaggered.

When I got to the Elizabeth Arden shop, I had to sit a long time in the waiting room. I had an idea that Rowena had planned it that way. She called out to me from the inner room when she heard me speak to the receptionist, and I answered so that the women waiting with me would know I belonged to her.

At last she appeared—flushed, radiant, smiling.

I stood up and she took my arm. When she felt my newly acquired muscles, a look of mock astonishment crossed her face.

"My hero!" she said.

We went to dinner. Somewhere. I could not have found the restaurant again if my life depended on it. It existed in the world of enchantment, softly lighted, with muted music and conversation in the background. We had cocktails, and much to talk about, and dinner, but I don't remember what we ate. We had wine. We talked and talked and laughed and laughed. Time stood still.

All at once I was aware that a good deal of time *had* passed. I straightened up.

"I don't want to sound like a character in a 'B' movie," I said. "But my ship sails at dawn."

Rowena smiled, and placed her hand over mine.

I called for the check. I could and I would pay for this.

We went out into the velvet evening. I hailed a cab.

There are some moments in life that are indescribable.

# 26

OUR MISSION WITH the British Home Fleet came to naught, and I found myself back on shore duty, this time in the office of Dr. Palmer, chief of medicine at Boston Naval Hospital. The enlisted men waiting to see him, with visible anxiety, were lined up on chairs in the corridor outside his office. Dr. Palmer was unfailingly polite to each of them, especially the most awkward, listening to their symptoms gravely, never suggesting that he thought their symptoms imaginary or the end product of homesickness.

One morning he called me into his inner office. He was seated at his desk, with papers in front of him. His usual calm, patrician manner could not quite conceal his excitement.

"We have been given permission to use a new drug," he said. "Sit down and I will tell you about it."

I sat down, attentive. A British bacteriologist had isolated a substance from a type of mold that so far had proven to be effective against certain bacteria, principally the cocci (as for example gonococcus, the bacterium that causes gonorrhea). So far the drug had been tried on animals, and on consenting prisoners in penitentiaries. Dr. Palmer's hospital had been given a limited supply of this substance to try on patients.

"Your service record shows that you saw duty in the venereal disease ward at Norfolk," Dr. Palmer said. "We can use your help."

The new drug, called penicillin by Dr. Alexander Fleming

who discovered it, after penicillium, the mold from which it had been extracted, was to be given to a few older patients, who suffered from chronic gonorrhea or arthritis and certain disorders of the prostate.

No way had been found to synthesize the new drug, Dr. Palmer went on to explain. And no way had been found to slow its passage through the body. It might be excreted in the urine in fifteen minutes.

My contribution was to supply each patient with a urinal and to instruct him in the value of collecting his urine. If the urine was saved, the penicillin in it could be extracted and used again. On no account must the patient use the bathroom, the head, to urinate.

I am afraid that, in spite of the gravity of Dr. Palmer's talk with me, I did not realize the importance of the project. I went about my small share in it with punctilious absentmindedness, as I had learned to perform all my navy duties. I distributed the urinals as instructed. I gathered them up each morning and took them to the laboratory. My mind was elsewhere. I was busy at the time making a fool of myself over a pretty young actress I had met, whose beauty outshone her artificiality. My thoughts were of love and romance, not of urinals.

The experiment took only a few days. After it was finished, Dr. Palmer called me again to his inner office. He was holding a sheaf of medical reports, which I recognized as the records of the patients under the penicillin treatment.

Dr. Palmer waited until I had approached his desk and stood in front of him. He looked up from the reports he held, his face transformed with a wondrous smile.

"They are all cured," he said.

His eyes were bright with tears.

# 27

I FELT NO joy when my orders came to leave Boston. I felt no sorrow, either. My navy experience had taught me to accept whatever came to me. I did not possess time. The navy possessed time, my time and theirs.

The navy was not a bad life for a young man. Healthful regimen. Discipline. Role models in abundance. Camaraderie. Security. Food, clothing, housing, even spending money was supplied. Yet every once in a while you would be reminded that you were not a free man. A giant hand, reaching down when you least expected it, plucked you out and made your life miserable. The worst thing of all was being subjected to small-minded, mean-minded men who had power over you because of superior office or rating. There was absolutely nothing to be done, no reprisal, no way to vent your frustration.

Once the pretty young actress I was enslaved by in Boston invited me to the play in which she had a role. The day before the performance, I went to a Chinese laundry in town, stripped off my dress blues, and asked them to press them for me. In the process, my liberty chit slipped out of the pocket and could not be found. A frantic search of the premises failed to turn it up, and I had to present myself at the gate of the hospital compound without my pass. I was called to captain's mast and sentenced to three days' confinement to the compound, and three days of scrubbing latrines. I did not mind the latrines so much; after all, I was familiar with latrines in all shapes and sizes, but

I minded missing the play and my date afterward with the pretty young actress. Even as I opened my mouth to try to explain to the captain, I was shouted down by "Silence!"

When my new orders came through, the actress came to see me off at the train station. I was surprised. Apparently I had underestimated her, or I had underestimated my own charm, which was difficult for me to do at that time. She even brought me a present. It was almost impossible to buy a bottle of whiskey in those days. The alcohol was needed for the war effort. But for some reason it was possible to buy a bottle of Southern Comfort. Maybe it was hard to distill alcohol from it, or the Old Dominion threatened another civil war. Anyway, she brought me some Southern Comfort. It was in a gift bottle with a silver cup screwed to the top, so that when you opened the bottle, you had a cup to drink from.

We bade a passionate farewell, and I boarded the train and found myself a seat, and opened the window to wave good-bye to my love.

The train began to move and no sooner had I settled in with amorous afterthoughts, opened the bottle of Southern Comfort and poured myself a drink, than with a clash of the coach door, into the car strode a brand-new Ninety-Day Wonder, fresh from the shell. He even smelled new, with his crisp whites and with the gold braid that proclaimed him to be God's annointed, a lieutenant (j.g.). The Ninety-Day Wonder was a product of the war. The increased demands for navy officers far outstripped the previous leisurely procedure for supplying officers. Before the war, it had taken four years to produce an officer and a gentleman. But now hatcheries had been set up to produce an officer in ninety days.

He approached me; looking straight ahead, without breaking stride, he reached out and plucked the silver cup from one hand and the bottle of Southern Comfort from the other and threw them out the open window of the moving train, and without a word moved briskly on.

I sat, stunned, and prayed for peace to descend upon me. I tried, but failed, to unclench my fists and arrange my fingers in my lap in the lotus position—for serenity. I prayed! God Almighty, I prayed, to keep me from leaping from my seat,

147

tearing off its armrest, and running after the young lieutenant to bash his brains out!

I did not want to end up being slammed in the brig on my arrival in Norfolk, on charges of drinking in transit while under orders, and of assaulting an officer. So I turned, in desperation, to my favorite peacetime memory, a memory that was like money in the bank, that I could draw on when needed.

My first novel had been published while I was still at Brentano's, the year before I had joined the navy. The result was a disappointment, and was best forgotten, but the publishers had given a publication party at the Rose Room of the Hotel Algonquin. There the ebullient host of the hotel, Frank Case, had taken me by the arm and led me to a glittering round table at which sat the most sophisticated literary people in town and said, "This is the author for whom the party is being given. Who the hell are you?"

Laughter, happiness, success, friends. That was the world I would go back to. After the war.

IN WARTIME the ordinary civilian, going about his business at home, reading the newspaper, listening to war reports, has a good chance of knowing more about where the troops are and what they are doing than the troops themselves.

We had been assigned to an enormous convoy out of Norfolk, somewhere in the Atlantic, going—where? Even the captain didn't know. We were sailing under sealed orders. One evening, at twilight, I climbed the mast and counted 101 ships, and more over the horizon, all carrying supplies and war matériel somewhere. I had known the stormy North Atlantic on the destroyer, which was capable of great speed. Now I was to experience the comparatively tranquil Atlantic, south of that area, traveling at the slowest speed of any lesser vessel in the convoy, which was thirteen knots. We hardly seemed to be moving.

The year was 1944, and we had been assigned to play a small part in the larger drama of the landings in Normandy and the invasion of Europe, but we didn't know that.

Our LST was a brand-new ship, which we had "commissioned," the navy term for equipping and outfitting a ship. Running short of enlisted personnel, as well as of officers, the navy had given me a couple of boosts in rating. I was still an enlisted man, but I had been assigned two assistants of lesser rating. I was in charge of the sick bay, the health and welfare of the crew, and of the one hundred marines we carried as passengers. The navy had completely run out of doctors. So as a result, I was the ranking medical person aboard. I tried not to think about that.

Nowadays we hear cries about the extravagance of the military, but then it was not apparent in the meager supplies doled out to our ship. We even had to make our own pills. Wearing aprons we would spread out a mixture of phenacitin, caffeine, and aspirin on papers in front of us, scooping up the mixture into gelatine capsules to be used for everyday complaints. I drew the line, however, when it came to hemming the towels for the operating packs. We were sent a roll of fifty yards of toweling, out of which we were to make fifty towels with double hems, so that a loose thread would not find its way into a wound. Since at that point we were still tied up at the dock, I went to the shore telephone and called the wife of the admiral of the yard, whose name I found in the base telephone book. I explained my predicament, a station wagon picked up the roll of toweling in the afternoon, and fifty towels, each double-hemmed at both ends, were delivered without a word the next morning.

We had to make operating packs, large and small, which we assembled as instructed by the manual, and since we didn't have an autoclave in the sick bay, I baked them in the ovens in the ship's galley. The head cook became my rough-and-ready buddy. He was a law student from Boston, an Irishman named Dan O'Connor. When I presented myself on arrival in Norfolk by saying, "I am your pharmacist's mate," I must have seemed a ludicrous figure. A silence fell over the room, and finally Dan O'Connor said, "If we'd known you were coming we'd have baked a cake." That was the beginning of a beautiful, lasting friendship.

I had had a good chief on the destroyer, who treated me with the contempt that was my rightful due as a yardbird, but I respected his dedication and I wanted the sick bay on the LST to be as good as his sick bay; so to this end I drove my two assistants to understand and respect what a proper sick bay should be like. We also had to equip the officers' wardroom to serve as an operating room. There was a light already in place above the table, and a large storage box that we had to fill with operating packs, morphine Syrettes, rolls of gauze and adhesive, and the necessary instruments for routine surgical procedures, plus a few bottles of Old Grand-Dad (now I knew where the whiskey had really gone).

As we sailed to destination unknown at a leisurely, rolling pace, the ship's routine went on as scheduled. Sick call was held in the morning and in the afternoon. Chow was served, breakfast, lunch, and dinner. The bos'un's pipe was held in the morning, and lights out at night. We sailed under blackout conditions. The crew's quarters and the officers' wardroom and the bos'un's locker and the sick bay were gathering places after dark. The lights would go out inside when the hatch door was opened and went on when the hatch was closed.

We gathered in the sick bay, a few privileged souls—Dan, the bos'un's mate, the gunner's mate, the motor machinist's mate, a few men in charge—to shoot the breeze and relax. Dan would bring a roast chicken from the galley and a jug of orange juice, and on special occasions I would break out the medicinal alcohol. Medicinal alcohol was not used in our sick bay for medical purposes. Merthiolate was good enough for that. I had learned this from the chief on the destroyer, who was an old navy drinking hand.

The chief used to say, "See you on the sun deck." We were

on a perpetual cruise on our LST. We did our laundry and hung it to dry about the ship. We soaked our navy caps in Clorox to the desired whiteness and old salt look. I used to present myself in the galley with a soup bowl, like a mendicant, and ask Dan to give me my rations before he touched them. "I will cook them on the Bunsen burner in the sick bay," I said. To which he responded by putting bolts in my mattress cover, or by pouring a pailful of cold water down my back while I was in the shower.

We passed through the Sargasso Sea, a comparatively still body of water in the Atlantic, where enormous islands of submerged algae flourish.

It was during this time that one of my assistants, Nick, made a Ouija board for diversion. It is very difficult to find any wood around a modern warship, but he came up with a piece of plywood on which he lettered the alphabet in a semicircle, with YES and NO at either end. He made the little tripod out of the lid of a cigar box, and its legs out of cutoff swab sticks from the sick bay. We had some incredible experiences with the Ouija board.

But before I share them, I confess my reluctance to do so. I will set the details down and let the reader draw his own conclusions.

To begin with, as a good little Roman Catholic boy I was taught that the Ouija board was sinful, the handiwork of the Devil. We spoke in hushed tones of those who had one in their house. I imagine that Dan O'Connor had the same background, but in the beginning we regarded it as a game. Because the nights aboard the LST were endless and blackout conditions made moving freely about the ship difficult, the Ouija board seemed a welcome diversion.

Two people sat at a table, the Ouija board between them. Each rested the fingers of one hand on the tripod, and waited. When the tripod moved it was supposed to point out letters on the semicircular board and, in cases where a yes or no answer was sufficient, indicate that word. We had all the time in the world. We waited. The Ouija board was asked where our destination was. Where were we headed? The tripod spelled out NAPOLI. (We ended up in Naples, but no one on board knew that.) We were impressed. It took time, endless time, but the

151

Ouija board spelled out answers to personal questions, named names, and when I addressed the board and asked if it had something to say to me, told me to JUMP SHIP. Not a very practical answer in the middle of the Atlantic.

Dan O'Connor became a convert. It may have had something to do with the feeling that what we were doing was wrong, or sinful. He decided on controls to determine if anyone was deliberately moving the tripod on the board. He would be in charge, with pad and pencil, to write down the letters. The two seated at the table were to be blindfolded.

This is where the story gains in incredibility. The board talked, it ran at the mouth, the tripod whizzed around, telling us who we were speaking to—in one instance it was a sailor who had been drowned, giving the date, the location, the circumstances. On other nights we were talking to "Kind Spirit," who answered all sorts of personal questions. The Ouija board became our obsession, more real than the actual world. We couldn't wait for the sessions. Dan brought a pitcher of reconstituted orange juice from the galley; I broke out the medicinal alcohol. We bent our heads over the table, addressing the board as if it were a living person, getting back lucid answers. I still regarded it as a game until one night when Dan finally grew tired of writing down an endless stream of letters and said, "It's no use. It's saying the same thing over and over again and it doesn't mean anything." I was sitting at the table with Kansas, my other assistant. I removed my handkerchief blindfold and asked Dan to show me the pad. I looked at the stream of letters, and at length asked Dan for his pencil and drew two lines through the letters. It said, perfectly, without missing a single letter: THEMISTOCLES/THEMISTOCLES/THEMISTOCLES.

We were stunned.

Now our entire small group became obsessed with the Ouija board, living for our nightly sessions. The days were stultifying, hellishly boring. The same rolling, the same snaillike pace. The ship's routine became automatic—muster, chow down, pass the time—except in the sick bay where our little group gathered. The board worked best when Kansas sat at it. It didn't matter who sat opposite him. The tripod spun around to face one of us when Kansas touched it. Kansas finally rebelled. It made him sleepy, he said, and the long periods when he sat blindfolded at the board were boring. We pleaded with him after trying everyone else in every combination. It only worked well when Kansas sat at the board.

By that time we "listened" to different "voices," or so it seemed. They came through the board laboriously, spelling out words, but we learned to differentiate between different "voices." We resisted calling them "spirits." There was "Kind Spirit" who had first talked with us. This one was feminine; we recognized her personality by the answers she gave. Then there was the drowned sailor. He was masculine, rough, unlettered, as we recognized his messages. Different "voices" came and went. We never did determine who had said THEMISTOCLES.

One night a very different feminine "voice" answered. She was quite chatty and replied to our questions readily. The tripod spun under Kansas's hand. I was sitting opposite him. At length I asked whom we were talking to.

A long period followed with the tripod busily working at the alphabet. Kansas's head nodded. At length Dan, who was standing over us taking dictation, said, "It's saying the same thing over and over again." I took off my blindfold and asked to see the pad Dan had written on. The succession of alphabetical letters made no sense to me. I handed it to Kansas, who had also removed his blindfold.

Kansas, looking at the pad, went white, dead white. He didn't say anything. Suddenly he jumped up from his chair and made for the hatch door. He undogged the door frantically and, still without a word, plunged out, leaving us in total darkness.

Dan then closed the door, which turned on the light, and we looked at each other.

"Let's go after him," Dan said.

We opened the hatch door and went out into the darkness, splitting up for the search.

The LST had a long, wide, empty deck where we were carrying two top-secret craft. Since the craft were covered and secured with wires and line, we had been unable to determine what they were. They were just another mystery in the larger mystery that surrounded us, but they made good places to hide.

It was a dark and moonless night, warm, and the air was still. We searched, calling "Kansas," "Kansas," until finally I found him. He was squeezed behind a stanchion, almost invisible, but my eyes having grown accustomed to the darkness, I saw his whites, which gave him away.

When I went up to him, he didn't move, or speak. "Kansas," I said, in an apologetic tone, "we are sorry if anything upset you. We won't make you sit at the Ouija board ever again. I promise that. Please come below and tell us what happened."

He followed me silently. When our little group had gathered in the sick bay we closed the door, dogged it, and turned toward Kansas in the light.

"Tell us what happened," Dan said in a reasonable tone of voice.

Kansas looked down. He didn't say much at any time, and his words always came hesitantly, as he spoke in the idiom of his time, before the word "guy" became common usage.

"I didn't tell you fellas," Kansas said, looking down, "but I was married before. When I was very young. My wife died. That was the name I used to call her."

We stood frozen, speechless. After a moment we gathered up the Ouija board and the tripod, and the pads and the pencils, and went out into the darkness.

We went to the stern of the ship and threw them all overboard, leaving them to bob away in the phosphorescence of our wake.

# 29

A FEW NIGHTS LATER the bos'un came to me in the sick bay wearing a troubled look, his cap pushed back on his head.

"I don't want you to tell anyone else, but the bow doors are leaking, Doc, and I don't know what to do about it. I've got the pumps going. All we can do is pray."

If the bow doors kept on leaking, we would sink, alone. Because our ship was too badly needed, we had skipped the routine shakedown cruise. Now here we were with the bow doors leaking.

I looked at Boats' troubled face and I felt oddly calm. We stood there for a moment in silence, and then Boats turned away, muttering something about how he had to check the pumps.

It was sack time. I closed the sick bay and went below, undressed, and got into my bunk. The odd feeling of calmness persisted, and I fell asleep. It was a good sound night's sleep, one of the best I ever had on the LST.

In the morning we were still rolling along at our leisurely pace. I sought out Boats.

"What happened?" I asked.

Boats smiled. He was his old healthy, ruddy-faced confident self. "Oh, she cured herself," he said, his smile broadening.

Two days later we made our first landfall in Oran, Algeria, nineteen days after leaving home port. Oran was another world to us. The harbor was faced with huge stone walls on which were painted in large white letters, VIVE DE GAULLE! VIVE DE GAULLE! VIVE DE GAULLE! We did not know who De Gaulle was. We tied up. It was late afternoon. The off-watch had liberty, but since I had the duty, I did not go ashore. Later, when I read Albert Camus, I regretted that I had not seen the setting for his novel *The Plague*.

Now that we were in the Mediterranean we seemed more a part of the war. The convoy had been dispersed as had the passenger marines—when, where, and to what ports we did not know, just as we did not know what had brought the convoy together in the first place. Now as part of a fleet of LSTs, we resumed normal cruising speed. The air seemed brighter, more charged, and we had our first air attack.

My battle station was in the officers' wardroom, alone. We had general quarters routinely, and I always liked going to my battle station, which would be the largest first-aid station in time of combat. I enjoyed the luxury of the leather sofas, the magazines lying around on scattered tables, the air of civility after the spartan amenities of the crew's quarters. I would pour myself a glass of ice water from a pitcher on the sideboard, select a magazine, and sit down in a comfortable leather-upholstered chair with a small table beside it, to read until the all-clear sounded.

But this time it was for real, and I soon discovered the drawback of the officers' wardroom as a battle station. It had no portholes, no way to see outside. I endured the forced isolation for as long as possible, then I stepped outside into the narrow passageway that ran midship from port to starboard. At that very moment a plane swooped so low over the ship that I could see the pilot. He was alone in the cockpit, and he turned to look at me. For an instant our eyes met and then he was gone. I stepped back into the wardroom. In telling this tale I realize what simple affairs some of the planes were that fought in World War II. I remembered the planes that my father worked on at Glenn L. Martin, and this plane resembled them. The pilot sat in an uncovered cockpit, wearing a helmet without goggles. I could see the expression on his face, as startled as mine must have been. It was a reconnaissance plane, we learned later. The men were at their antiaircraft guns, but not a shot was fired. Soon after we were called from general quarters.

When we arrived at our next port, we still didn't know where we were. We would be there for several days, and eventually found out that the ship was tied up at Karouba, the port city of Bizerte, in Tunisia. We were given the freedom of the dock and the shipyard, but the city of Bizerte lay off bounds to us. It was in ruins. Our planes had bombed it to rubble in their effort to drive the German Army under General Erwin Rommel out of North Africa. Although some walls still stood, the Army Corps of Engineers had not yet had time to go over the city, and it was dangerous to walk there.

We were thirteen ships in the port, all LSTs. The captain informed me that the senior pharmacist's mates, the hospital corpsmen, from every ship had been called to headquarters, which had been set up in one of the few buildings left standing in Bizerte. A bus would call for us in the morning.

The bus came, and we senior pharmacist's mates boarded it. We went through the ruined city to get to headquarters. It was a sobering thought that our planes had destroyed the city. Our planes, piloted by our men. We had never seen a devastated city before and it was indescribable, like a picture of some pock-marked Mars. I had seen some of the cities of England and Scotland in my duty on the destroyer. This had been before the destruction wrought by the buzz bombs later in the war. But Bizerte was flattened. Some of the citizens were visible here and there, going about their lives. It was apparent that living went on in some of the cellars and basements.

The headquarters building, which turned out to be the city hall, buzzed with activity. We were shown into a conference room, and presently an admiral in the Medical Corps came to address us. He sat down and looked at the thirteen of us soberly. Some of us were bearded, and the first thing the admiral said was that the beards must go. "Shave them off, and tell the men of your crew to shave them off. If they are burned, it hampers treatment to have a beard. Tell your men to keep their arms covered at all times. Wear work shirts, buttoned at the wrist." I myself had even tried to grow a beard in the long tedious days crossing the Atlantic. After a week of cutting and primping and turning this and that way in front of the mirror, with scissors in hand, I had shaved it off. It didn't do anything for me except make me look like a Sunday-school picture of Jesus Christ.

Now the admiral became serious, leaned forward in his chair. "You have ten days," he said, "ten days in which to turn your ships into hospital ships, to receive the wounded off the beaches. You have perhaps noticed the brackets that have been welded to the bulkheads of the tank decks. They are for stretchers. Each ship must be capable of receiving three hundred wounded men, to take them to a neutral country for hospitalization. A doctor or doctors with their staff will come on board with the wounded men, but meanwhile you must prepare the ship to have them. You have ten days." He didn't tell us what beaches, in what country.

He went on to explain the details to his awestruck and silent and intimidated audience. The officers' wardroom would serve as the number-one operating room, as intended, but a second operating room must be made out of the ordnance room, with an operating table and an operating light installed. A supply depot would be set up somewhere in the ruins of the city. We would go there each day to equip the various first aid stations and the medical supply boxes. We had ten days.

It was a solemn group that went back on the bus. We didn't know each other, and it seemed unlikely that we would ever meet again. I had learned that in wartime many of the social amenities were dispensed with. We had no conversation.

As I walked back to our ship through the yard, I noticed that our crew was playing a pickup baseball game on a diamond they had marked off in the shipyard. There was much laughter and shouting, and I felt a sudden surge of anger. It seemed unthinking and uncaring of them to be having a good time. This involuntary surge of anger was the preamble to a period of stress and tension that ended disastrously. I realize now I should have joined in the baseball game. I should have sought out relief and release for the tension building inside of me. The boys playing that pickup baseball game on the dock at Bizerte were as overwhelmed as I was by the circumstances in which life had placed them, but for a moment they were forgetting their woes. I carried mine onto the ship.

The next day I found the supply depot that had been set up in the ruined city. The leading hospital corpsmen whom I had never thought to see again were all there, fighting and yelling to be heard above the din in their desire for supplies.

It was not that easy. This was still the navy, in spite of the war, in spite of the heat, which was a monstrous 104 degrees the entire ten days we were there. Things had to be done the navy way. There were questions to be faced back home. The taxpayers had to be satisfied that they were not being cheated, that there was no corruption, and that things were not given away. Forms had to be filled out, for every roll of bandage, every surgical forceps. Forms, some in duplicate, some in triplicate. I had learned how to do this under the chief on the destroyer.

The supply depot itself was clearly recognizable in the rubble; it was an instant navy building, like a Quonset hut. In spite of the preparations, and the navy had prepared for this major operation for months, there would not be enough supplies to go around. The loudest voice, the clearest, most perfect forms were given preference. I did not have the loudest voice, but I had nearly perfect forms, so I finally made my way up to the counter to one of the supply personnel. He filled out my order as well and as generously as he could, and he told me to come back. Back I went to fill out more forms.

A sense of urgency had gripped the ship. Everything was being made ready for the coming operation. I put Nick in charge of the second operating room, the former ordnance room. I put Kansas in charge of filling the supply stations with medical equipment that I managed to squeeze out of the supply depot. We finally used up the last of the double-hemmed towels in the operating packs that the admiral's wife and her friends had hemmed overnight while we were commissioning the ship.

I went ashore every day to do battle with the supply depot. We needed blood plasma and morphine Syrettes to go in the medical supply chests. There were simply not enough to go around. My friend Dan worried about me. I was driving myself too hard.

We had a liberty together, and he made me go on it. There

was a French resort town, relatively untouched by the bombing, twenty-five kilometers away. Other crew members had been there and recommended it. The town was called Ferryville, and the road between it and Bizerte was a dangerous and desolate stretch. Signs in French told us that the area was mined—KEEP OUT! A ruined house, looking lonely and macabre, was plastered with these warning signs. The retreating Germans had done everything they could to cover their tracks. We stood in the road outside the gates of the compound and waited for a truck to pick us up. The truck might be hauling supplies or rubble, or a working party of prisoners-of-war, mostly Italians, members of the army that had helped the Germans. The rule was that trucks had to stop and pick up servicemen. We finally made it to Ferryville.

It looked like a stage setting or a movie set with façades and nothing behind them. A travel agency boasted an awning and signs in its window advertising cruises, but it was empty. Sidewalk cafés flourished along a main street faced by buildings and houses that looked as if they had been put up for the day. Dan and I sat down at a café. We managed to convey to the waiter that we wanted something to drink, and he brought us cheap red wine in glasses that had been made of cutoff Perrier water bottles, the edges sanded so as not to cut the lips. We drank the wine. We watched the passing show. A semblance of normalcy prevailed. People laughed and flirted and talked. The café tables were crowded. Dan said I got quite drunk, and he had to take me back to the ship. It is true that I don't remember returning.

Finally the ten days were up. Our job was completed, or as nearly completed as we were able to make it. We sailed at night. The air was cool. I felt hot, feverish. The next morning I was really sick. We stopped at Sicily and I tried to pull myself up out of the hatch to look at it, but I felt even worse. A forward compartment had been prepared as a quarantine area in case it was needed. It had a bunk bed in it. I decided to sequester myself there. On the third night I got up, feeling like hell, to go to the head, and my right leg gave away and I fell to the deck. I dragged myself to bed. Polio was in my mind. I had all the symptoms—fever, diarrhea, weakening of the muscles. The next morning I told my assistants of my fears. They went to the captain, who sent word back to calm myself. I was exaggerating. I would be all right. The next day we would be in Naples.

See Naples and die, was all that I could think of. We had never been to Naples. The war was still going on in Italy. We arrived at night, and my condition had worsened. It was decided to try to get me ashore and to a hospital. By radio, the captain located an army hospital on a hill. They would send an ambulance to the dock. The trouble was that in the darkness we didn't know where the dock was. Dan O'Connor, my friend who had poured cold water down my back while I was in the shower, who had put bolts in my mattress cover, took charge. Everyone was afraid to come near me, for fear of contagion. Dan told the coxswain to lower a small boat. He came in, packed up my gear, and put it in the seabag, which everyone was afraid to touch. He got two seamen to rig up a Stokes stretcher to lower me over the side. They lifted me onto the stretcher, strapped me down, and, feet first, lowered me over the side to the small boat. I was dimly conscious, I was barely aware that Mount Vesuvius was erupting, a small eruption that made a red stain on the night. We set off in the darkness to the shore. After a while we stopped. I heard a voice, the coxswain's, say, "We are lost."

At that moment an air raid began. The sirens sounded and the antiaircraft guns from the shore went into action. They gave us enough light to find the dock and the ambulance to take me to the hospital.

**30**

AT THE HOSPITAL in Naples I was put to bed, with the bars raised on either side. I was agitated, constantly moving, constantly in pain, half-delirious. When they came to put a screen around my bed, as I knew was done when a patient was dying, and the priest came with his holy vessels, I was caught up in a paroxysm of anxiety. At the time I enlisted I had written *Roman Catholic* on the form where it stipulated religion, out of deference to my parents, so I knew that the priest was going to give me Extreme Unction, the last rites.

With an effort, I raised myself in bed. "But I am not dying!" I shouted.

"Quiet, son," the priest said, going on with his Latin words.

"But I am not dying!" I shouted again. "My time has not yet come!"

"Quiet, son," the priest said, going on with his ritual. "You are disturbing those around you."

I did not die. There were seven of us in that room, all stricken with the same virus. Four of us died. We were tended by an army medical unit from Toledo, Ohio. The doctor who saw us and the nurses who tended us were very kind. While the man next to me lay dying, the doctor pleaded with him in a soft, familiar Ohio voice. "You must not die," he said. "You have a wife and children waiting for you at home. You must not die."

162

The nurses, in shifts, kept him alive all night with artificial respiration, but at dawn they let him die. He died on a final long exhalation of breath. The nurse went to the casement window and opened it, to let his soul escape.

The building we were in was the palace of a ducal family. I was there for a month.

In our lifetime we are all destined to know catastrophic illness, in ourselves or in others close to us. So I won't dwell on that life-altering attack of polio with its subsequent crippling. The passing of the years, and the suffering and the death of those near and dear to me, has lent it perspective. But I like to remember a few acts of kindness that were shown to me in my suffering—not Pollyannaish, perfunctory, greeting-card acts of kindness, but real acts of kindness such as can come only from a loving heart.

Gratitude Number One: Dan O'Connor, who physically helped me and packed up my gear when everyone else was afraid to come near me or to touch me or anything of mine for fear of contagion. Dan got Boats, the bos'un, to lower the small boat that took me ashore at Naples, and he stayed with me until I was in the ambulance.

Gratitude Number Two: The nurse at the hospital in Naples who gave me a little kerosene camp stove to be placed beside my bed, and on which a pot of hot water was brought to boil in which she dipped sections of old army blankets to wrap around my paralyzed right leg, to prevent contraction, which was very painful. The "Sister Kenny Treatment," as this procedure was called, was still a matter of controversy, but when I graduated to a physical therapist to help me walk again, I was that much ahead because my leg had not contracted.

Gratitude Number Three: The cook in the same Naples hospital who was a native of the city but had lived for a while in Brooklyn. (I never saw her, but I get this information from the day nurse.) I was terrifically hungry. I was running a fever constantly, and I had to feed the fever. All that was available was army C rations, dished out of the cans and served on a regulation compartmented tray, but I ate everything and scraped the tray clean. The Neapolitan-Brooklyn cook observed this, so before she went home at night, she would slip in the back door of my hospital room, where no one was permitted to go for fear of contagion, and wordlessly hand me a generous slice of good homemade, crusty Italian bread on which she had spread jam or jelly from the army rations. Silently she reached for my hand from within the curtain of my bed; silently, hungrily, I took the proffered slice of jelly bread; silently she withdrew; silently I devoured it. Sometimes I think that that bread and jelly saved my life.

Gratitude Number Four: The young army corporal who was with me on the hospital plane to the United States. This was before jet travel and we had to make it in three stages. It was a cargo plane, interior empty except for brackets. A forklift raised us up to the plane on our stretchers. Aboard the plane were army nurses in trousered uniforms who would care for us en route.

At our first stop, Casablanca, we were carried to a convent where beds had been set up in a large, cool, quiet room. With the blinds pulled down over open casement windows, we were supposed to rest before the long second flight over the Atlantic. I was still running a fever and I was restless and in pain, but the boy next to me, an army corporal, sat on the side of his bed and talked with me. He was being flown back to the States on an emergency basis to have an artificial eye put in the socket where his right eye had been before the socket closed. He had been in a landing craft approaching shore. Natural curiosity had made him look out of the slit in front of the boat, and a stray, freakish bullet got his eye.

"I don't need a rest," he said to me. "I will sit here on the side of the bed while you rest, and if I can bring you anything, like a drink of water, you let me know."

Our second stop was Bermuda, where we came down, briefly, for refueling.

The third and final stop was Palm Beach, Florida, where a luxury hotel had been vacated and given to the army for use as a hospital. You have no idea how depressing a *grand luxe* hotel is after all the help has gone. But the army's medical personnel made us as comfortable as possible overnight, and the next day we were dispersed to various service hospitals, I to the naval hospital in Jacksonville.

BUT I HAD A FRIEND in the White House. Literally. Our president, Franklin Delano Roosevelt, my commander in chief, had been stricken by an attack of polio when he was still a young man, as I was, but he had gone on to lead an active, successful life. Even before he had become president, Roosevelt had found a retreat in Warm Springs, Georgia, where he could swim in a natural, spring-fed pool. After he became president he continued to go there to seek relaxation and renewal of spirit even if the waters of the pool didn't have any miraculous healing quality. Naturally the spotlight, both national and worldwide, was turned on this remote hamlet in Georgia.

President Roosevelt, as we know, was a gregarious man who liked the company of others. He was also warm and compassionate. So, to make a long and complicated story short, he bought a resort, and with the help of influential men who were close to him, he set out to transform it into the Warm Springs Foundation, a place for the treatment and research of poliomyelitis, sometimes known as infantile paralysis.

I was to be sent there.

I had done my share of crying in Naples when I discovered that I could not stand and I could not walk. Now that I didn't care what happened to me, I had become as helpless as a bag of potatoes. Let others handle me. Let others push me around.

165

So I didn't know what kind of behind-the-scenes activity sent me to Warm Springs. I never knew. I don't know to this day. I was too sick to care when it happened, and later I was too grateful and reticent to ask.

In Florida I was lifted by hospital corpsmen on a stretcher through the open window of a train, and I spent the night in the lower berth of a sleeping compartment. A hospital corpsman sat with me through the night as the train went to Georgia. At the tiny railroad station at Warm Springs I was put into an ambulance. I did not realize it at the time, but I had said good-bye, temporarily, to the navy and all of its cohorts.

Needless to say, I was very sick. I ran a constant temperature and I was in pain, only dimly aware of what was happening around me. I was taken to the receiving hospital at the Warm Springs Foundation and put to bed.

In the morning I was seen by the chief of medicine, Dr. Bennett, and the chief physical therapist, Miss Plastridge, both cheerful, competent professionals. They evaluated me physically. My right leg was zero. My left leg was seventy-five percent. I had lost muscle use of fifty percent around the middle of my body.

Miss Plastridge, who had written the entry for poliomyelitis in the *Encyclopedia Britannica*, was an optimistic and encouraging person. She started right off with the ego boost that she must have used for everyone, but it fell on fertile soil. "Polio is a disease that is contracted only by exceptional people. People with a highly organized central nervous system." She mentioned Sir Walter Scott and a few others, including the president. "It is caused by a virus that destroys the nerve cells in the spinal column that transmit the impulse from the brain to the muscles. You will never regain the muscles that are lost, but we will try to make you compensate. That is the word. Compensate. You will learn to have other muscles do the work of the muscles that are lost." She explained that they would keep me in the receiving hospital for a few days until my fever had abated and I had gained some strength from going on a special diet.

\*    \*    \*

Warm Springs no longer exists as it was then. The development of the polio vaccine by Dr. Jonas Salk made the facility obsolete. As the need for it diminished, the Foundation fell into disuse. It was too remote, too sequestered to serve as a general hospital. Finally, James Roosevelt, the son of the president, gave it to the state of Georgia.

But in 1944, when President Roosevelt was alive and still in office, while polio epidemics still raged sporadically and unchecked, Warm Springs was a wonder to behold. There was no other place quite like it in the world.

Situated some seventy miles from Atlanta in the pine-forested hills, it gradually became a self-sufficient community. The original pool had been replaced by a large, glass-enclosed, heated pool; there were exercise rooms, therapy rooms, wards for the patients called "halls," as in Builders Hall and Kress Hall, there were recreation rooms, doctors' offices, a large dining room, smaller dining rooms for committee meetings and heads of state, conference rooms, and kitchens. There was even a brace shop where necessary orthopedic equipment could be made on the premises, a schoolhouse for younger patients, a library, a small convenience shop, a chapel.

At some point, an architect, Eric Gugler, had been called in to make a coherent whole out of these disparate parts, which by themselves formed a kind of rectangle. He surrounded this rectangle with a wide, colonnaded, 18th-century walkway, thereby defining it. The whole effect was reminiscent of the University of Virginia, which Thomas Jefferson had designed.

At the far end of the rectangle was the receiving hospital. At the other end, the entrance to the Foundation, stood a great hall which was called Georgia Hall because the state of Georgia had given it to the Foundation. It was tall and imposing, with massive Doric columns in front and French doors. A semicircular driveway approached the entrance, with a fountain in the middle.

Georgia Hall was furnished in the style of a great country house. There were drapes at the windows, rugs on the polished floor, a grand piano. There were mahogany writing desks against the walls. There were mahogany card tables, upholstered sofas and club chairs. On the walls hung portraits in oil, in handsome frames, of distinguished benefactors and doctors who had made the place possible. There were lamps, but the great room was softly lighted. The whole impression was of southern antebellum elegance, old money, good taste, good family, careless luxury.

Some years after I was there, I met a woman who had been born and had grown up in the village of Warm Springs as the daughter of a poor but strict Christian family who allowed very little diversion on a Sunday.

"I used to press my face against the windows of Georgia Hall on Sunday evenings, and see you all in there, laughing and talking, playing cards, with someone playing at the grand piano, and I envied you. Yes, I envied you in your wheelchairs."

I began to emerge from the acute stage of my illness. The fever abated. I grew stronger. Thanks to the good nurse in Naples who had administered the Sister Kenny Treatment, I had no contraction in my right leg. I could begin physical therapy immediately. The head of the brace shop, bringing a large sheet of brown paper, came to measure me for the leg brace, tracing the outlines of my afflicted leg on the brown paper. All orthopedic equipment was custom-made. For young patients new equipment had to be made as they grew. For adult patients equipment had to be adjusted as the limb atrophied from lack of muscle use over the years.

While the leg brace was being prepared, with frequent fittings, I was provided with a wheelchair and assigned to one of the physical therapists, a beautiful, tawny young woman with whom I immediately fell in love. She introduced me to the famous pool, enormous, heated, glass-enclosed, with padded headrests in place. There, in bathing suits, the patients were helped to lie on their backs and do the required exercises submerged, floating, assisted by the physical therapist, who was also in a bathing suit. I looked forward to these sessions. They were the nearest thing to making love that I had known for some time.

My civilian clothes had arrived and I soon found myself involved in a social life with the other patients and several members of their families, many of whom had rented the summer houses that remained from the old resort. I had been informed that I did not have to wear a naval uniform at Warm Springs, even though I was kept on the books and drew my regular navy pay. I had written a letter to my sister Jane, who had the best clothes sense in the family, and asked her to buy me some flannel trousers, shirts, ties, and a well-made sport jacket. She had performed her assignment very well, and I was in business.

It has been my observation in life that those who are disciplined, who are working toward a goal, and who are well-mannered, particularly the latter, are better able to cope with adversity. Such people try to "fit" calamity into their lives and they try not to disrupt, any more than necessary, the even tenor of their ways. They go about themselves by believing that "nothing is as bad as it seems." And it isn't. Only death is final.

These were the sort of people whom I met as patients at Warm Springs. They were polite, cheerful and disarming in their wheelchairs. They came from places like Indianapolis and Warren, Ohio, solid citizens with solid backgrounds. Most of the patients were about my age. Many of them were women, some married, some with children. At a time when only actresses like Marlene Dietrich and Katharine Hepburn wore pants, these women wore trousers to conceal their leg braces. For reasons that escaped me, young fathers were treated at home, possibly because it was thought their wives would attend to them. Between pool and exercise, and exchanging of the time of day, there was much laughter among the patients, never any talk of personal limitations.

My leg brace was finished, and I stood up for the first time. It was a frightening experience, even with the crutches provided me, even with people at hand. I felt like a tower constructed out of glass blocks, at any moment about to crash and collapse. I took a tentative step or two.

My physical therapist, Marjorie, with whom I was in love, encouraged me to venture out on the grass of the rectangle. "If you fall it will be softer," she explained. She encouraged me to fall. Ultimately she demanded that I fall. "You will fall in real life, and you will have to pick yourself up. People who rush to assist you don't know how to help you, and they invariably do the wrong thing. You will have to fall, and pick yourself up."

So I did. Marjorie stood at a distance with her arms folded and told me how to pick myself up. "Raise yourself on your arms, at full length of your body." "Make sure your brace is locked." "Pick up one crutch with both hands, and slowly raise yourself up with your good leg." "Now, stand erect." "Stoop over for your other crutch." After many exhausting sessions, I succeeded.

We dressed for dinner, not formally but in our best clothes. We were served in the dining room at tables of four or six, by white-coated waiters. This was before the civil rights movement, and there were a lot of "colored boys" everywhere. They were called "boys" no matter what their age. The general-purpose "boys" were called "push boys" because they pushed wheelchairs for patients who could not manage to do it themselves. They were always within calling distance, and they responded with alacrity, politeness, and good cheer.

At dinner the conversation was animated, with talk of families at home and the humorous episodes of the day. Never about our personal problems. After dinner we congregated in Georgia Hall for more conversation or bridge. Someone played the grand piano. As a result of these social evenings I acquired a roommate when I was ready to leave the hospital.

A rotund Frenchman, with two leg braces hinged at the knee, and two upper-arm braces, he was confined to a wheelchair. But his face was alive with humor and he spoke English with a delicious French accent. His attitude was, and I tried to copy it: Things are too serious to be taken seriously. His life had become a grand gesture in the face of absolute adversity, and I admired him enormously.

He was Alain Darlan, the son of the commander of the French fleet, Admiral Darlan. Alain was an officer in the French navy. He had been in North Africa, serving under his father, who had been assassinated in 1942. Alain was stricken with the same virus that I had been, the so-called Egyptian virus. He had collapsed while giving a ceremonial dinner for the Bey of Tunis in silken tents. Some thought it was merely the heat. But he had been completely paralyzed. Alain was in the hospital when the

170

Allies were driving through North Africa. When the Allies overcame the city, everyone fled and Alain was put in the ward with the insane, who could not be moved when the hospital was deserted.

The word reached Roosevelt about the admiral's son. The president dispatched a destroyer to get him. The destroyer eventually brought him, his mother, his wife, and a French doctor to Warm Springs, where Madame Darlan rented a house on Pine Mountain, near the Little White House.

After we became roommates, Alain told me that his muscles had become atrophied, by long lack of care, into a fetal position. At Warm Springs they had "knicked" all of his atrophied muscles. He had contrived to get a hand mirror, with which he watched his wife and doctor as they became lovers. He shrugged as he told me this. "They ran away together. Who could blame them?"

His mother remained in the rented house on Pine Mountain. I had never been to France, but I was assured she was a Frenchwoman typical of her class and generation. Madame Darlan dressed conservatively, and she always wore a black toque, morning, noon, and night. (Years later I met the French couturière Elsa Schiaparelli, who wore an identical black toque.) She spoke very little English, and she called me "Beel." She encouraged my friendship with her son.

Although we were of different nationalities and a wide gulf existed between our assignments and ranks in our respective navies, Alain and I had much in common, besides both being in wheelchairs. We were exactly the same age and had been educated by the same religious order, he in France and I in Cleveland—the *Société de Marie*, which Alain could pronounce correctly, unlike me. As I was ready to leave the hospital, he invited me to share his room in Builders Hall. I learned many things from him: to make light of my disability, to accept it and make the best of it, and always to be cheerful.

Our room was like a room in a small hotel, or, more exactly, like a room in a college dormitory. There were two beds, two small bureaus, a closet divided into two, and an adjoining bath.

We shared what used to be called a "body servant," a local

171

black boy named Raymond. I had the use of my upper body and I could dress and take care of myself. At Warm Springs the shower was in a special room that was completely tiled inside. A white enameled wheelchair waited outside the door. I transferred myself from my own wheelchair to the white enameled one, using my arms to lift myself. The knobs of the hot and cold shower were within reach and I had a glorious shower.

Alain, on the other hand, was completely dependent on Raymond to give him a bed bath, to dress him, to assist him in the bathroom.

Life became very social after I left the hospital. The population at Warm Springs was constantly changing. People came to be treated for several weeks. Then they would go home, returning after a few months or a year later. Some of the patients knew each other from previous visits. The younger ones sometimes arrived with their families, who rented one of the summer houses of the old resort. There were dinner parties, served by local help and the ever-present push boys.

I remember a dinner party given by an attractive and obviously successful couple from Des Moines, who had brought a young daughter to Warm Springs to be treated. She was in the children's ward and they wanted to be with her, but evenings alone in their rented house, with the tragedy of their daughter, were not to be endured, so they gave parties.

The dinner party was very proper. There were eight of us, with cocktails before dinner, place cards, and the hostess signaling from the head of the table when you were supposed to turn from the partner on your left and make conversation with the partner on your right. A push boy had pushed me up the sidewalk from the Foundation. Some hostesses did not want wheelchairs at their tables. He had then carried me to the chair indicated by the hostess. The dinner was a success. The food was delicious, the conversation sparkling. Yet I suddenly realized that I was helpless. From the table up I looked acceptable with white shirt, tie, and jacket, but I could not rise and walk away.

After dinner the push boy returned me to my wheelchair and I was taken for more conversation into the living room. I felt momentarily insane, as though I could not waken from a nightmare.

A very different and more positive note was struck after a champagne breakfast given by the Danverses, a couple very much like the pair who had hosted the dinner party—young, attractive, successful, with a daughter who had been stricken with polio. They had rushed Belinda to Warm Springs as soon as she was out of the acute stage of the illness and fortunately for all of them, her case was a light one. She needed a few weeks of therapy and continued surveillance, but the only long-range consequence would be that she would have a special shoe with a slight lift, and she would have to learn to walk with this shoe without throwing her leg out of balance.

Naturally the Danverses were overjoyed. Nothing would do but a party! Not an evening party, but a Sunday champagne breakfast after service in the chapel, to which everyone who was capable of coming was invited.

The Sunday service in the chapel was unusually well attended, the patients in wheelchairs with push boys, and everyone sat patiently through the service before heading for the Danverses' house.

It was a splendid occasion. Preparations had been made on the porch and on the lawn. A local cook had been called in. There were scrambled eggs, sausages, and homemade biscuits. Every table had a brimming pitcher of orange juice. And, of course, there was champagne. Gleaming, frosted ice buckets held the champagne bottles, their foil-wrapped tops visible over the ice. I dutifully ate some scrambled eggs and some sausage and a biscuit, and afterward accepted a long-stemmed glass of champagne from my host. It had been a long, long time since I had had any champagne, and it tasted like a gift from the gods. It was so good, I drank it perhaps too hastily, and the genial host, ever on the watch, filled my glass again. About halfway through I realized I was in trouble. My head began to swim and I could see two hosts. I knew I had to get to my room and my bed. Alain had not come. I think he thought it was more than he could handle, and it developed that it was more than I could handle.

I looked about for a push boy. There was none visible, for a wonder, or perhaps it was my suddenly undependable vision that was playing me tricks.

The sidewalk beyond the lawn led down to the Foundation, and Builders Hall was just to the left when you entered Georgia Hall. I decided that I could get there on my own. The imperative fact was that I had to leave.

I made it out to the sidewalk. Everyone was having such a good time that no one noticed my leaving. The sidewalk was gently sloping. I pointed my wheelchair straight ahead and tried to guide it down. The slope was more than I had bargained for. The wheelchair picked up speed. I tried to restrain it with my hands on the wheels, but soon I was frantically trying to hold the chair on course with my hands. I did all right for a while. The wheelchair wavered as it gained speed, and I lost control of it and veered off onto the grass. The sudden stop in the grass propelled me forward, and I sailed out of the chair and landed in a heap.

I fell so loosely that I was unhurt. I lay like a child, curled on my side. It was comfortable in the grass. I began to laugh. I was drunk on champagne, paralyzed, and couldn't pick myself up. In my inebriated state, it seemed the greatest joke in the world. There would be a push boy along any minute. As I lay there laughing in the grass, it came to me all at once that I did care, very much, what happened to me. I had accepted this crippling blow, which would mark the rest of my life. I wanted to see what would happen next. I wanted to live.

# 32

MY MOTHER CAME to visit me at Warm Springs. She was still beautiful. She did her best to conceal her heartbreak for me, from me. She still wore a Da Vinci half-smile, as though she knew some delicious secret about life. I learned later that my elder sister, Coletta, who had volunteered for army communications, was in the hospital with pneumonia at the same time I was in the hospital in Naples. Mother and Father were notified both times, but they could get to neither of us. My mother fitted my description of people who are best able to cope with adversity and calamity and did not speak of their anxiety.

She fitted right into the scene at Warm Springs and made several lifelong friends. Her days were filled with exchanging family news with the patients and the parents of the patients. She seemed to have been there forever. I never knew where she stayed and didn't think of asking. She came the day after Thanksgiving. She had stayed to roast the turkey for family members at home.

Alain and I had settled into a routine. Mother found us, if not the odd couple, certainly a very strange one. To while away the long afternoons I had subscribed to two correspondence courses from Kent State University in Ohio—Russian One and Philosophy One. Now that Russia had become such a power, I wanted to speak the language, but I hadn't taken into account that to learn a language you must hear it spoken. I struggled with the assignments. I had never done very well with phonetic symbols in the dictionary, and after a while I gave it up. I had learned how to say "Good morning, Comrade," and "Good evening, Comrade." I settled for that.

The philosophy course was a different matter. Alain Darlan had matriculated in philosophy at the Sorbonne, and he was amused at my assignments. The professor would give me certain questions by mail and grade me on the replies I mailed back to him, after consulting the textbook he had sent me.

Alain looked forward to my questions and my answers and the professor's comments on my answers. He could hardly repress his glee. Finally he proposed a philosophical question himself, for the two of us to ponder. Supposing, he said sententiously, supposing, for the sake of philosophical ruminations, there was a log floating down the Mississippi River, and on the log there were two ants. How would the ants view the world? What would they understand of the universe? The cosmos?

It wasn't difficult to imagine the identities of the two ants floating down the Mississippi on a log, as we lay on our separate beds during the enforced rest period after lunch. Alain was fascinated by primitive America. He had a shortwave radio on which he listened to world news at night, but kept tuned to country-and-western music during the day. His favorite tune, which he learned to sing in his French accent, was "Don't Fence Me In." I understood why, just as I understood that the two ants on a log were really him and me. We spent many lazy after-lunch sessions elaborating on the philosophy of the two ants and their perspective on life, on the universe, and on the cosmos.

Mother was friendly with Alain and with Madame Darlan, but they were really outside her orbit. She spent with me what free time I had from my routines in the afternoon and evening. We gorged ourselves on happy reminiscences, laughing together about the past. We didn't talk about polio or the future, which was very much on my mind. Mother had talked at length with Dr. Bennett and Miss Plastridge. She had come to fortify me and fortify herself with an exchange of love. She succeeded very well.

\*    \*    \*

We had postponed celebrating Thanksgiving at Warm Springs. There was a tradition that President Roosevelt would spend Thanksgiving with the patients at Warm Springs. That year, 1944, the president had been at the Yalta Conference and had returned to Washington exhausted. He wired, Would we be willing to postpone Thanksgiving for a few days? We would indeed. As the day approached, everyone was caught up in the excitement—patients, staff, and families of patients. Mother had been invited with others to go to the station at Warm Springs to greet the president. She was very pleased about that. What stories she would have to tell when she got home!

The day came, the appointed time for the president's arrival. I waited impatiently for the greeting emissaries to return. Mother finally entered our room during the rest period after lunch. She was upset and pale, and she tried to conceal her emotions.

"The president is dying," she finally said, stricken. When they had lowered him from the train on a stretcher, he looked like a corpse. "The president is dying." She would say no more. In a moment she kissed me and left in order to compose herself.

Mother had planned to return to Ohio the next day. That evening she was shaken and nervous. The talk at dinner, and after dinner in Georgia Hall, was all about the president's condition. Mother was very near to tears.

The morrow dawned bright and sunny. There was good news from the Little White House. The president had rested comfortably. The recuperative powers that he always felt at Warm Springs had reasserted themselves. Let the planning for Thanksgiving continue, three days hence.

Mother was rosy and smiling when she left later in the morning. I don't remember what we said at parting. It was very emotional and lies buried deep.

**33**

IT IS IMPOSSIBLE to describe our emotions when we saw President Roosevelt in his wheelchair. The outpouring of empathy, of admiration, of love! We wanted to be near him, to touch him, but we were constrained by an unspoken agreement to treat him as one of us.

The president sat at a long table at the end of the dining room, facing us at our smaller tables. An air of festivity filled the room. We had the traditional Thanksgiving fare, from turkey to pumpkin pie, although we didn't eat much because we were so filled with happiness.

We had planned a little skit after dinner to entertain the president. A space was cleared immediately in front of his long table, the chairs were pushed back to form a little stage.

I no longer remember what we performed, but I was part of it. The small entertainment was forgivably amateurish from beginning to end. Different people did different funny things, intentionally or unintentionally. My contribution was to come on as Stalin, wearing a fake black moustache and my navy pea jacket buttoned to the collar, and say "Good morning, Comrade," and "Good evening, Comrade" in Russian.

After the entertainment the president spoke briefly and extemporaneously. The words were not recorded, but the intimate and loving manner in which he said them remains in my memory.

When dinner was over, the president took up his place, in

178

his wheelchair, inside the double doors of the dining room, to have a few words with each of us as we left. I remember that his handclasp was warm, his manner concerned, and his smile sincere.

On principle, I have never taken part in any discussion of President Roosevelt as a man or as a president. That is sacred ground to me.

The president stayed on for a few days, but we didn't see him again until he left when he wanted to say good-bye to all of us in front of Georgia Hall.

It was early in the morning, but we were ready in our wheelchairs beside the semicircular drive that led up to Georgia Hall. The president had come to see us, and now he would go back to his duties. He appeared, driving his convertible with hand controls. The president was very proud of his car and of being able to drive it, and he looked very dapper behind the wheel. He stopped and sat and smiled at us. There was chitchat with those closest to him, and finally he looked directly at me and said, "Where is Alain?"

When I had left, Alain was still being dressed by Raymond. "He will be along in a minute," I said. I blurted it out, surprised and taken aback at having the president address me. I even forgot to call him "Mr. President."

He continued to talk to me. "Next time I come back," the president said, "I will stay longer."

Alain came out then, and Raymond wheeled him beside the president's car, to have a few words of farewell.

The next time he came back, President Roosevelt did not leave. The peace and serenity he had always sought at Warm Springs had claimed him at last.

# 34

Now THAT MY mother and the president had gone, Alain and I resumed our exercise and play. We became bridge friends. Alain loved any game of cards. Early on he had established the Saturday night practice of going to his mother's house on Pine Mountain to play a game of cards that he had learned in boyhood named "Liverpool Rummy," which I had never heard of but which he taught me to play.

Our Saturday nights developed their own routine. The push boys came for us shortly after dinner, and wheeled us up to Madame Darlan's house. The card table was set up in a small room next to the dining room. We played Liverpool Rummy at the card table, and Madame Darlan sat in semidarkness in the dining room, wearing her black toque. Promptly at ten o'clock she appeared with a tray of coffee in cups and a plate of little cakes. She did not join us in our refreshments, but she went back to the dining room to her semidarkness and straight-backed chair. Shortly after that the push boys came for us. Madame Darlan and I had a moment of chitchat, in my broken French and in her broken English, and then Alain and I were wheeled back to our room in Builders Hall.

Raymond would undress Alain and then leave us alone. It was time for Alain to wrap his head in Turkish towels, which I presume was a French custom he entrusted to no one, to protect him from the insidious night drafts. (Oh, those Georgia night drafts are mean!) The result, with the ends tucked in firmly and neatly, resembled a turban, for his ears were free. That finished, we turned off the lights from switches within reach of our beds and settled down for Alain's world news, news of the war, from his shortwave radio.

Beside the radio, which was on his bedside table, was a large, silver-framed photograph of his father in the full regalia of admiral of the French fleet, taken on the bridge of his flagship. Next to him stood a smiling General Eisenhower, again in the uniform that befitted his rank. Alain never mentioned his father, and I didn't ask about him. I took my very real and tragic problems about my condition and my future into the darkness with me, and I am afraid I did not listen to the war news, which now seemed unreal to me.

In between news bulletins, Alain reminisced about his days before he had been stricken with polio. His father had taken an entire floor in the Hôtel Georges V in Paris, to be the family home while they were in Paris. The summer residence, the family seat, was a villa on the Bay of Saint-Tropez. Alain was totally uninhibited and unselfconscious about his memories of Paris under the German occupation. He made it seem like the most natural thing in the world. I didn't interrupt, but I wish I had listened more closely as the details poured out—Göring in box Number One at the Paris Opera . . . or was it Goebbels? . . . Names flickered in and out of the conversation . . . how Corrine Luchaise really felt about Otto Abetz (who were they?) . . . Pierre Laval . . . Vichy. . . . More descriptions . . . the splendor of the inside of Hitler's private train. . . . On the night the newscaster told excitedly about how the Allies were advancing toward Paris, Alain muttered, "Fools!" "Fools!"

I forbore to ask him who the fools were.

I much preferred Alain's happier, sunnier memories of when he was a young man in Paris before the war. He had known the French novelist Colette. He had been a frequent caller at her apartment, where she had trained her beloved cats to use the toilet. One day he had gone to the bathroom. When he opened the door and was confronted by an outraged female cat perched on the edge of the toilet, he retreated, flustered. He said, "Pardon me, Mademoiselle," and backed out of the bathroom, closing the door.

This story reminded Alain of the count of Paris, the pretender to the French throne, whom he also knew. "You always back out of his presence," he said. "You never turn your back on the king."

And, "When we recover, we must take a trip to Marrakech. It is such a beautiful place. I know the sultan."

Daylight brought reason and purpose. With my new appetite for life I had a goal. I made up my mind that I wanted to walk by Christmas. With a leg brace, mind you, and two crutches, but I wanted to stand erect and walk on my less than perfect legs.

Under-the-armpit crutches were frowned on at Warm Springs because they led to bad posture. The crutches that were favored were called "Canadian" crutches, which didn't support you under the armpits but extended only halfway up the upper arm, ending in a semicircular, padded band of steel for added support at the back of the arm. With Canadian crutches you stood erect. At first I found it unnerving to stand erect after such a long time and feared toppling over backward. But the physical therapist held me by the back of the belt until I had gained confidence. Soon I was walking endlessly, back and forth across the exercise room; outside I fell again and again on the grass, deliberately, and picked myself up.

In the exercise room there were four sets of steps. They included architects' steps, wide steps, narrow steps, and carpenters' steps, those found in old houses built by the owners. In other words, all steps were not equal, and I had to learn how to navigate them, which was fairly easy going up with my body weight leaning forward. But coming down I was faced with a descent in which I might fall. There were handrails on both sides of the steps, and I switched hands going up and coming down as the handrail had to be on my stronger side. I practiced these routines again and again. I was young. I felt my strength returning. I walked and walked and walked with my Canadian crutches.

After a brief rest and a shower and dinner, we played cutthroat bridge in Georgia Hall. It has forever spoiled me for playing bridge with any civilized person. Alain and I made formidable partners. We didn't draw for partners. Players had to take the two of us. We shouted and laughed and made insulting remarks to our opponents, we gloated shamelessly over our victories, we shamelessly ground down losing opponents. We had terrific fun, to balance the effort of the day, all of us, winners and defeated alike.

I walked into Georgia Hall for Christmas dinner. I *walked*. I had waited until everyone was seated and had been served. I wheeled my chair into Georgia Hall, locked its wheels, reached for the Canadian crutches slung over the back of the chair, stood erect, locked the leg brace at the knee, took the crutches, and walked in and took my place in a chair at my table, without comment. I don't remember eating. I was filled with happiness.

Alain Darlan remained at Warm Springs after I left. We kept up an on-again off-again correspondence. I was writing a novel. Alain was writing a book about his father. Madame Darlan had returned to France. Alain had married his physical therapist. I wrote to congratulate him. It was a splendid arrangement. Phyllis, the therapist, was a single woman with a growing daughter. Whether she was widowed or divorced I don't know. In any case, she and he needed each other. I wrote him that I was jealous of their connubial bliss. Alain, with his little family, returned to France and sent me a joyous letter from his villa on the Bay of Saint-Tropez. I responded, telling the couple how happy I was for them, but I had private misgivings. I think Alain was completely unprepared for the France he returned to. The newspapers were full of accounts of what happened to collaborators. Women had their heads shaved in public, men were shot.

Sometime later he sent me a copy of the book he had written about his father, *L'amiral Darlan parle,* in French. It was published in 1952 by Amiot-Dumont in Paris as part of *Le livre contemporain.* Unfortunately, my French was not up to reading it. On the half-title page, Alain wrote a loving message, including the words *In memory of our days as roommates, Bill, and the glory of being "polios."*

183

I wrote him at once to thank him for the gift copy and to tell him my own news. I had no reply. I wrote him again, after a considerable time had passed. Again there was no reply. By that time we had worked up a reasonably efficient grapevine among the former patients at Warm Springs and their families. I sent out word that I wanted to know why I hadn't heard from Alain. After a time, news came back, having been passed from letter to letter from a member of a patient's family who had been to France. They had all died, Madame Darlan and Phyllis shortly after they had returned to France. And then finally, Alain.

While I had no direct word of their deaths, or the manner in which they died, I am a romantic. I think Alain, who lived in a world of fantasy with a silver-framed picture of his father and a smiling General Eisenhower on the bedside table beside him, died of a broken heart.

ROBERT FROST HAS said, "Home is where they have to take you in when you have to go there." So naturally I went home to Ohio when I left Warm Springs and was discharged from the navy, even though I had not lived at home for ten years before the war. My parents took me in, on my Canadian crutches, lovingly. They had moved to a retirement house near Lake Erie. It was really a summer cottage that my father had insulated and renovated for year-round living. They had added an extra bedroom for guests, never expecting any of us children to come home again, but they hid their heartache and the disruption of their plans behind a gala homecoming.

My father had turned the guest room into my room. He had built a desk against one wall, surrounded by bookshelves. There I wrote a novel.

In my despair I had turned again to Voltaire and was determined to write a pastiche of Voltaire's *Candide,* my hero being a young navy officer who had lost his leg in action. I made him an officer so I could laugh at the navy caste system of officers and men, and get out of my system all the resentment I had felt in being an enlisted man. The main theme was the futility and the absurdity of war, and there was a romantic subplot. Since then I have, oddly enough, taken pride in my navy days, and I have forgotten the alleged injustices that were shown me. I had begun the manuscript of this novel while a patient at Warm Springs, and at home, under the loving care of my parents, it went quickly.

But I was alone in this room prepared lovingly for me. For the first time since I had been stricken I had no others around me—no nurses, doctors, other patients, and I had ample time to reflect on my condition.

To a lesser or greater degree, there is something wrong with all of us. We wear false teeth, or eyeglasses, or hearing aids, or pacemakers. We have arthritis, or rheumatism, or Parkinson's disease, or multiple sclerosis. Sometimes we go to body-repair shops and have our noses bobbed, or our ears pinned back, or our faces lifted. You can buy false eyelashes in Woolworth's. The norm, in fact, is so uncommon that it may not even exist.

The word "cripple," as *Webster's New Collegiate Dictionary* will tell you, comes from Middle English as well as from Old English, and derives from a word meaning "to creep." (If you press on and look up the word "creep" in the same dictionary, the last definition given is "an obnoxious or insignificant person.")

The word "Cripple" is defined in modern usage by Webster as: "1: a lame or partly disabled person or animal. 2: something flawed or imperfect."

In the line below, the word used as an adjective describes something worn out, with a cross-reference to the word "inferior."

If you attempt to seek refuge in the word "disable," as defined in the same dictionary, you will read: "disable 1: to deprive of legal right, qualification, or capacity. 2: to make incapable or ineffective; *esp:* to deprive of physical, moral, or intellectual strength." It adds that "disable" is a synonym for "cripple."

My own reaction to all of this has been to tell the bastards to shove it!

But there is a very real human issue at stake here that must be thought through. We are animals, in our most primary reactions, and one of our most primary reactions is to reject, if not to destroy, any "flawed or imperfect" member. It is an involuntary instinct. It is in all of us.

Margaret Mead, a family friend, once took the time, with her wonderful lucidity, to elaborate on this theme for me.

"Ours is a very competitive society," she said. "When you are crippled, you are removed from competition. You are a threat to no one."

First there is the coming to terms with being crippled—an acceptance of that does not come easily. Shortly after I came home I read in a news magazine that an orthopedic doctor had discovered that lost nerve impulses might reroute themselves in an already paralyzed person who suffered a secondary serious accident. This physician was now going to experiment with the use of air hammers on paralyzed limbs, to see if the same effect might be achieved.

I wrote to this doctor and offered myself as a guinea pig. I was accepted. I wanted to be independent again, and so I insisted on going alone by train to Philadelphia, where the doctor would perform his experiment.

While I was under a general anesthetic, my right leg was battered by an air hammer from my hip to my toes. When I awoke in the morning in considerable pain, I was running a temperature and my swollen right leg was black and blue from top to bottom.

But there was no need for my staying in the hospital. The

temperature, the pain, the swelling were all to be expected, and the beneficial effect, if any, would not be evident until later when the leg began to heal.

Besides, I had made plans to go on to New York City, where my literary agent, Don Congdon, had planned a party. I had begun to write short stories, successfully. Margarita Smith, the fiction editor of *Mademoiselle* magazine, then the most prestigious showcase for promising young writers, wanted to fete her two discoveries of the year, of whom I was one. It was an occasion I was not going to miss. So I forced my swollen leg into my leg brace, took up my crutches, and went to New York, and to the hotel room Don had reserved for me. That evening, feeling like death warmed over, as a friend used to say, I went to the party at Don's apartment in Greenwich Village.

When Margarita Smith arrived, she brought with her what seemed to be a young boy of twelve or thirteen. He wore a cardigan sweater, and his straw-colored hair hung in bangs over his forehead, his complexion resembled the color of Roquefort cheese.

"That is Margarita Smith," Don said.

"Is that her son?" I asked.

"No," Don said. "That is Truman Capote."

He was my fellow discovery of the year for *Mademoiselle* magazine.

Capote was then working at *The New Yorker*, and as he regaled us with tales of his adventures there, I forgot my discomfort and my fever. The evening went on, with drinking and anecdotes, until someone suddenly decided that all who were left at the party should go on to the Hotel Drake.

There, in the semidarkness, and the gabble of conversation, it suddenly all caught up with me. I needed to go back to my hotel room. I needed to go to bed. I whispered to Don, asking if he would leave with me to help me get back there.

He interrupted the others at the table to explain what I had been through, how I felt, and why I must leave.

Truman Capote at once focused all of his considerable force upon me. Why hadn't I told them before? Why had I suffered in silence? Why had I let them put me through such discomfort?

"Do you have any sleeping pills?" he asked.

"No," I said.

"We will get you some," he said.

The waiter was summoned, the bill was paid, we went to the street, and we piled into a taxi. At Truman Capote's direction, the cab driver took us from one friend of Capote's to another, ringing doorbells, waking them up, calling back and forth at suddenly opened windows. In between these stops, Truman Capote sat wedged beside me in the crush of the taxi and tried to comfort me.

At last our mission was accomplished. Two Seconal tablets were wrested from some unwilling victim. The taxi took us to my hotel, and everyone tucked me into bed.

Our ways parted after that. I never saw Truman Capote again. But when I read later that he was giving a party at the Plaza Hotel for several hundred of his closest friends, I did not doubt that statement for a moment. He had a genius for making friends. He had made a friend of me forever.

The use of my leg was not restored after the experimental pummeling with the air hammer. However, sometime after, my own doctor made a rather surprising discovery in his examination of me. The experimental treatment with the air hammer, which I had told him about rather sheepishly, had an unexpected but favorable result. The scar tissue that formed after the damage done to the leg helped support my hip and made it possible for me to walk, with my leg brace of course, but without the dip to one side that was characteristic of so many victims of polio.

I was happy to settle for that.

# 36

THINGS HAPPEN VERY quickly when you are young and hungry for life. I was stricken with polio in North Africa in 1944; in 1945 I was released from Warm Springs, Georgia; in 1946 Simon and Schuster published my novel, *All for the Best.* In 1947 I was married.

Now, about Kitty.

When we met, she was sitting in a canvas chair in the summer house of mutual friends near my parents' retirement house. She was wearing tennis shorts of a soft and faded pink, with a shirt to match. Her fair hair was drawn up and back in a Psyche knot. On her feet were sneakers. Her long, slender, tanned bare legs were stretched out in front of her, crossed at the ankles, and she was smoking a cigarette carefully, putting it down in a little china ashtray beside her, for she was knitting. Afterward I wondered what had happened to whatever she was knitting, for I never saw it again; it could have been the skein of her life before she met me, put aside and never to be picked up again.

She looked at me and I stopped in front of her, balancing myself on my crutches, knowing her at once, although I had never seen her before, for, as Proust has said, the image of the beloved is engraved upon the retina of our eye.

I moved to a chair beside her to sit down, but she held up her hand, and everyone laughed as she pointed to the rafter over my head where a pigeon sat.

"We went into town for dinner last night," she said. "When we came out of the restaurant we found the pigeon on the curb, with an injured wing, so we brought him home. Why don't you sit over here."

I moved to the chair on the other side of her and sat down, awkward with my crutches. I was introduced to her. She had a married name, and my heart sank. But we talked, and I could not stop looking at her. The perfect profile. The proud and lovely head. The hair drawn upward and back. I wanted never to stop looking at her, and after I had returned to my parents' house I called our mutual friends to ask if there was a husband, and if so where had he been. No, there was no husband was the answer. There had been a divorce. There was a small son, but no husband.

The next day I telephoned her. "I must see you," I said.

We arranged to meet that evening at a café nearby called The Peppermint Lounge. I could make my way there. It was a spare place with a bar and little tables, and not much light, but what light there was was pleasant for it came from small lamps fitted with rose-tinted shades.

We had a drink together. I said, "I think I'm in love with you. I think I fell in love with you the first moment I saw you. Is that ridiculous?"

She looked at me. She smiled. "I don't find it ridiculous," she said. "Tell me about it."

I told her. We talked. We talked endlessly. I told her everything. Of my dreams for myself, of the work I wanted to do—of my present despair. She listened, her eyes never leaving my face. If I paused, she urged me to go on. We talked until the barkeep asked us if he might please go home.

A worn path led to the water's edge, and we began to make our way down it, slowly. The night was bright with stars. The moon stood high. In the air was the scent of summer breezes over fresh water, like a door opened onto remembered innocence and happiness.

We stopped when we came to the grassy bank where it fell away to the beach. I was able to lower myself to that, and we sat there for a long moment in silence, listening to the soft murmuring of the water below.

Finally I spoke. "I haven't any right to love you," I said, "now that I'm damaged goods."

She turned to me and reached out and touched my face. She brushed a lock of hair back from my forehead. "You must let me decide that," she said.

I took her in my arms and carried her backward with me to lie in the grass. I arched the upper part of my body over her, supporting myself with my hand. My head was above hers and I looked down at her. Her eyes glowed softly in the darkness.

She left the next day, with her son, Brent, for New York, cutting short her visit, our mutual friend told me on the telephone, because of an urgent call from her office.

I was not to learn until later that she had created this emergency herself, hoping to resolve a problem before it could be fully formed. It was not by chance that she was alone with her small son. When one has been so badly hurt in the past, it is best to avoid future involvement. The freedom and security she had achieved were hers, and she had worked hard for them. She did not want them threatened.

I knew nothing of this. All I felt was my sense of loss at her leaving. But sometimes the furies that pursue us tire, and in the interlude that follows a more benevolent providence intervenes.

My novel, *All for the Best,* was published soon afterward to favorable reviews. A telephone call came from New York University, asking me if I would care to teach a class in creative writing, in their department of journalism.

I took up my crutches, and returned to New York.

# 37

THE HOTEL ALBERT was so shabby that even the mice shunned it. But at least it was on Washington Square, near the university, and I could walk back and forth. If I used my imagination and looked at the neighborhood with a neoromantic eye, I could almost imagine that it was the Left Bank in Paris.

I was supposed to consider myself lucky, as I did, to have found any place to live at all. Housing was still so tight in post-war New York that one was allowed to stay only five nights in any hotel, including the Albert, where under ordinary circumstances even overnight might have seemed excessive. I had been given permission to live there by lying in such a complicated manner that my memory, out of a sense of stubborn integrity, refuses to recall the details.

However, I was now a confident young man. I had to be. There is one uncomfortable certainty in life that you can count on, whether you like it or not. No beautiful woman ever has but one admirer. Kitty was seeing me, but she was also seeing others. I was back in competition.

But where ignorance is bliss, 'tis folly to be wise. I needed her. Perhaps she did not need me. My task was to make her want me, if not to need me, and, wanting me, need me.

I planned my strategy. I would undertake to convince everyone, including myself, that I had no physical handicap or that at the very least I was not to be identified by it.

I trained myself to walk with a cane, a long leg brace, and

192

a hip that did not dip to one side. *Love* can work miracles. I was a handsome young man. (If you are a handsome young man who is crippled, and threatened with removal from competition, you are allowed to say this about yourself.) I was a war hero. I would never feel sorry for myself. I would turn my lousy hand of cards into an asset.

I had accumulated back pay coming to me from my time at Warm Springs. I spent it. I went to a specialty outfitting shop and bought a fine cane of dark, polished wood, with a gold band for initials, to replace the institutional-looking cane I had first acquired. I bought shoes imported from England, hand-lasted, since they would better hold the metal bracket in the heel of my shoe into which my leg brace must fit. I went to Brooks Brothers for suits, shirts, ties, socks, a coat, and a hat. In those days men still wore hats, and I bought a bowler because I thought it went so well with my mahogany cane and my polished English shoes.

I felt that the importance of grooming could not be over-estimated. It seemed it would be much more difficult to dismiss a disabled or handicapped person if he was well-dressed, even expensively well-dressed, than if he was slovenly or indifferently groomed. I went regularly to the barbershop at the Biltmore Hotel, for the works.

I felt a need to be impeccable, to turn aside, if I could, that instinctive withdrawal we feel in the presence of someone who is physically imperfect. I bathed and shaved with care each morning. I scrubbed my face. It is my impression that with the invention of the aerosol can, many a man simply does not ever wash his face. He sprays on the foam, scrapes off the beard, wipes off the residual foam, and rushes to work. We are becoming a race of men with dirty faces.

Of course, I didn't want to give the impression that I had been dressed and groomed by a mortician to be laid out, so I strove for an air of casual elegance, or elegant casualness, with a handkerchief thrust carelessly into the breast pocket of the jacket of my suit. I wore my bowler hat slightly tilted to one side.

My life rule became: Dress well. Scrub your face. Brush your hair. Walk erect. Hold your head high. Never hurry. Never let yourself be hurried. Never invite pity. Laugh.

193

In spite of this, it was to be a long campaign.

On days when my schedule permitted, I would go to Kitty's office to meet her and walk home with her the few short blocks from her office to her apartment.

Her beauty and slender elegance was of the sort that caused people to turn after she had passed. One warm evening, shining in memory, she wore a linen suit in light yellow, with white piping at the lapels. She was always immaculate. Her housekeeper put out a fresh pair of white gloves for her each morning as she left for the office. With my new sartorial splendor and my suitor's arrogance, we made a very handsome couple, and I don't mind saying that we enjoyed the effect we made.

Kitty was a brilliant woman with a highly demanding job in public relations for charitable organizations. She worked hard to support herself and her small son, Brent, without any other help. Sometimes she would be so preoccupied with her business affairs that it would be difficult to get her to leave the office at the end of the day.

So, on this particular evening, in order to make her pay attention to me, I decided to be outrageous.

"It's fortunate for you that you're so beautiful," I said. "Certainly you could never get by on your brains."

She stopped. I stopped. She looked at me for a moment in shock. Then she began to laugh. She laughed until she had to reach out to me and grasp my lapel for support.

"That's just what I've always *hoped* someone would say to me," she said. "So much has always been expected of me."

When her laughter had subsided we stood for a moment together, touching. We looked into each other's eyes.

I wasn't home yet, but I had made points.

MEANWHILE, I HAD an ambivalent relationship with the students in my class at New York University. Most of them were men about my age, attending school under the G.I. Bill. They were mainly New Yorkers—from Brooklyn or the Bronx. Anything west of the Hudson River was to them *terra incognita.*

They were street-smart. They knew everything, including the fact that you couldn't get anywhere unless you knew someone with influence in the profession you wanted to enter. They hooted when I disagreed with this.

All the faithful there were absolutely convinced that you could not have a story published, or anything published, no matter how well-written, unless you knew an editor or one of the owners of the publication.

I explained that I had been published without knowing anyone of influence. You just submitted things, and waited. It took time, and you had to be patient, but that was the only way it was done.

Baloney. They weren't buying that. They weren't from the country. They knew the score.

I couldn't persuade any of them to send any of their writing to a magazine, no matter how highly I might praise the work. No, they said shrugging, it would simply be a waste of their time and money.

At one point I asked everyone in the class to write a story of true experience; if they were war veterans, then perhaps they should write about the most moving and vivid experience they had had in the war.

Many of the contributions were exciting. There was one written by a former navy fighter pilot that described his feeling of being one with the plane when he flew, almost as if he were in the womb, sustained by its control systems. I asked him to send it out. I suggested he send it to *Esquire* magazine, where the editor, Arnold Gingrich, was on the alert for new, young talent.

He laughed and turned away.

I took the manuscript from him. "I will mail it for you," I said. "I will show all of you how it is done."

To the next class I brought two nine-by-twelve manila envelopes and postage stamps. I had taken the manuscript to the post office to have it weighed so I would know what postage was required.

In the presence of the class I addressed one envelope to the student at his home address. I folded it in half. With a paper clip I attached the postage necessary for the return of the manuscript should it be rejected. I put this with the manuscript of the story into the second manila envelope, which was addressed to *Esquire* and had postage attached.

Two weeks passed. Then, one day as I came to class, the former navy fighter-pilot student came racing down the hallway toward me, wearing a beatific expression and waving a slip of paper.

I stopped with a feeling of excitement. *Esquire* had taken the story!

The student stopped, breathless, in front of me. He thrust the slip of paper into my hand. "See!" he said, with an air of triumph. "Didn't I tell you? I knew this would happen!"

The piece of paper he had thrust into my hand was a printed rejection slip.

People who took rejection so happily and claimed it as a vindication of their convictions were not exactly my kind of people. In class we argued a lot. Once, backed to the wall by the students' foolish and limiting delusions, I tried to retaliate. "You're just a bunch of hicks," I said. "You are far more provincial than I am. I grew up in Euclid Village, Ohio, but I know about New York. You grew up in New York, but you don't know a thing about Euclid Village, Ohio."

This stopped them, but it didn't change them. They knew better. They weren't born yesterday. You never got anywhere unless you knew somebody, and that was that!

Meanwhile, on fair days I walked back and forth between the Hotel Albert on University Place, and New York University on Washington Square, with my leg brace and my cane, going up and down curbstones, walking along the level sidewalk, mainly without incident, except for one memorable occasion when I myself forgot the rule about giving assistance to someone who is handicapped.

The rule is simple: It is best to wait to be asked. Or, if assistance is indicated, to ask the person first if you may help him. To rush in without permission, to touch someone, aside from posing a threat is also an invasion of the privacy and dignity on which we all must pride ourselves.

On one of those fair days I was walking back to the Hotel Albert from New York University. A young man was walking ahead of me. He was a familiar figure to those who lived in the neighborhood, although I did not know him and had never spoken to him. He was also a veteran of World War II. He was blind. He made his way along the street with his white-tipped cane, feeling the sidewalk before him. I caught up with him just as he came to the curb of a cross street.

"Let me help you," I said, and reached for his arm.

The moment I touched him he struck out at me with his stick so viciously and with such force that I almost fell.

I stepped back to compose myself. He could not have known that it was a case of the lame trying to help the blind, and I did not try to explain that to him. I accepted the rebuke I had earned.

Now it was possible for me to go about the city by subway or bus. The subway seemed less hazardous, odd as that may sound in this dangerous day. But because you had already paid your fare before getting on the subway, you could usually find a seat, or a pole to grasp, before the train started up again. When you boarded a bus, on the other hand, you had to pay your fare before you sat down. By that time the bus had started on its lurching way, and you had to grasp a seat or anything else at hand, like another passenger, to steady yourself.

Then subways were not thought to be places of peril, and you could assume that your fellow passengers were decent people. I was once nearly frightened out of my wits by the unsolicited assistance of strangers who wanted to be helpful.

I had gotten up to stand at the train door, ready to get out at the next stop. When the train stopped, the car was on a curve and the space between the car and the platform was a little too wide for me to step across. I stood in place, thinking to get off at the next stop, but two fellow passengers, seeing me looking as if reluctant to get off, sprang into action. Without a word, and as if they had rehearsed it, they took hold of me, one on either side, under the arms, and stepping forward, lifted me onto the platform. They stood me there, like a Barbie doll, poised perilously on my cane. The two men then jumped back into the subway as the door closed, and it rushed on, leaving a turbulence of air behind it in which I fought to maintain my balance.

As I moved more widely about the city instead of merely walking back and forth between University Place and Washington Square, I learned that the three major hazards were dogs, small children, and beautiful young women, not necessarily in that order.

Some people think that dogs are as intelligent as human beings, or maybe even more so. Dogs are faithful. Dogs have been known to pine away on their masters' graves. They have gone for help for an injured master. They bring brandy in little kegs around their necks to men lost in snowstorms. But for me, I regret to say, dogs lack a certain perception about people. They sometimes jump on you if they feel friendly, and they will sometimes run between your legs, even when they are on a leash. Also, many dogs are trained to fear a stick, and they may feel they should attack anyone walking along with a cane. In such instances I found it best to stand still, grab something to hold on to, and yell. (The master or the mistress of the dog would always say, smilingly, "Oh, he wouldn't hurt you for anything! He's just being friendly," in a tone of voice that suggested that you were probably such a coward you shouldn't have come out of the house in the first place.)

Children are darling and unpredictable. Sometimes they like to run at you and grab you around the knees. In that case it is best to pitch forward, letting their little bodies cushion your fall, which may even remind them not to do *that* again. But mostly children are inattentive. They are busy being children. Their minds are outside of their bodies, in the Land of Oz or outer space. They run and they don't always look where they are running, and they are much too preoccupied to listen. Again, I found it best to stop, grab the nearest stable object or person, and yell until help came, or until the danger was past.

The trouble with beautiful young women, if one can call it trouble, is that they are not used to *looking;* they are accustomed instead to being looked *at.* And they usually learn by instinct, if they are very beautiful, the old Hollywood rule for the public appearance of a movie star: See no one, and smile a little.

In New York City, beautiful young women are always in a hurry. They never just walk. They are always rushing to an appointment with the hairdresser, or a lover, or a model agency, or a motion picture producer. So, seeing no one and smiling a little, they press onward, confident that a passageway will open before them, which is all very well unless a part of the passageway is occupied by someone who can't move very fast.

I found it necessary to watch all beautiful young women closely. I had always done that, but it saddened me to have my way of looking at them change from appreciation to awareness, as if Siva the Creator had suddenly become Siva the Destroyer. A beautiful young woman is always a threat or a danger to a man, but on crowded city streets it is a different game, and I often wished that a referee was at hand to blow the whistle.

Beautiful young women often travel in twos, laughing, talking, walking rapidly, seeing no one. The Red Sea may part for them, but the unstable of foot are advised to cling to the walls. Sometimes, when walking in twos, one young woman suddenly decides to split from the other one, but in doing so she may not have finished her conversation with her friend, so she proceeds for some paces backward. This is when I yell.

\*      \*      \*

In my travels about the city, I could not find the New York I had left. I was, in fact, in a different terrain. New York University was at Washington Square. Kitty's apartment, where I spent as much time as I was allowed, was near Gramercy Park. All of this was Downtown. My life before in New York had been Uptown. The line of demarcation was Forty-second Street.

One Saturday afternoon I summoned up my courage and resolved to pay a visit to Brentano's. I chose a Saturday afternoon, hoping that my return would provoke as little attention as possible, because on Saturday afternoon the store would be filled with customers.

I need not have worried. There was no one left in the store to remember me, or for me to remember; I might have been a specter, returning to the scene of a former life.

As I went through the Annex into the main store, seeing no one that I knew, my heart sank deeper with each step. There were stacks of nonbooks everywhere, the sort that you could look at but that you didn't have to read—books on art, on architecture, photography, interior decoration, picture books on places such as Charleston and Williamsburg. And, horror of horrors, there were stacks of paperback books. They had never been in the store in my old bookselling days.

The worst was yet to come. Mr. Brentano's corner had been ripped out. The shelves that had held his precious collection of old and rare books had been removed, and in their place were mounted glass-fronted cabinets in which were displayed alleged "museum copies" of jewelry and artifacts, all looking rather tacky.

The staff that was present, although louder than we used to be, were as always young and confident, with a rather superior air, marking time on their way to higher things, condescending to serve as salespeople to the ignorant.

I turned toward Forty-seventh Street, thinking I would leave without making my presence known to these people who did not know me. But suddenly I saw in the corner inside the door, where she had always been, Miss Guggenheim behind the counter in the stationery department. She would know where Rowena was.

I went up to her and identified myself. She was painstakingly copying out an order for personal stationery, carefully transcribing the name and address from a letter onto an order form. She looked up and acknowledged me without changing her expression. She did not express any surprise or any emotion at all at my sudden reappearance.

"Where are the Brentanos?" I asked, somewhat foolishly.

"Mr. Brentano, Senior, is gone," she said. "He passed away."

I was prepared for that after seeing his private corner removed. "And Mr. Brentano, Junior?" I asked.

"He retired," Miss Guggenheim said. "He sold the business. I don't know where he is." She did not look up from her work as she spoke.

"And Rowena?" I asked, my heart almost stopping.

In the instant before she replied, I had a feeling that Miss Guggenheim was like the chorus in a Greek tragedy, forever in one place, watching the scene, marking the passing of time, the characters coming and going, explaining this to the onlooker.

"Rowena is dead," she said without looking up.

For a moment I could not move. I wanted to ask where? When? How? And then suddenly I knew I didn't want to know the answers.

I moved. I turned. And as quickly as I could I left the store, using the entrance on Forty-seventh Street.

There was a sound of great roaring in my head. When I reached the street I turned to the side of the building and leaned my forehead against the stone until I had regained my equilibrium.

**39**

I WANTED TO give up my teaching and write. I longed to get out of the city. Surely everything would be easier and better in the country. But I could not persuade Kitty. I had learned of her misgivings about marriage. She did not want to be hurt again.

As if in compensation, the nature of my life changed remarkably for the better, oddly enough through one of my students at the university. He was a veteran who had lost a leg in action. He stopped at my desk one evening at the end of the class and said, "Did you get your free car?"

"My free what?" I asked.

"Your free car," he said.

"What free car?"

"Haven't you heard?" he asked. "Don't you belong to any veterans' organization?"

"No," I said.

I didn't belong to any veterans' organization because I didn't want to be a member of any group whose opinions or politics I might not agree with. However, veterans' organizations kept their members informed of their entitlements, which meant that I was often penalized for my hauteur, as any snob should be. I consoled myself by thinking that many of the good things in life, such as the right not to have to belong to any group, were expensive.

However, this time I was saved from my folly by my student. The good senator from Maine, Margaret Chase Smith, had sponsored a bill, passed by the U.S. Congress and signed by the president, which provided that anyone who had lost a limb, or the use of a limb, while on active duty during the war was to be given a free car.

I got in touch with the Veterans Administration, and after consulting my records, they told me that I was indeed entitled to a free car. I could spend up to a certain specified sum, and they would reimburse the dealer. I picked out a black, two-door Oldsmobile sedan. But I had never learned to drive. This ignorance didn't trouble the Veterans Administration at all. The New York City Police Department, which had driving instructors on its staff, would teach me to drive.

Every afternoon I went to the spacious grounds of the Kingsbridge Veterans Administration Hospital in the Bronx, where a young police officer in uniform sat beside me in the car and taught me how to drive with an automatic shift. He was such a very young man—a cadet police officer, I suppose—that I wondered if he had begun to shave yet. At any rate, he was patient with me. In fact, he was almost insulting.

"How am I doing?" I asked him one afternoon.

"Very well for an older man," he said.

The day I drove the Oldsmobile home to Kitty's apartment, alone, I felt as free as a bird. I was now more mobile than I had been when I had two good legs. It seemed a compensation for my disability, but I suppose Margaret Chase Smith had known that it would be.

That evening Kitty, Brent, and I went out for a drive up the East River Drive to the Triboro Bridge. Although the young police officer had been a very good teacher, he had not taught me how to slow down at the approach to a curve, and then accelerate into it, so we took the approach to the Triboro Bridge at full speed and went whirling around its outer edge as if we were on some new and particularly frightening concession at an amusement park. Brent yelled with delight. Kitty clutched my arm. We lived, and I didn't forget *that* lesson.

The city was now our oyster. We could go anywhere and with my special parking permit park anywhere except in front of a fireplug or a theater. If we went to the theater, one of the mounted policemen in that district, seeing the parking permit on my windshield, would lead us to the nearest available parking place on the street and wait until we were safely parked. Sometimes Brent even got to stroke the muzzle of the horse when we got out of the car.

I was almost resigned to city life. Almost. My exasperation with my students hadn't lessened. It was a bore to read story after story, and to work with the writer to help him improve it, knowing that it would never find its way into print, no matter how fine it was, just because the writer knew better than to send it to some unknown editor for rejection. (The course in short-story writing was an indulgence for most of these students. Their major studies were in more practical subjects such as advertising or copywriting, which would lead them one day to a safe haven on some nice dead-end street.)

But home is where the heart is, and it was a pleasure to go to Kitty's apartment. In the evening with the lamps lighted, and Brent in bed, we talked to each other in nonstop conversation.

"We must talk until we know each other completely," Kitty said. She was arranging daffodils, carefully placing them in a glass flower holder at the bottom of a crystal bowl.

"I can't ever seem to do this right," she said, "hard as I try."

"It looks perfect to me," I said, watching the graceful way her silk skirt caressed her legs when she turned.

"I suppose it will have to do," Kitty said, with a last touch at the flowers.

"It's always so hot in these city apartments," I said, getting up to open a window. I could walk about the apartment now without my cane, balancing myself on my braced leg like Long John Silver and his peg leg. I moved about, restless but happy. I was too warm. My face glowed as if it had been oiled.

"I don't know whether I can do that," I said, going back to sit on the sofa.

"Do what?" Kitty asked.

"Give myself completely," I said. "There is a part of me that I cannot give to anyone.

"Maybe it has something to do with my writing. I can talk

about that, you know, but I cannot tell you how it is done. I don't even know that myself." And so then I told her my theory about the compost heap, and why I believed so strongly that no creative person should ever go through psychoanalysis.

"In a compost heap," I said, "all of the grass cuttings and the hedge trimmings and the prunings and the weeds are heaped up high until the weight carries them down and they decay and heat is generated, and from this new things will grow. We grow out of our past. The creative person creates out of the heat of his past experience. If the compost heap were spread out under the sun, it would simply dry up and nothing would come of it at all."

"It sounds unpleasant," Kitty said, snuffing out her cigarette.

"If I gave all of myself to you there would be nothing left of me," I said. "As much as I love you, there is a part of myself that I must keep for myself. You do understand that, don't you?"

"I will try," Kitty said.

After a moment of silence, I said, "Isn't there some part of you that you cannot share with anyone else? Some private part of you?"

Kitty stretched her arms above her, and after a moment of equal silence, she said, "Sometimes I am so tired I don't know. The last few years haven't been easy for me."

She said she felt like a juggler trying to keep all of his tenpins in the air at the same time, never being able to relax for a single minute, with Brent, her job, the apartment.

"Yet change frightens me," Kitty said. "What would we do? Could we make it on our own?"

"Of course we could," I said. I felt vigorous, successful, in control of my life. I had got it all together at last, and we were steaming down the track, full speed ahead. My writing was going well. It was selling.

"There are whole areas of my life that have never been developed," Kitty said, "because of the pressures. I've never had time to run a household, or manage it. I've always had to hire someone else to do that so that I could earn the money to keep it going. I've always thought I might like to do that. But can we?"

A woman novelist, a friend, had said to me after meeting Kitty, "Why do you want to marry this woman? This woman who has been married before and has a child?" The novelist was charming, compassionate, and warm, and meant no offense.

"Because I want the responsibility," I had said. It was enough. The question was answered.

I had given some years to the service of my country, and I was proud of that. But I had to make up for those years. I wanted to be a family man in my own house. It would be a gamble to pull up stakes and leave the city, and who knew if we could make it? But the success of that challenge would be my fulfillment.

Now I turned toward Kitty, to answer her question.

"This apartment has been home for you and Brent for a long time, I know. But for me it is just a place where I came after I found you. And how lucky I was to have found you! But now I'd like for us to have a house of our own, for our new life together."

"I have dreams too," she said, "that go beyond just keeping house."

"What sort of dreams?"

"I see a big house," Kitty said, leaning back in the sofa. "A big, old house, with lots of waste space, and in this house there would be rooms with doors to close. You could paint with water colors in one room, and when you were tired of that you could just leave, and close the door, and go to another room where you might sew, and make a dress. You could close the door on that when you wanted to, and then go outside. There would be gardens, flower gardens, and inside of course there would be an enormous, old-fashioned kitchen where you could bake, or cook, or make bread, or anything."

She stopped and looked at me. "Could we do that?" she asked. "Could we?"

"We'll never know if we don't try," I said.

She got up and walked a few paces back and forth. She turned and faced me.

"If I am to be married," Kitty said, "I want to be married to a writer, not a teacher."

I stood up and came around the coffee table and faced her. We held each other at arms' length and looked long at each other. We embraced.

WE WERE TO be married in September. It was then late spring. We planned a small wedding because Kitty believed second weddings should be as inconspicuous as possible. Still, some preparations had to be made. Preparations. Kitty began to make lists. I had never thought of myself as an ordinary man. But I did what an ordinary man would have done. I left town.

In my defense, I had applied for a summer session at the MacDowell Colony, the refuge for artists in New Hampshire. I had been accepted. I was working on a novel. (This would be my refrain all my life. I was always working on a novel.) It was to be my third novel, and the third novel, as other novelists know, is important. It demonstrates whether the writer had the right stuff.

The MacDowell Colony had separate studios, where you stayed all day and where no one was permitted to disturb you. You lived there in dormitories or rooms, in a kind of monastic withdrawal. Husbands and wives, sweethearts, fiancés and family members were forbidden to enter except on weekends. I wanted very much to go. Kitty said she wanted me to go, whatever she may have really thought.

The MacDowell Colony was a godsend for university instructors. I had learned that university instructors are busy all the academic year. They have classes to prepare for, papers to read and to judge, a number of egos, easily bruised, that are entrusted to them, and it behooves them to move gently—firmly, but gently—all the time looking back to see if they have left any victims in their wake to whom they must attend with various forms of succor. The MacDowell Colony was made for them, a place where they could breathe without someone breathing down their backs.

So, I was beautiful and engaged and I used Vaseline Hair Tonic when I set out for the MacDowell Colony in my merry Oldsmobile. I didn't know what to expect of the artist's life. Would it be birdsong and evensong, madrigals and vespers? I was ready for anything. I had been a loner in my writing. Now I was about to meet and work with colleagues. I resolved to keep an open mind.

The buildings and the setting of the Colony were reassuringly simple. We were welcomed with sandwiches and coffee on this open-house day, with Colonists arriving at all hours—a friendly gathering, with people talking and introducing themselves. Our attention was directed to a notice on the bulletin board. Mrs. MacDowell, who was still living then, with her plain dress and her plain Puritan shoes with the silver buckles, had requested that the Colonists go to church, in a body, the following day, which was Sunday. This unusual request was explained by those who had been in residence before. It seemed that the previous week a poet had chosen to sun herself in the nude on the stone wall beside her studio, in full view of workmen repairing a roof nearby. Second, a young male composer had seduced a boy of fourteen on the village green. I had thought that young boys who allowed themselves to be seduced kept their mouths shut about it, but this village boy had blabbed everything to his father. And it had taken twice as long as the estimate to repair the nearby roof. The poet and the composer had left the Colony, but not under a cloud. To whom much is given, much must be forgiven, etc. The poet was well-known for her love poems, so that explained everything, and it was also well-known that a lot of men, in the top echelon of all the arts, were homosexual.

We had homosexuals in those days. The self-confident, self-righteous, garrulous gay had not yet appeared to demand and take up his rightful place in the cowed and cowering populace. Mrs. MacDowell had also had her troubles with her husband, the composer Edward MacDowell ("To a Wild Rose"). There were rumors about him and other women. Mrs. MacDowell had decided to rise above all that, and concentrate on the arts. We were to do the same. The next morning we all went to church, in a body. Everyone behaved, both the Colonists and the church-goers. That was the end of that.

The daily routine at the Colony was engagingly simple. We slept in the main building. A separate building was supplied for the women artists. Breakfast was either in the dining room of the main building or in your studio. Lunch was brought to your studio and left at the door in a basket. There was a menu that you could mark in the dining room before going to your studio: sandwiches or a salad, fresh fruit, a thermos jug of tea or coffee. Dinner was served at six-thirty in the dining room of the main building.

I was assigned to the studio in which Thornton Wilder had written *Our Town*. The village in the play was assumed to be Peterborough, the village nearby, so they must have seen their share of odd and queer characters. I saw Thornton Wilder's name on a plaque inside the door on which we were supposed to sign our names, and I signed proudly. I settled down happily with my typewriter and my novel, which was about a sensitive young man who was tormented by religious scruples even while deflowering a pretty young girl in the hayloft of his family barn.

A few days later a fellow writer with whom I had become acquainted told me that the man who delivered lunch to us in an old jalopy was "as crazy as we are," or "crazier." He wouldn't elaborate on that but advised me to see for myself.

I made it a point to stand beside the open door, at five minutes to twelve the following day. On schedule the old Ford arrived. I waited until the man had come up on the porch and placed my lunch basket beside the door and then I cleared my throat and stepped outside and said, "Hello."

The man, a local man, friendly and not averse to a little conversation, returned my greeting, pushed his cap back, and said, "I see you're in the cabin where Thornton Wilder wrote *Our Town*."

"So I have been told," I said. "I'm very proud to be here."

"You see that tree over there?" the man said, pointing to a pine tree.

"Yes," I said.

"Well," the man said, "Thornton Wilder read every line of *Our Town* to that tree."

"He did?" I said.

"Yes," the man said, and spat for emphasis. "And if the tree didn't like the line, he took it out."

So saying, the man turned on his heel, and left the porch and boarded his old jalopy, and waved to me, and drove off.

Cooped up as we were all day, with no one to talk to except the lunch man, not allowed to visit one another, we treated dinner time like feeding time at the zoo, but feeding time to animals who could talk. Interested as I am in food, I don't remember a single thing we had to eat the entire summer. We talked and ate, devouring each other across the table, and when we finished we moved to the living room, where we grouped around the fireplace and the talk grew even more heated.

I was in my Transcendentalist Period. I had read with interest Emerson's theory of the "oversoul," in which thoughts and ideas are believed to float around us overhead. At any one time, or so I understood, many people harbored the same ideas, and if you wished to share these ideas and thoughts all you had to do was, figuratively, to reach up and pull them down from the constant stream passing above. Now, at the Colony, I found this theory substantiated. We were a motley group—writers, poets, sculptors, painters, composers—but in our conversation we found, excitingly, that we were all trying to do the same thing, have a creative response to those thoughts and ideas that

210

were streaming, as in a millrace, above us. We had some fine fights. We shouted and laughed, and cried. We went to bed, exhausted.

I had nightmares. I dreamed one night that I was crawling through a long pipe, forcing my way through to a light at the other end. I woke up to find I was curled up on the small bedside table, a feat which I could not have accomplished when awake. I carefully uncoiled myself and went back to bed, but I didn't sleep the rest of the night.

I fell in love with Kay Boyle, one of the fairest flowers of the American expatriate group in Paris. At our first meeting, filled with memories of her superb short story "The White Horses of Vienna," I said, "I feel I have always known you." She came forward without a word and took me in her arms and kissed me. I never told Kitty about Kay Boyle. She wouldn't have understood.

We used to sit on the front porch of the main building at five o'clock, after our work was finished, and gossip. We took Carson McCullers apart. It was easy to take Carson McCullers apart. It is also easy to view Carson McCullers's life as a tragedy, but this would not be fair to her. Carson viewed it as a huge joke. There was always a wicked smile on her face. She kept drinking and she kept having strokes. She wouldn't stop drinking. She greeted the guests at the door of her house with a welcoming drink in hand, bourbon and branch, and saying, "Have a toddy for the body."

Kay Boyle had a particular memory of Carson that rankled. She had rented a villa somewhere in the south of France. Carson was there, but she was supposed to have vacated the villa the previous day. When Kay arrived, with her family, she found Carson in bed.

"I have had a stroke," Carson said. "You aren't going to throw me out, are you?"

Kay shrugged in telling the story. "What could I do?" she said. "I couldn't throw her out. She spoiled our summer, of course."

Kay had been married several times, and she had several daughters, whom she had named after fruits.

I met her daughter Apple when she came to visit her

mother. Kay was married at that time to Baron Munch-hausen, who was young and personable and spoke flawless English.

I met him during intermission at a very tedious recital at the Recital Hall on the grounds of the Colony. It was an obligatory attendance for everyone. Every artist was expected to display a portion of his work, preferably whatever he was currently working on, before he left the Colony. This recital was the work of a composer in residence.

Once I threw a book, hard, at a composer's head during one of our evening after-dinner discussions. All of the composers at the MacDowell Colony composed in the twelve-tone scale. I don't know what that means exactly, but it made for some pretty tiresome music.

There were three categories of studios at the MacDowell Colony. Studios for writers were simple affairs, but studios for painters and sculptors had skylights and soaring interiors, to accommodate larger work. Studios for composers came with a grand piano and a bust of Beethoven on the mantel over the fireplace. The bust of Beethoven was always turned against the wall. I once asked a composer (in the twelve-tone scale) why the bust of Beethoven was always turned against the wall, and he said, "Because with Beethoven everything came to a stop. It wasn't possible to compose after Beethoven. We had to start over again, from the very beginning."

This composer I threw a book at said that I was not an artist. I had just sold my first story to a so-called popular magazine, *The Woman's Home Companion,* for five hundred dollars, which was top price in those days.

"You are not an artist. You sell to magazines," he said. So I threw a book at him, a heavy one, *Roget's Thesaurus.* Not much has been heard of him to this day, and I regret having thrown the book at him, but not very much. An honest five hundred commercial dollars was better and more respectable, I thought, than the sleazy grant the composer was there on.

I was soothed next day over lunch by Cordelia, an anthropologist whose studio was through the woods next to mine. We had taken to having lunch together, on her porch or mine, after which we went back to work.

An anthropologist is not normally thought of as an artist, but Cordelia had written a borderline book about actors and dreams, so she was allowed in under the wire. Often I was silent during lunch, thankful for her presence but involved with the hero of my novel, which was called *Into the Labyrinth,* who had unexpectedly turned into a one-way son-of-a-bitch, a real bastard. I was having trouble with him, and I let Cordelia's conversation about her anthropology department flow over me. I didn't know if Cordelia's anthropology department existed in the real world, or if it was an anthropology department in the sky. These vague conversations between people who never quite make a circuit with each other are commonplace.

At any rate, the things that went on there! Bisexuality, it seems, was rampant. When a new young male anthropologist turned up, bets were taken on who, she or he, would get him.

"Dr. Smith did, of course," Cordelia said. "He always did."

Cordelia's studio was a composer's studio, given to her, I suppose, because they had run out of composers. It was a large, spacious room with a grand piano and the bust of Beethoven on the mantel turned dutifully against the wall.

Cordelia and I decided, in a burst of genius, that instead of reading a portion of our work we would give a cocktail party together at Cordelia's studio. No one would object. A party was an option, sometimes a welcome option, to being on display with one's work. We would have the cocktail party at five o'clock when the Colonists returned from their studios, before the cook came and rang the dinner bell at six-thirty. The cook wanted to get home. Very neat. The guests would leave for their dinner, and that would be that.

We explored the studio. The piano could be pushed back. There was a long, large table, presumably for spreading out of musical scores, that could very well serve as the bar. I turned the bust of Beethoven out to face the room. He seemed to breathe more easily. The date was set—a week from Saturday—and we would announce it at dinner. Everyone applauded when we did.

Kay Boyle was enthusiastic about the party. She had a young protégé in residence. I had a feeling Kay always had a young protégé somewhere on the premises. I would have happily been her protégé, if I hadn't already been spoken for. Anyway, her current young protégé, whom I'll call Fred, was a painter and a sculptor who had been given the most desirable of painters' and sculptors' studios. It was of stone, with wooden rafters and beams and a fireplace at the end of a long room. The proportions were especially pleasing to the eye. I had been there once before, and Fred had transformed the place. He did paintings or prints in colored inks on large sheets of Japanese rice paper, and he had hung them from the rafters. He also did sculpture, in wet plaster—table sculpture, which looked like beautiful, tinted cow flops, and these were on display about the room. Kay told us he had a wonderful collection of Thelonious Monk records and a record player, and the party could continue there after dinner. What could be nicer?

Cordelia and I went to the village the Saturday before the party and stocked up on potato chips and crackers and nuts, and then we went to the liquor store. Liquor was less expensive in New Hampshire than in New York, so we bought generously. Everything that was left over we could divide and take back to New York. In the liquor store I spied a bottle of imported French dry vermouth that I could not get easily in New York, and I told Cordelia that I would pay for that. Little would be used at the party, and the bottle would last me for years, considering the amount of vermouth that I mixed in my martinis.

The cocktail party was a great success. Everything was freestyle, the bar, with ice and glasses from the kitchen of the main house, and bowls of comestibles sitting about everywhere. Knowing the deadline, everyone pitched in and poured himself a generous drink. Soon the decibels rose to shattering heights. When the dinner bell rang, everyone put down his glass and ran. I told Cordelia to go ahead while I made a quick check to see if all the cigarettes were out. My eye traveled over the drink table. My French vermouth bottle was *empty*. Absolutely empty! I stood for a moment in silent shock. They must mix martinis very differently in New Hampshire than they do in New York, I concluded, shaking my head and hurrying on my way to dinner.

The party continued after dinner in Fred's magnificent

studio. It was a cool evening, and a fire had been laid in the fireplace. Shadows danced on the walls and on Fred's paintings. The guests danced, Greek style, hands on shoulders, single file, the length of the studio, to Thelonious Monk. It was an unforgettable evening.

The next morning, at seven o'clock, Kay Boyle knocked on my door, looking sad and resigned.

"Come on, we have cleaning up to do." While I scrambled into my clothes, Kay explained what had happened. Fred was an alcoholic, trying to quit. *He* had drunk my bottle of vermouth.

His studio was a shambles. A friend had been called and had picked up Fred, but not before he had wrecked the studio and destroyed all of his art. The Japanese rice-paper paintings were in shreds, the sculptures had been smashed. In silence, Kay and I took up brooms and dustpans and did the best we could, emptying Fred's dream into the trashcans.

Kitty was coming for the next weekend. She would stay at the inn in Peterborough. I would meet the train and we would have dinner and the evening together, as well as Sunday morning. I would bring her to the Colony for lunch, and show her around, and show her off, and then I would take her back to the afternoon train to New York.

All went as planned. Late Sunday morning I brought her to the Colony. She was wearing a Chanel suit of palest lavender, piped in white, white gloves, and a two-strand pearl choker tied with a velvet ribbon. She wore no hat, but her blond hair had been arranged in a chignon at the back of her head.

The Colonists fell apart. Lounging around the luncheon table in their usual thrown-together attire, they lapsed into a deep, catatonic silence. All you could hear was chewing.

In the brief social gathering in the living room after lunch, I could see that the composer I had hit on the head with a book had Kitty in a corner and was talking earnestly and breathlessly to her.

"He implored me not to marry you," Kitty explained as I took her back to the inn. "He said you were too violent."

Out of the corner of my eye I could see that she was smiling.

"Well, he made me damn mad," I said defensively.

"I gathered that," Kitty said, still smiling.

At the inn she gathered her things together and I took her to the train. We were comfortably silent. We had had a good weekend, a miraculous time together in which we had pledged, anew, eternal devotion to each other.

"I enjoyed the Colony," Kitty said. "The others were very polite."

For some reason I felt oddly defensive, as if they were members of my family who had been shown up in a bad light.

"They're really not bad at all," I said. "Actually they are pretty nice, in their own sort of way."

The train came then, and I kissed her and put her aboard and stood outside her window until the train pulled away. I would miss Kitty, but I was glad I was not going back to the city yet. I thought about the writer who had called my attention to the man who brought our lunches.

"He is crazier than we are," he had said.

Later, the writer had said, "I am really comfortable here, much more comfortable than I am in the outside world. I hate the weekends when the civilians come to visit." Come to think of it, I hadn't seen him at lunch. Kay was away with her baron, and Cordelia did not show. I, too, would be happy to be back isolated in my studio. I, too, was more comfortable at the Colony than I was in the outside world.

The civilians versus the crazies.

Who was I? I had never given that much thought.

I was not a civilian.

I was "violent."

I was not really fit for any organized, civilized society.

I was an artist.

I stood and watched the train depart.

**41**

Kᴵᴛᴛʏ's ᴍᴏᴛʜᴇʀ ʜᴀᴅ given up her apartment in the city and moved to a nursing home in White Plains. It was an easy drive from New York City, and I went to see her when I came back from New Hampshire, a meeting arranged by Kitty. Her mother received me on the upstairs porch of what had formerly been a tree-shaded private house among other large houses in a suburban setting.

Kitty's mother had quite a number of things wrong with her but she was not visibly uncomfortable, and we sat in comfortable wicker chairs on the porch. Kitty and I were to be married in a Presbyterian church nearby so that Kitty's mother could attend.

"Kitty's father is dead," her mother said to me in a conversational tone. She was an agreeable woman, pretty, with white hair and an easy, authoritative air. You could see that she had lived her life well. "So, in her father's absence, I suppose I must talk to you about the responsibility of marriage."

She fell silent. She looked at me. I looked at her. She began to smile. I began to smile. We both ended up laughing. So that was that. We spent a pleasant half hour chatting about the upcoming wedding and about her grandson, Brent, who had not yet come into focus for me. I had been too busy courting his mother.

Terry had reappeared, my old delinquent friend, of whom I was very fond. I asked him to be my best man. As a man who had real buttonholes in the sleeves of his suit so he could unbutton the sleeves and roll them up in case of a duel, he seemed an appropriate choice. Kitty had asked her younger sister to stand with her at the ceremony.

As the fateful day approached, I rented a small reception room at the Roger Smith Hotel in White Plains. I ordered a bottle of champagne, chilled, and tray with half a dozen champagne glasses. Present were Kitty and I, Brent, Terry, Kitty's sister, and their mother. I don't remember anything about the ceremony except that I was very nervous, which I tried not to show. We six adjourned to the room in the Roger Smith, where I opened the bottle of champagne and passed around the glasses, even giving a small sip to Brent. Kitty's mother, looking very pretty in a flowered print dress, accepted the glass of champagne from me, saying, "Now don't expect anything sensible from me after I drink this." I wanted to say, "Don't expect anything sensible of me during the entire day," but I was unable.

The way to feel married, as I said afterward, is to start your wedding trip with a small boy in the backseat.

We set out in our Oldsmobile for Ohio, feeling happy all around. But a small boy is never still. His mother knew this, so as soon as we got to the open country, we played a game called "Road Cribbage." I don't remember exactly the rules of the game ("Don't expect anything sensible out of me during the entire day"), but there were certain points for a cow and certain points for a horse. You held your breath if you passed a cemetery. A red traffic light stopped us in front of a cemetery, and looking in the rearview mirror, I thought Brent would explode.

After we tired of Road Cribbage we were quiet. I suddenly realized Brent was unusually silent. I looked in the rearview mirror and what I saw needs some explaining. Kitty's mother, knowing we were on our way to Ohio where a party would be held by my family, who hadn't been able to attend the wedding, and by Kitty's cousins, at whose house we had met, had ordered individually boxed wedding cake slices, fifty of them, from a caterer. Now Brent had discovered the carton containing them, and he had emptied out on the seat all fifty pieces of boxed wedding cake slices.

"What are you doing back there?" I inquired, mildly.

"Oh, I'm building a castle," Brent replied, busy.

I smiled. I was silent. Building a castle out of pieces of wedding cake. I would settle for that.

# 42

WE HAD BEEN married for less than a month when Kitty told me she wouldn't go out with me anymore unless I stopped hitting taxicabs with my cane.

I had always regarded the taxi as my natural enemy, but in post-World War II New York, with its many shortages of services as well as of goods, the taxi driver had become a kind of petty tyrant who enjoyed the use of his power. Sometimes he would take you where you wanted to go, and sometimes he couldn't be bothered. He would ask where you wanted to go before you got into the taxi, or while you were getting in, and if the destination didn't please the driver, you would have to get out or be left standing at the curb.

Sometimes taxi drivers took childish delight in trying to frighten you. They might come racing to a screeching halt, just inches from you, as you crossed the street with the light. Or sometimes they would round a corner so closely that they could wipe the polish off your shoes. Or they might decide to flip their Off Duty signals on, all at once, while you were trying to hail one of them, and speed unheedingly by you, in flocks, like swallows flying back to Capistrano.

It was my custom, in any of the above instances, to deliver what I thought was a well-deserved rebuke by hitting the hood of the cab, if I could reach it with my cane, hoping to leave a dent.

On this particular evening we had come down from the apartment to go to the theater. At the curb in front, I hailed a cab with my cane, useful for peaceful as well as aggressive purposes. When the taxi pulled up to the curb, I told the driver where we wanted to go. He shook his head.

"I'm on my way home," he said. "That's in the opposite direction. I won't turn around."

So I hit the hood of the cab sharply with my cane as the driver pulled away. At the time, it seemed the only reasonable thing to do. But when I turned around, I was alone. Kitty had gone back upstairs.

When I got back to the apartment, Kitty was taking off her gloves. "I won't go out with you again until you stop hitting taxis with your cane," she said.

Kitty reminded me how I had hit a composer of music in the head with a book while I was at the MacDowell Colony.

I wanted to point out to her that there was a difference between the hood of a taxicab and the head of a composer of music in the twelve-tone scale, but at that moment I couldn't remember just what it was.

"Don't you think it is about time you got over this rage of yours?" Kitty asked.

I was silent. Hadn't I been all through this before? I knew of the rage of the crippled. I had looked at it and I had examined it and I thought I was over it.

I looked at Kitty. "I didn't know it was rage," I said.

"It is," she said.

"I thought it was just exasperation," I said. "Everybody gets mad at taxis."

"Not everyone has a cane to hit them with," Kitty said.

I looked down again and was silent for another moment. "If I think about that," I said, "can we still go to the play?"

"I want to see *Mister Roberts* just as much as you do," Kitty said. "But you must *promise* to think about it."

"I promise," I said.

220

Kitty kissed me lightly on the forehead and pulled her gloves back on. We went down to the street again, found a more reasonable taxicab driver, and went off to see *Mr. Roberts*. We laughed a lot that night.

So I became a reformed taxicab hitter. I was becoming adjusted to marriage! Or, if you like, I was learning that marriage is a series of giving up self-directed actions for the rewards of a larger life.

Another area of my marriage in which I needed mouth-to-mouth resuscitation, besides rage or violence, was fatherhood. The little boy who had never been quite in focus because I was looking at his mother, suddenly came into sharp, hard-edged view.

I wrote a novel about my adjustment to my stepson, Brent, and his adjustment to me, that I called *This Is Goggle*, which was one of my most successful books. My confusion, my bafflement, my feeling that I would never live up to fatherhood, although written humorously, by God's grace, was apparent on every page.

I find that the first impression I had of Brent, after we returned from our wedding trip to so-called family life in the New York apartment, is still valid. So I will quote from it.

> As I understand it, in my ignorance of such things, it is possible that little girls of ten are different. They like to be seen in new dresses, and often they are pretty to look at, and have curls, and they are made of sugar and spice and everything nice, and sometimes they help with the dishes. On the other hand, little boys of ten, as everyone has always known, are made of snips and snails and puppy dogs' tails, and if you are the parent of one never ask for whom the policeman calls; he calls for thee.
>
> Our Goggle at ten stood maybe four feet high and he weighed about as much as a bushel of potatoes. There used to be a series of marks in the doorway to his bedroom in our apartment in New York, measuring the turbulent years like notches on the stock of a

shotgun, but we moved away from there, to the ill-concealed relief of our neighbors, and I have forgotten his exact height. I do remember that he seemed to be made of some sterner stuff than his poor mortal parents. Something like vulcanized rubber, for instance, or the plastic they make these new dolls from—which feels like human flesh, as the advertisements say, but is washable and unbreakable and will not crack. If Goggle bumped into you he left a bruise, and a session of roughhouse with him before bed was rather like commando training, only more exhausting. He was never sick. Bacteria shunned him.

He had stubby black hair like hog bristles, and his nails were worn down below the quick, and there was a wart just below his right elbow. He walked on his heels the way small boys do, especially barefooted, and especially on Saturday mornings when Papa wanted to sleep. You couldn't escape the sound of his voice anywhere. He hated to lose any game, whether Chinese checkers or baseball, and he only did lose, of course, when the other guys wouldn't obey the rules. His face, if we call it that, was generally contorted with some sort of violent emotion or commotion—anger, or laughter, or passionate interest—and this, together with his constant movement, gave the impression that he lived inside himself only with the greatest difficulty. Most of himself was somewhere else, around the corner or somewhere, but when he was finally caught up within himself at night he fell into such deep and instant sleep that not even the United States Marine Band could have wakened him.

He was always soiled but never what you might call dirty. His face was smudged and his hands were rough and grubby and when he undressed at night and took off his socks there was a dust shadow around his ankles, but even so, looking at him, you knew you'd never again in your whole life be as clean as he was. His idea of a bath—although I don't suppose you could say that a bath was ever his idea—was to run the tub full of water and then float lazily there, humming to himself, until steps were taken ("Good God, Goggle, aren't you ever coming out!"), and then to leap out quickly and rub the soil from himself onto a clean towel, which he dropped on the floor. He disdained soap. Who needed it?

In his bedroom his clothes were deposited in little moist, sodden mounds, like cow droppings; socks and underwear here, jerseys and corduroys there. If they were not retrieved at once, subsequent layers of culture, such as parts of airplane models, and hub caps, and comic books, and old carburetors, covered them quickly. It all looked and smelled rather like a bird nest, and when I tried to think of what might be an appropriate motto to hang over his door I discarded the idea of "Abandon All Hope, Ye Who Enter Here" in favor of "What Hath God Wrought?"

We longed for simpler pleasures. Surely everything would be easier in the country. We were not alone. Everyone was leaving the city. It was the time of the postwar exodus to the suburbs and the country.

Apart from White Plains, the territory around New York City was largely unknown to us. Kitty knew the countryside of Lancaster County, Pennsylvania, and I knew the countryside of northern Ohio around Euclid Village. We knew what we wanted, but we didn't know how to go about finding it. Our few attempts were ludicrous and inept and discouraging. Real estate agents and realtors led us to wonderful fantasies, like Levittown. We wanted an *old* house. Finally one weekend, we hid in the apartment, taking time off from our elusive search.

And that weekend it happened! If you read about it in a novel, or saw it in a movie, you would say that things didn't happen like that in real life.

The telephone rang before dinner, and on the telephone was a friend who had called because he needed comfort. The story was about his mother. She was in her early eighties, and she was living in the old family house because she wanted to be independent.

"I went over the house completely last spring," our friend said. "I put everything in tip-top shape. I even had a new furnace put in. But now Mother can't find the thermostat."

His tone of voice was despairing, troubled. It seems that his mother had become cold and she didn't know how to regulate the furnace, so she tried to build a fire in one of the fireplaces. But the flue wasn't open in the chimney and the house filled with smoke and his mother ran to open the windows and the doors, and the neighbors called the fire department, and . . .

We asked our friend if he didn't want to come over and have a drink with us.

"I'd like to," the friend said, "but Mother is here. She is safe and she admits at last that she shouldn't be alone in the house, and we are happy to have her here with us and safe, but what am I going to do with the house?"

"Sell it to us!" I said immediately.

"Stop," Kitty said, on the other line. She had picked up the phone in the kitchen and I was in the living room. "This isn't a time for our problems," Kitty said to me. "Ralph is talking."

There was silence on the other end of the line. Finally Ralph spoke. "I would be glad to show it to you," he said. "I suppose I'll have to sell it. But it's kind of difficult to think of giving up the old homestead . . ."

RALPH'S FAMILY HOMESTEAD was old and ugly. Ugly and *old*. Victorian. After we moved in we were told that it was the *one* house in the village that no one wanted to live in. But we loved it. It had wonderful waste space, a lot of rooms with doors you could close when you got tired of *that* project. It reminded me of the old haunted house in Euclid Village; it reminded Kitty of parental houses. It was surrounded by neglected gardens, and it was filled, absolutely filled, with an accumulation of furnishings and clutter that no one had thrown out in generations. But when we saw it we knew it was our house. Rockland County was within driving distance of New York City, so we wouldn't be cut off from our friends and professional ties.

We were content to wait until the house was emptied. It took a long time. It took a long time for Kitty to give up her job and reassure her clients that they would be properly taken care of. I said good-bye to my classes at the university without emotion, but not without some gratitude. The university had served me well while I courted Kitty.

It snowed the day before we moved. Three or four inches. But in the morning the sun came out, and the streets were cleared, and the moving van arrived on time.

We had worked out a plan. Kitty would go ahead in the car, with table lamps and a few precious things she wouldn't want broken. She would be at the house when the moving van arrived, to direct where things should be placed.

Brent would ride in the truck with the driver, which was what he wanted to do.

I would stay behind to supervise the moving of the furniture and to see that everything was left in good order when we vacated the apartment. I would come out later, with a friend who worked in town but who lived in the same village.

Everything went well until it was time for me and Brent and the moving man to leave.

"Where is my cane?" I asked.

It was a familiar cry. Now that I had learned to get about in the apartment without it, I usually forgot where I had left it when I wanted to leave. All hands would turn to in the search, and the cane would usually be found hanging on a doorknob against the wall, or under the bed, or on the floor back of the sofa.

This time, however, the moving man turned white.

"It was the first thing I packed," he said. "It's up front in the trunk, behind all the furniture."

I looked at his blank, bland, suddenly guilty face, and I began to laugh. Nothing could upset me on this happy day.

I went to the telephone where it sat, unhoused, on the floor. I called a neighbor, and she came over with a mop and her handy household saw, and sawed a length for me from the handle of the mop that I would need for a cane.

The moving man and Brent left. I called for a taxi to take me to the office of our friend.

It was dusk when we pulled into the driveway at the old house. There were no curtains or drapes at the windows yet, but all the lights had been turned on and the windows cast golden rectangles of color on the violet-colored snow.

As we got out of the car and made our way toward the porch, Kitty stood in the doorway, waiting, with the light behind her.

It snowed all night, but stopped before dawn, and when we wakened in our new bedroom upstairs, early, for of course there were no curtains yet at the windows, the rays of the rising sun, reflecting from the snow, had filled the room with a rosy glow. We lay there warmly together, drowsily, filled with wonder, as if awakening to the dawn of the world.

"I don't believe I have ever been so happy in my life," I said at last.

"How beautiful it is," Kitty said. "It is like being inside a pearl."

WE WERE HAPPY in the old house in the country. Under Kitty's hands it bloomed and came to life again. She painted walls and scraped floors and hung curtains; she did all manner of things that she had no idea she knew anything about at all. A part of herself went into the house, so that in the end it exhaled a fragrance that was like her own. In the spring the gardens would become hers; she would take care of that when the time came. She was always busy, absorbed, unaware of herself.

And Brent had found a friend. On the very first day of school a hand had shot up in the back row of the classroom he was shown to, and a cry went up, "Brent!" It was Hatfield, a friend he had known almost since infancy, when their mothers had enrolled them in the same day-care nursery before going off to their respective jobs. Hatfield, called "Hat," took up residence in our house as a second home. We were very happy to see him. His mother had not given up her job when they moved to the country. She commuted every morning to the city with her husband, Hat's stepfather, and Hat was left alone. Until we came along. "You never have one boy," Kitty said. "I have learned that. Friends materialize."

At about this same time Brent's grandmother, Kitty's mother, sent a substantial birthday check from her nursing home, enough to buy a bicycle. He and Hat pored over the Sears, Roebuck catalog until they found the perfect bicycle.

"Why don't you go into the village," I asked naïvely, "and buy a bicycle?"

The two looked up from the catalog with scornful eyes. "Buy a bicycle that other guys have *handled!*"

In due course the pristine bicycle that other guys had not handled arrived in its crate, and it was lovingly, reverently unveiled. And the boys had their freedom because Hat already had a bicycle. The village was theirs, the vicinity was theirs, the township was theirs. They brought back strange reports, but their most common goal, and common it was, was the village dump where all sorts of treasures awaited them. They even found hats—a top hat and a Spanish-American War hat that they wore triumphantly.

We enjoyed the accounts of their exploits. No more city streets. No more city policemen. No more apartment elevators and apartment cellars where a boy could get into trouble. No more street gangs.

In the country everything came together. After a while we realized that a different atmosphere pervaded the house. One of tranquillity. I was awfully tired of being the heavy father, a role which fitted me badly, and Kitty was very tired of being the peacemaker. We began to relax in each other's presence. Soon, wonder of wonders, we began sometimes to treat Brent with benign neglect. A young boy needs a lot of that.

Our days in the country fell into a pleasant and familiar routine. After we got Brent off to school, in "a spray of Rice Krispies," as I noted in *This Is Goggle,* Kitty and I kept out of each other's way during the day. I had writing to do, and Kitty had her work laid out. I had chosen a workroom upstairs in the back, a secret room with a passageway and two doors you could close. Going there, I picked up the threads of the story or the novel I was working on and shut myself blissfully away.

When I disappeared into my workroom, Kitty was off on a multitude of errands, to visit painters, decorators, auction houses, furniture stores, for our house, which she was getting into shape.

Lunch was unheard of; it was something you sent out for

from your office or went out for with a business client. I opened a can of soup and made a plate of sandwiches. That was all right with me. Conversation would have spoiled my train of thoughts. Leaving the sandwiches out after I had my lunch, I went back into my workroom.

Brent didn't come home for lunch. The school had a hot lunch program in which the mothers participated in shifts, including Kitty, however ineptly.

At that time Kitty was a stranger to the kitchen. She had been raised in fair affluence in which she was not allowed to go into the kitchen, and later, cooking was something that she never had time for. At six o'clock I covered my typewriter, washed my face, put on a clean shirt and a necktie and a jacket, and went into the kitchen to get out the ice for cocktails.

We prepared dinner together. I had come from a cooking family. Plain meat-and-potatoes cooking. Brent would play outside until the last minute before dinner. We carried the food into the dining room and sat around the table. And then the dam broke. All of the pent-up conversation poured out. We never finished our conversation. We had to interrupt ourselves, Brent to do his homework (oh, loathsome word!), we to clear the table and do up the dishes.

By spring the interior of the house was finished, or as finished as ever a house is. It was too early to start gardening. Kitty turned her attention to cooking. She had had a housekeeper in the apartment in New York, but now she was free at last, in her own house, in her own kitchen. She was tired of poor cooking, institutional cooking, simple cooking. She would teach herself how to cook! She turned to it with all of the energy and drive she had put into her professional career.

For a while the kitchen was a laboratory, workplace, shop. Kitty bought all the necessary equipment. She bought all the primary cookbooks and ranged them along a shelf in the kitchen. She bought files for recipes, which she kept in a desk she had bought for the kitchen. She bought loose-leaf notebooks, for work in progress. She even bought apothecary scales and weights and measures, and laboratory beakers and measuring cups. Some recipes, especially old ones which she had begun to collect, as well as foreign ones, gave measurements in grams, by weight, or by ounces. And she was absolutely adamant about one thing. The recipe, any recipe, had to be made exactly as written the first time, after which you could experiment a little if you wanted to. But it had to be absolutely right the first time! The research had to be completed, the laboratory work done.

Soon wonderful smells began coming from the kitchen, penetrating even the closed doors of my workroom. Tantalizing, alluring smells that made it almost impossible to work. We started to have wonderful dinners, dishes that I was unaccustomed to, dishes that I had never heard of, never tasted before. There was a certain ritual with which we began each dinner. "It will be better next time," Kitty said.

Brent and I put our foot down about that. It reflected on our judgment. We thought it was delicious the first time.

Some friends, two at first, then four, began to be invited to share the *coq au vin* with red wine, the chicken with white wine, the heavenly broiled fish.

To cater to my meat-and-potatoes background, Kitty turned out a wonderful roast loin of pork, perfumed with olive oil and thyme, with pan-roasted, glazed potatoes. Or, on special occasions, she might produce a towering standing rib roast of beef with Yorkshire pudding. I helped with that, lifting the roast to a warm platter to rest, pouring the hot fat in the roasting pan into a measuring cup for the Yorkshire pudding.

She taught herself to make sauces, using the apothecary scales and all the laboratory equipment. Disciples, friends, came to watch and learn from her. I once overheard her in the kitchen telling a very young friend, "You can get married if you can make Hollandaise sauce and mayonnaise." I carried this advice, thoughtfully, to my workroom. This was well before the days of the health revolution and the diet scare, so presumably this pretty young woman now has a fat and happy husband with a cholesterol problem.

Kitty also made a wonderful curry sauce—which she spooned over a scooped-out tomato holding an artichoke heart—as well as trifle from leftover pound cake. (She used to hide the pound cake so it *would* be left over.) The greatest triumph of all in the dessert category, at least to my taste, was a stupendous vanilla Bavarian cream in a ring mold, with nut meats and candied fruit arranged in the bottom of the mold so they would be on top when the dessert was unmolded.

Kitty gave a dinner party to celebrate, after several preliminary efforts, her successful presentation of chicken breasts in white wine sauce with white seedless grapes, called Chicken *Veronique.*

She planned a triumph, at which I was a willing helper. Also dragged into service, to don an apron and serve the night of the dinner, was faithful, patient, long-suffering Eva May, who did our heavy cleaning well as that of some of the neighbors.

Kitty planned her dinner party so she would be absolutely through in the kitchen, ready for Eva May to take over, with plenty of time left to bathe and dress, put on her face, arrange her hair, and be sitting in the living room before I opened the door for the first guest.

We had cocktails, then everyone was directed to the dining room. There was a moment of silence, and then the magic happened. I popped the wine cork, the guests laughed and talked, and Eva May served flawlessly.

After the successful dinner party, a sort of food fatigue set in. Kitty didn't want to go near the kitchen for some time. She had completed her apprenticeship, and ahead of her stretched, endlessly, three meals a day.

I fixed dinner the following night, hamburgers and baked potatoes and sliced tomatoes.

"It won't be better next time," I said.

Next day Kitty went out and surveyed the garden. Over the weeks of late winter and early spring she had cleared the tangled growth and defined the flowerbeds. She had made paths. She had set out shrubberies and bulbs, and planted seeds, all according to a plan she had drawn on paper. Now, she had to wait for Nature to do her work.

She came back into the house and began reading Jane Austen.

School was threatening to close for the summer. An upheaval in our lives. Hat was going away to spend the summer in Maine with his mother and stepfather.

"What will I do?" moaned Brent.

I had finished a long and complicated story. It was the best thing I had ever done, I said, as I did at the end of any writing project. "Or the very best I could do." Familiar postpartum blues followed, characterized by a vague unrest, and thoughts of mortality.

It was a time of crisis, a minor crisis, to be sure, but nonetheless real. Something must be done.

At that very juncture a letter arrived, out of the blue, and we were saved again through a friend. We had friends, this time in North Carolina, who wrote us that Wade, the husband, had fallen down the cellar steps and broken his leg. It was a clean break, and it was healing nicely, and the prognosis was good. But they wouldn't be using their cabin in the mountains this summer. Instead, they were writing to a few close friends to offer it. Wade, a fisherman, had built the cabin by a trout stream. It was very primitive and had none of the amenities. It was no place to spend a carefree summer. They would offer it, but we probably didn't want it.

I telephoned, to forestall any of their other friends who might get there first, and insisted that we did want it for the summer, very much. We had worked hard to find a new life for ourselves in a new community, and badly needed a change of scene.

But the cabin was without anything, we were told. No electricity, no plumbing except a john and a bathtub that you could put water in, but it drained out on the ground. You had to heat water on the kitchen stove. No gas. The kitchen stove was wood-burning and had to be stoked.

"It sounds heavenly!" Kitty said, and she meant it. She had always wanted to cook on a wood-burning stove, especially since she had tried her hand at *haute cuisine*.

"Thank you very much," I said over the telephone. "We'll take it."

We were about to embark on an adventure that had unexpected, profound effects on each of us, an adventure that drew us closer together, so at last we made a family.

232

# 45

IT RAINED ALL night before we reached the cabin. It had rained the day before, and the day we arrived. The cabin, halfway up the mountain, was all that we hoped for. It was one with the wilderness, looking as if it had always been there. Inside it was bone clean. All of the unimportant things had been eliminated, but the necessities were at hand. Kerosene lamps, filled with kerosene. Wood beside the stove in the kitchen and beside the fireplace in the living room. Clean bedding piled on the beds. We gloried in it. We made up the beds. I built a fire in the fireplace. Kitty built a fire in the stove to heat soup and coffee to go with the sandwiches, which she set out on the all-purpose table using dishes she had found in the open cupboards.

And still it rained. It made a pleasant symphony for the first night's sleep in the cabin, but by the following morning the trout stream that tumbled by our door had risen high enough to carry away the footbridge, with a noise like a tree falling. We went out on the porch to survey the damage. Our car was on the other side of the stream.

"We wanted to be isolated," I said, looking at the distant mountains dissolve and reappear in the rain, like a series of Japanese prints.

The Branwells, a family of hill folk, lived at the top of the mountain. We had had them explained to us in a letter from our friends before we set out. The mountain people are kind, the letter told us, and we might persuade the Branwells to help us in cutting wood or bringing in supplies, but we must not patronize them or regard them as lesser people.

Suddenly there was a noise on the steep, narrow path that led down to us from the Branwells', and while we watched, a row of figures emerged in a single file from the rhododendron. They were the Branwells, and we could see what the letter from our friend meant. To our city eyes they looked very much like comic-strip hillbillies.

First in line was Mr. Branwell. After him came a girl of about seventeen; after her, three small children. Each carried something in his hands, and a dog brought up the rear, like a guard. They came up to the porch and put down their burdens. They had brought us two freshly killed, dressed broilers, a gallon of fresh milk, a pound of newly churned butter, corn, string beans, squash, onions.

"It will help you until you get to the store," Mr. Branwell said. "When the rain stops I will bring down Prince, my horse, and pull the footlog back across the branch. We knew the bridge would go."

Gratitude is difficult to express, particularly if it is felt deeply and toward people so strange to us that we hardly knew how to speak. Were we to pay for these things? Sometimes the only way is to ask. And so while we sat together on the porch, echoing our thanks, I did just that. "Can we pay you for this?" I asked, hesitating over the words.

Their composure banished our indecision. "We brought these things to you," the girl said. "But you can buy things from us after this, if you like."

In the conversation that followed we learned to identify our callers. The teenage girl was Mary, youngest daughter of the family, unmarried; the children were those of her sisters. The small girl with the lovely pensive face, wearing a Kate Greenaway pinafore and a Kate Greenaway expression, was the daughter and only child of one sister, Martha. The two little boys, Henry and "Tiny," were the sons of another daughter, Molly.

And then there was the dog. I did not recognize his breed. He had thick hair, gray and curly, and a blue muzzle and dark eyes. In the shy silence of the front porch I sought him as a topic of conversation and I noticed that as he lay with his eyes open, his legs twitched, and every now and then a strong tremor passed through his body. "Is he ill?" I asked. "Why does he tremble?"

"He is a psychoneurotic dog," Mr. Branwell said.

I thought I had not heard him correctly and I looked at him with an expression of bewilderment.

"He is from the veterans' hospital," Mr. Branwell said.

"Oh," I replied, as if I were thoroughly familiar with psychoneurotic dogs from veterans' hospitals, but bewilderment must have remained on my face because Mr. Branwell explained further.

"The hospital is five miles over the hills," he said. "Bully—we call the dog Bully—came over one time with some friends of Molly's husband, and since then he comes to see us every once in a while. He was mascot for a group of flyers. He doesn't speak English."

"He doesn't?" I asked.

"At first we thought he was deaf," Mr. Branwell said, "but then we realized he was a foreign dog and didn't speak our language.

"Molly's husband was killed in the war," Mr. Branwell added.

There was nothing to say to that, and we said nothing.

"These are his sons," Mr. Branwell explained. "He was killed near Luxembourg, and he never saw Tiny here. Tiny's a mean one."

From his tone and the expression on his face I gathered that the word was spoken in affection. Tiny had found the rocking chair on our porch, and with feet extended was now busily occupied in rocking back and forth as violently as he could. He smiled broadly, showing pink gums and white little boy's teeth, but in that smile you could see the man that he would be, and the man that his father was.

"He calls me Pa," Mr. Branwell said. "He's a mean one. He gets mad, just like that. Sometimes you don't even know why. And then he goes into the parlor and sits in his rocking chair and rocks. It's an old chair and we were going to throw it out, but Ma says it's his chair now and he can have it."

Tiny smiled. On the floor Bully twitched again and Mr. Branwell leaned over and ran his gnarled hand softly over the uneasy haunches. "I could pet him to death," he said, without looking up.

When I remarked that farming on top of a mountain must be difficult, Adam Branwell smiled and said that they liked the view. "And we are safe from the atomic bomb," he added, pronouncing it atom-ic, not a-tomic.

The Branwells left, shyly, but Mr. Branwell returned after supper, showing himself in his most vulnerable light, as if to test our understanding. He was almost drunk, with a Mason jar of corn whiskey in the pocket of his overalls. It was impossible for him to completely submerge his instinctively good manners, and he waited until my wife had left the room to put Brent to bed before he offered me a drink. "It is mountain dew," he said with a wink.

I asked him to wait until Kitty returned. "She needs a drink," I said. "We traveled far yesterday. And she has never tasted mountain dew either."

I admit I was rather concerned about his visit. It was dark and we were alone with only the light of the kerosene lamps and the burning log in the fireplace to show us the outline of Mr. Branwell, tall and uncouth in his overalls, his black hat at his feet, his tobacco-stained teeth revealed in a smile.

But Kitty was not alarmed. When she came back into the room, she brought some woman's magic, and all at once we were not strangers before a fire, but a man and his wife in a new home to which a neighbor had come to call and welcome us. We drank some of the liquor he had brought us in kitchen glasses, and when our eyes smarted at its potency, Mr. Branwell rose to demonstrate it further. On the hearthstone of our borrowed cabin he poured a small amount and put a match to it. Limpid blue flames danced above its surface. Afterward we said it was then Mr. Branwell had dedicated our cabin.

And then he talked.

"I take the Charlotte *Observer* because it has the best foreign news," he said.

And, "Bear fat makes the best bread. Ma always used bear grease when she baked."

236

He said, "Dewey is not politician enough to be in the White House. Even a good man has to be a politician to be president."

And, "You must learn to know the touch-me-not which grows along the branches. You put the leaves in sweet milk and pour it down the dog's throat when a rattler strikes him."

And finally, "On our mountain we raise everything we need but baking soda and flour. We are safe from the atom-ic bomb."

While the stream was high, Thomas Branwell came down to fish for trout. He looked like his father, and like him he dressed in overalls; and in his pocket, along with a can of fishing worms, he carried a plug of chewing tobacco. He was twenty-five, and he was a little boy.

"You don't need to worry about Tommy," Mr. Branwell had told us, as an afterthought when he had started back up the hill the night before. "He was sick when he was little. They say it was meningitis, and his mind never grew up after that. But he's a good boy. He won't hurt nobody."

Brent found that out for himself. We had forgotten to tell him about Tommy, but when Tommy came down to fish we found them together, sitting back on their heels, like Rousseau's noble savages. Tommy fished and Brent watched.

"Like to fish?" I asked Tommy.

"Yep."

"Catch anything?"

"Nope."

After that the conversation died. It might have been easier to make a further attempt if Tommy hadn't turned to look at me every time I spoke. His eyes were mild and clear and incredibly blue, but they were intimidating because they were so pure. I had once seen a deer with eyes like that. He had been born and raised in a game preserve and he had never heard the hunter's gun.

("I like Tommy," Brent said later. "He's fun to be with. He always smiles.")

Tommy's fishing technique was something to watch. He carried his worms in a Prince Albert tobacco can in his rear overall pocket. He would pull the empty hook from the water, shake his head, reach for the tobacco can, extract a worm, and then he would hang it over rather than through the hook until he had achieved a nice balance. Back into the stream went the line. In a moment he would pull out the empty hook again, shake his head, reach for the tobacco can, etc. In this sort of friendly fishing, in which neither worm nor fish are disturbed, there is eventually an end to the worms, and when this point had been reached, Tommy threw away his tobacco can, searched for flat stones where he was sitting, and practiced skipping them in the water. He skipped one stone nine times before it reached the opposite bank. Brent was rightly impressed.

"Tommy's a good boy," the voice of Mr. Branwell said behind me. I had been so interested I had not heard him approach. He had come with Prince to pull the footlog back from the side of the stream where the current had left it. The great, lumbering workhorse looked as if he had been placed there by Picasso, in a collage, perhaps, to achieve a disturbing sense of juxtaposition with the forest.

But no one else thought the scene strange. Tommy arose to help, and he was a good assistant who spoke little and cheerfully obeyed instructions. They worked slowly and well, Mr. Branwell, Tommy, and Prince, entertaining us with a running conversation.

"Tommy won't drink beer no more," Mr. Branwell said, laughing.

"Nope," Tommy said, emphatically shaking his head, bracing the log, which Prince would pull across the **stream**.

"I had him in town," Mr. Branwell said, "and before I knew what was happening—I was talking with neighbors, you know—they had bought him three glasses of beer. Had to hold his head while he threw up. Old lady gave me hell when I brought him home. 'Getting our son drunk,' she said. Tommy wants no more beer."

"Nope," Tommy said, still smiling and shaking his head.

Mr. Branwell smiled too, and suddenly I saw him in the round. In his smile as he looked at his son was the same protective kindness I had seen when he looked at Bully, the dog,

238

and at Tiny, his fatherless grandson. It was there also when he looked at me, where I stood by the stream, leaning on my cane, unable to help.

When the bridge was up, the world was ours again, and we went on Sunday to have dinner with the Branwells. We had to drive down through old streambeds and around the base of the mountain, and start up from the bottom on the other side where the Branwells had their road. After we reached the top I realized that my neck was so stiff from strain that I could scarcely turn it; I had never driven up a dirt road which circled a mountain, so that at every turn there was nothing ahead of the car but space. Stones rattled away under the tires, and sometimes the car skittered nervously over loose gravel. It was a road on which you dared not hesitate and could not turn back, and there was a curious sense that the normal landscape had unaccountably tilted up because you passed cows grazing in perpendicular pastures and corn growing in neat rows at a forty-five–degree angle.

At last we came to a clearing near the top, and there was the Branwell house, rising up on a stone base, with a tin roof slanting down over dark-stained batten board. The scene was like a diorama in a museum, cunningly contrived to operate with hidden wheels. Chickens ran helter-skelter from the car, dogs barked, and from his pen the pig groaned. Woodsmoke rose lazily from the chimney, ascending upward into limitless space, and all around as far as the eye could see stretched the mountains as God had made them.

The Branwells came to meet us. Mr. Branwell, deliberately, and Tiny, running, the other children in shy eagerness. Mrs. Branwell stood framed in the doorway with her hands folded in her apron.

There is a woman like her in every family, preserved in memory or in a dim daguerreotype. She had a mother's face, and when I had studied it long enough at discreet intervals, I knew what brought my eyes back to it. It was a round face, and soft; there were no lines in it yet, but the eyes held, like a mirror, the hope and sadness and questioning of life. They were quiet, and they were so innocent that one knew the end of the world was a long way off, but there was no resignation in them. No challenge, either, just acceptance and a belief that someday the answer to everything might still be made known to her.

"I declare," she said, "I meant to come to see you long before this. But it seems like I'm so busy now, what with beans to can, and tomatoes, and the cows to be milked every day."

We went into the living room and sat down. We met Martha, the little girl's mother, whose husband was gone away somewhere, and Molly, the girl whose husband had been killed in the war. Everyone was rather quiet, from shyness we thought; not until after dinner did we understand what presence lay in the room.

We had, as Mrs. Branwell explained, a simple country dinner. There was homemade sausage, and meatloaf, and a large platter of fried chicken. There was macaroni baked with cheese, and mashed potatoes, and hot biscuits. There were garden beans, and sliced tomatoes, and corn on the cob, and pickled cucumbers, and fried okra. There was cake, and there was pie, and there were pitchers of milk for those who did not like coffee, and for any unfilled corners there was homemade jelly to eat with fresh bread.

Afterward, when we were back in the parlor, Mrs. Branwell told us what occupied their minds. Molly was not in the room; she had gone into the kitchen to wash the dishes. With a glance in that direction to make certain that she would not be overheard, Mrs. Branwell told us they had received word that Molly's husband's body had been sent back from overseas. It was, in fact, in New York City, and it was now only a matter of days before it would arrive in North Carolina.

Mr. Branwell shook his head. When he spoke we could tell from the tone of his voice that he was repeating an opinion he had often stated before. "It is a mistake," he said. "The boy should lie where he fell. And how will we know it is his body in that sealed coffin? How will we know there is anything in it at all?"

I hastened to report that from my own past observation I knew that the Graves Registration Corps was one of the most efficient and conscientious units of the military. "You may be assured it is he," I said, with all the emphasis I could muster.

Mr. Branwell still shook his head. "It isn't good," he said. "It stirs up old feelings."

Here Mrs. Branwell spoke up. "Tiny," she said, pointing to the small, smiling figure, even now rocking violently in his own chair, his sturdy little legs stuck out in front of him, "was born on one day, and the telegram came the next."

"Had I been there," Mr. Branwell said firmly, "she would not have had the telegram. They brought it to her in the hospital."

"They said it was orders," Mrs. Branwell said mildly, the look of innocent questioning even stronger in her eyes. "They said it had to be delivered in person." She paused. "Molly hasn't had a well day since."

"And she wanted her husband brought home?" I asked.

"Yes," Mrs. Branwell said. "It was her wish."

Molly came into the room at this moment, and she heard what we were talking about. "We have to be ready," she said. "He may be here any day. We have to go to the cemetery."

I spoke then, tactlessly, the question that was in my mind. "Why did you want him brought home?" I asked.

"For the boys," she said without hesitation. "The oldest doesn't remember him, and Tiny never saw him. When they are grown up I can take them to the cemetery and I can say to them, 'There is your father.' "

As I met her clear eyes, I reversed my conviction about such things. "Yes," I said, "I think he would like to be brought home. I think he would like to lie here in the hills he had always known."

Before we left their house I told Molly and her mother, in the conventional, helpless way one says such things, that if there was anything we might do to help them they must not hesitate to call upon us. When such a thing is said among the people I have always known, it is generally accepted in the manner of its delivery, as a sort of coinage of kindness. But the next morning Mary Branwell came down the mountain with a message from her mother. Since I had been good enough to offer my services, would I drive them to the cemetery so they might clear a place for his grave?

I would indeed. It touched me to be taken into their lives, for there were others in the hills with cars or wagons—kin, or neighbors long known. I drove, at the appointed time, down through the streambeds and around the base of the mountain, but when I came to the perilous road, they were waiting for me at the bottom. They had walked down in the hot sun because they sensed my uneasiness about it.

Mrs. Branwell and Molly wore bright-printed house-dresses. Mrs. Branwell carried, with a smile, an old hat of her husband's, to protect her from the sun. In his hand, Mr. Branwell carried tools. He had brought a hand scythe and hedge clippers, and we put these in the back of the car.

It was a bright day and we drove back into the mountains with an unaccountable feeling of holiday. The cemetery lay some ten miles distant, away from the highway, where the older people had lived. It seemed, as we drove, not so much a passage of miles as a journey backward into time. The Branwells delightedly pointed out to each other certain familiar landmarks. Aunt Jessie had lived there, for example, and down that road old Mr. Cooney used to walk in the evening on his cane, to catch a breath of air and talk with the neighbors at the store.

The houses here were more as I had imagined the houses of hill people would be like, with verandas supported by thin poles, the stone springhouses covered with creepers, the pink mimosa and lilac and myrtle in the yards. At length we came to the cemetery. The road into it was impassable. Rains had deepened the ruts made by the heavy hearse wheels, so we took to the open pasture and drove across it toward the grove of dark pines before which the tilted grave markers were discernible in a tangle of briars and weeds.

When we got as near as we could, we got out of the car, Mr. Branwell carrying the clearing tools, and made our way into the tangle among the stones. Only a few of the grave markers had been cut; what I had taken for stones whose legends had been obliterated by time had never been anything but rude markers. Now that the men who had placed them were dead, and those who had been present when it was done were gone, no one knew who lay beneath them. It was true that here and there were conventional monuments from the stonecutter's yard, bearing names and dates, and sometimes a few words. The stone on the grave of Mrs. Branwell's mother, for example, explained sorrowfully that THE JOY OF OUR HOME HAS LEFT US. But I was not to be deceived into thinking that where she lay was new burial ground.

"Every time they dig a grave here," Mrs. Branwell said, "they uncover others."

This bothered the Branwells; they did not like to disturb the rest of the dead, but one was buried here where one's fathers had been buried, and if an early grave was uncovered inadvertently, then it was reverently closed and another spot chosen. "No one knows who all these dead are," Mrs. Branwell said, "although we think that some are Indians who were friends of the early people."

We were standing, as we talked, at the edge of the Branwell plot; our job was to choose the spot where Molly's husband would lie, and clear it and mark it with a stake, which Mr. Branwell cut from a nearby tree. Old friends would come by to dig and make it ready.

"We'd better clear a path," Mrs. Branwell said, "because the Legion post is going to send some boys with a bugle, and there will be both families, too, to stand here."

They set to work. Mr. Branwell wielded the scythe, and Mrs. Branwell, her husband's old hat on her head, used the clippers to clear away the vines and brambles, which would slip away from the scythe's blade. Molly stood at the edge of the plot to watch them. "Here is old Mr. Lampion and his little colored boy," Mrs. Branwell said, pointing with the clippers. "We must not dig here, and over there, by Mama, are eight graves, but there is room there anyway, Molly, if you want him to be near the family."

Some family moments are too intimate for the presence of a stranger, and although the Branwells seemed to have temporarily forgotten me, I wished that I might have been anywhere else but where I was. I turned toward the pine grove behind the cemetery, cool and silent, so closely grown that the trees branched only at some height.

Molly's voice was clear and light when she answered.

"I want him over in that corner," she said. "I want him all to myself, so that I can do anything I want to with the grave."

When they had cleared the corner spot and marked it with the stake, and cleared a place for the mourners to stand, we returned to the car and drove away, out of the past and out of memory into the present. The sun was very hot, and beside me Mr. Branwell wiped the moisture of his exertion from his face, and Mrs. Branwell, in the backseat beside Molly, fanned herself with the old hat. We talked a little, quietly, as people do when not to talk is a dangerous thing.

When we reached the foot of the mountain they would not allow me to drive them up, even though I insisted. "We will bring the cows in on the way," Mrs. Branwell said.

They thanked me, almost too much, I thought. And then I drove away with the feeling one sometimes has that the episode was incomplete, that none of us had been able to conclude it with a remark that might have given it meaning.

I went on to our house thoughtfully, hoping that in conversation with Kitty I might resolve this feeling and give the day shape. She was in the kitchen, cooking supper at the wood range, but while we talked Brent came in to say that Mr. Branwell was on the front porch. "He wants to see you," he said.

There was a gravity in Brent's manner which suggested that if he did not prepare me for it I might not rise to the demands of a special occasion. I went to the door and found Mr. Branwell sitting heavily on the front steps of the porch.

I was relieved to see that he had a Mason jar of mountain dew with him, and I took a drink gratefully. We sat together for a while in silence. I wondered, not at the solemnity of his manner, which I could well understand, but rather at what had brought him down the mountain so soon after we had seen each other.

Then he said, "They don't like me to drink," and I began to understand a little.

"Who doesn't like you to drink?" I asked.

"My wife, the girls," he said. He was already a little drunk. But then it is very easy to get drunk in the sunlight at that

244

altitude, especially on mountain dew. "They say it isn't Christian," he said.

"They do?" I asked. And then it occurred to me how I might come to his defense, or offer him a defense for his own use. I felt it was very clever of me. "In the Bible," I said, "Jesus turned water into wine at the marriage feast at Cana. And wine of the very best quality, too."

Mr. Branwell shook his head. It was evident he had been presented with this defense before, or tried it himself. "That was only wine," he said. "It says nothing in the Bible about strong spirits."

We sat in silence a while longer. I sensed then that Mr. Branwell had come not only to share his drink with me, but also, even though I was alien to him in many ways, because I was a man and there are times when a man wants to be with another man, especially if he spends his life with women and children and a grown son who is only a boy.

"It isn't that I'm not a religious man," he said at length, his thoughts traveling some path opened to him by the liquor. "I believe in God. But this preacher, now, at the church where the women go, I've known him all my life. He was a mean one when he was young. He's got more than one bastard in this county. And then he was saved, you know. He didn't go to a school where you learn how to be a preacher. He just had the call. But when I go to be talked to about God, I feel that I ought to go to a man wiser than myself."

As I turned to look at him, I knew all at once why the gratitude of Molly and her mother had troubled me. It was because I felt they did not know where their true indebtedness lay, that familiarity had blinded them to the magnitude of this man. They did not seem to realize that only he stood between them, between Tommy, and Molly, and her fatherless sons, and the world.

But I could not say this; I could not even say what the mountain dew made me want to say—that perhaps a man wiser than himself would be difficult to find. Something other than natural reticence held me back, however, some subconscious feeling that in a world where so few men fulfill themselves, he must have his own reward. He did not need my statement about his stature, or my defense.

"Sometimes we can only help ourselves," he said, drinking again from the Mason jar and wiping his mouth on his sleeve. "Like Molly, for instance. It will take time. But I will bring her out of her darkness."

WE HATED TO see our summer come to an end. We packed the car reluctantly, mostly in silence, and we dawdled on the way home. We were like a holiday ship leaving port, trailing streamers of confetti, the confetti breaking, strand by strand. We didn't want to leave our memories, some of them sad and some of them joyful, but all of them profound.

It took us several days to travel the few hundred miles from North Carolina to New York. In spite of Brent's protests, we stopped at every antique shop and every secondhand furniture shop along the way. And we stopped in the late afternoon at a country store to buy a loaf of bread, and sliced ham and cheese, lettuce and tomatoes, cookies or cake, so we could prepare our meals in the motel room, and re-create once more the intimacy that we had enjoyed at the cabin.

But as we approached the end of the trip, a sense of urgency came over us. We suddenly wanted to get home. At dusk we didn't stop at a motel but pushed on, and it was after dark when we arrived.

I pulled the car around the house to the back in the darkness and stopped the motor.

"I'll go in and turn on the lights," Kitty said. "It will help you to unpack."

Kitty ran into the house, and Brent and I got out of the car and went behind it to unload the trunk. We began to unpack, piling the suitcases and boxes beside the car.

Suddenly I stopped.

"Brent, look," I said.

In the house, Kitty was going from room to room, turning on the lights. She had already turned on the outside light beside the front porch. It was a still, moonlit night. The stars were out. The house, in every detail, was outlined against the sky, coming to life as Kitty moved from room to room. Brent and I stood, silently.

Something miraculous had happened to the old house in our absence. Something magical.

It was home.